World Atlas CD-ROM

1. Running your *World Atlas* CD-ROM

Your *World Atlas* CD-ROM will run on both PCs with Windows and on Apple Macs. To make sure that your computer meets the system requirements, check the list below.

Minimum system requirements:

Acrobat Reader system requirements:

Windows
- R-class processor
- Microsoft® Windows 98 Second Edition, Windows Millennium Edition, Windows NT 4.0 with Service Pack 5 or 6 (Service Pack 6 recommended), Windows 2000, Windows XP Professional or Home Edition
- 64 MB of RAM
- 30 MB of available hard disk space (an additional 60 MB is needed temporarily during installation)
- Additional 70 MB of hard disk space for Asian fonts (optional)
- Web browser support. The Web browsers within which Adobe PDF files may be viewed are:
  – Internet Explorer 5.0 to 6.0
  – Netscape Navigator 4.5 to 4.77, 6.1
  – America Online 6.0

Macintosh
- PowerPC processor
- Apple® Mac® OS 9.1, 9.2, 9.2.2, 10.1.3, 10.1.5, 10.2
- 64 MB of RAM
- 30 MB of available hard disk space (an additional 60 MB is needed temporarily during installation)
- HFS formatted hard drive
- Additional 70 MB of hard disk space for Asian fonts (optional)
- Web browser support. The Web browsers within which Adobe PDF files may be viewed are:
  – Internet Explorer 5.0
  – Netscape Navigator 4.5 to 4.77, 6.1
  – America Online 6.0

2. Loading your *World Atlas* CD-ROM

To use your *World Atlas* CD-ROM, you will need to install Acrobat Reader if you do not already have it installed on your hard drive.

1. Place the *World Atlas* CD-ROM in your CD drive.

2a. If you have a PC, double click on the 'My Computer' icon, then double click on the 'World Atlas' folder. Double click on the 'Maps' folder and attempt to open one of the maps. If you are successful, you have a compatible version of Acrobat or Acrobat Reader already installed.

2b. If you have a Mac, double click on the 'World Atlas' icon on your desktop. Double click on the 'Maps' folder and attempt to open one of the maps. If you are successful, you have a compatible version of Acrobat or Acrobat Reader already installed.

3. If you cannot open a map, then proceed to the 'Acrobat Reader Installers' folder. On opening it, select your platform (Mac or PC) and proceed through the further folders until you reach the folder covering your operating system.

4. On finding the installer that matches your platform and operating system, double click on the installer and follow the on-screen instructions.

5. If you are unable to find either your platform or operating system, please go to the following website:
http://www.adobe.com/products/acrobat/readstep2.html

3. How to use your *World Atlas* CD-ROM

The *World Atlas* CD-ROM contains 47 world, regional and country base maps. The maps are 'text-free' PDF versions of the maps that appear in the accompanying *World Atlas* book. Lines of latitude and longitude are labelled. The names of physical features, town stamps, country and town names are not featured, allowing these maps to be used as a template for all sorts of homework activities. You can print the maps straight from the CD-ROM, then, using the accompanying *World Atlas* to help you, choose exactly which countries, towns and physical features you wish to label.

4. Contents of your *World Atlas* CD-ROM

The 47 world, regional and country maps are divided into nine folders. The number at the beginning of each file name refers to the page in the accompanying *World Atlas* where you can find the complete version of that map.

THE WORLD
16. The physical world
18. The political world

THE POLES
20. The Arctic Ocean
21. Antarctica

NORTH AMERICA
22. North America
24. Canada
26. Western US
28. Midwestern US
30. Southern US
32. Northeastern US
34. Mexico and Central America
36. The Caribbean

SOUTH AMERICA
38. South America
40. Northern South America
42. Southern South America

EUROPE
46. Europe
48. Northwestern Europe
50. The British Isles
52. The Low Countries
54. France
56. The Iberian Peninsula
58. Germany
60. The Alpine states

62. Italy and Malta
64. Eastern Europe
66. Central Europe
68. Southeastern Europe

AFRICA
70. Africa
72. Northwest Africa
74. Northeast Africa
76. West Africa
78. Central and east Africa
80. Southern Africa

ASIA
84. Asia
86. The Russian Federation
88. West Asia
90. Central Asia
92. South Asia
94. Southeast Asia
96. East Asia
98. Japan and the Koreas

AUSTRALASIA AND OCEANIA
100. Australasia and Oceania
102. Australia
104. New Zealand

THE OCEANS
44. The Atlantic Ocean
82. The Indian Ocean
106. The Pacific Ocean

5. Copyright details and disclaimer

Kingfisher Publications Plc
New Penderel House,
283-288 High Holborn,
London WC1V 7HZ
www.kingfisherpub.com

THE KINGFISHER
WORLD ATLAS

KINGFISHER

Kingfisher Publications Plc
New Penderel House,
283–288 High Holborn,
London WC1V 7HZ
www.kingfisherpub.com

Project Management: Picthall & Gunzi Ltd

For Picthall & Gunzi
Editor: Margaret Hynes
Designer: Dominic Zwemmer
Placename Consultant: Roger Bullen
Editorial Assistant: Carmen Hansen
Indexers: Jan Clark, Gill Cooling, Deborah Murrell

For Kingfisher
Managing Editor: Russell Mclean
Art Director: Mike Davis
Designer: Carol Ann Davis
DTP Manager: Nicky Studdart
Senior Production Controller: Nancy Roberts
Picture Research Manager: Cee Weston-Baker

Maps designed and produced by Anderson Geographics Limited, Warfield, Berkshire

First published by Kingfisher Publications Plc 2003
1 3 5 7 9 10 8 6 4 2
1TS/0504/TWP/CLSN(CLSN)/130ENSOMA/F

This edition produced for The Book People Ltd.,
Hall Wood Avenue, Haydock, St Helens WA11 9UL

The publisher would like to thank the following for permission to reproduce their material. Every care has been taken to trace
copyright holders. However, if there have been unintentional omissions or failure to trace copyright holders, we apologise
and will, if informed, endeavour to make corrections in any future edition.

Key: b = bottom, c = centre, l = left, r = right, t = top

6bl Corbis; 8t Lloyd Cuff/Corbis; 8b Lloyd Cuff/Corbis; 9t James A. Sugar/Corbis; 9b Jeff Vanuga/Corbis; 10bc Imagebank/
Getty Images; 10br Imagebank/Getty Images; 11tr Annie Griffiths Belt/National Geographic Image Collection; 12tr Darrell
Gulin/Corbis; 12b Laurence Fordyce/Eye Ubiquitous/ Corbis; 13tr Gary Braash/Corbis; 13bl Wolfgang Kaehler/Corbis;
13bc Wolfgang Kaehler/Corbis; 13br DiMaggio/Kalish/Corbis; 14-15 Bill Ross/Corbis; 14bl Adrian Arbib/Corbis;
14br Richard Bickel/Corbis; 15tc Robert Essel NYC/Corbis; 15tr Paul Almasy/Corbis

The publisher would also like to thank the following illustrators for their contribution to this book:
Richard Bonson 11b; Chris Forsey 7tr, 9tr; Jeremy Gower 10bl; Maltings Partnership 8bl; Janos Marphy 6–7

A CIP catalogue record for this book is available from the British Library.

ISBN 0 7534 1093 1

Printed in Singapore

THE KINGFISHER
WORLD ATLAS

TED SMART

CONTENTS

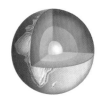

PLANET EARTH

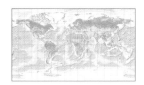

THE WORLD

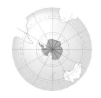

THE POLES

NORTH AMERICA

SOUTH AMERICA

EUROPE

AFRICA

ASIA

AUSTRALASIA AND OCEANIA

KEY TO MAPS

Settlements

■ **PARIS**   Capital city

● Halifax   Administrative region capital

○ São Paulo   Major town

○ Galway   Other town

Political and cultural regions

MEXICO   Country

Corsica   Dependent territory
(to France)

ARIZONA   Internal administrative region

TUSCANY   Cultural region

Boundaries

〜   International border

⋯⋯   Disputed border

– – –   Internal administrative boundary

Drainage features

〜 *Congo*   River

– – – *Warrego*   Seasonal river

〜 *Albert Canal*   Canal

✕ *Angel Falls*   Waterfall

Lake Taupo   Lake

Lake Mackay   Seasonal lake

Topographic features

△ *Mont Blanc 4,810 m*   Spot height of mountain

▽ *–8,605 m*   Spot depth below sea level

Balearic Islands   Island / island group

Thar Desert   Landscape feature / region

Seas and oceans

INDIAN OCEAN   Ocean

North Sea   Sea

Guinea Basin   Sea feature

Ice features

▲▲▲   Limit of summer pack ice

▲▲▲   Limit of winter pack ice

Land height

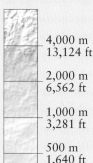

4,000 m
13,124 ft

2,000 m
6,562 ft

1,000 m
3,281 ft

500 m
1,640 ft

200 m
656 ft

Sea level

THE HOME PLANET

Planet Earth is roughly spherical in shape and measures 40,075 km around the Equator. As far as we know, it is the only planet that can support life. There are two main reasons for this. First, the Earth has an atmosphere that contains oxygen. Second, the planet is the just the right distance from the Sun. Planets closer to the Sun, such as Mercury, are too hot for life. Those further away, such as Mars, are too cold.

The Solar System

The Sun, our nearest star, has powerful gravity which attracts nine major planets, including the Earth, and countless minor planets, called asteroids. These, and other bodies, such as moons and comets, circle the Sun and form its family, or Solar System. The planets of the Solar System were probably created about 4.5 billion years ago from a cloud of gas and dust thrown out by the Sun when it was formed. The smaller planets nearer the Sun are made up of minerals and metals. The outer planets were formed at lower temperatures, and consist of swirling clouds of gases.

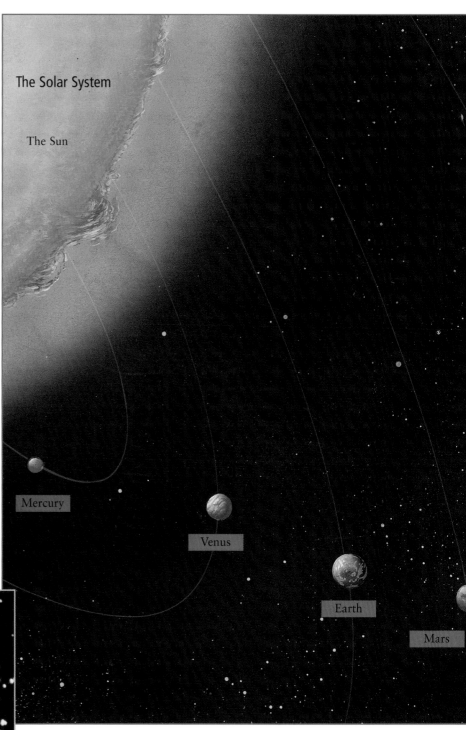

The Solar System

The Sun

Mercury

Venus

Earth

Mars

The Milky Way is an enormous, spiral-shaped galaxy of which our Solar System forms a tiny part. The galaxy contains at least 200 billion stars.

The Earth is the third planet from the Sun (above). It takes 365.25 days for the Earth to complete a full circle of the Sun.

The Sun and Moon

With a diameter of about 1,400,000 km, the Sun is more than 100 times wider than the Earth. Like other stars, the Sun is a great ball of gases. Although it lies about 150 million kilometres from the Earth, the Sun provides the light and warmth needed to make our planet suitable for life. The Moon lies about 384,000 km away from the Earth, and is our planet's closest neighbour in space. Its gravity is weaker than the Earth's, so it cannot hang on to any gases to make an atmosphere. However, the Moon's gravity does pull at our oceans to create tides.

Pluto

Neptune

Uranus

Saturn

Jupiter

Inside the Earth

Rocky crust

Outer mantle

Inner mantle. It is richer in iron than the outer mantle.

Outer core of molten iron and nickel

Inner core of solid iron and nickel

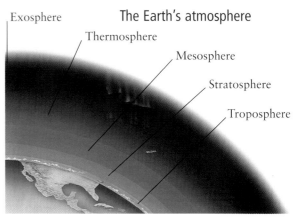

Exosphere

The Earth's atmosphere

Thermosphere

Mesosphere

Stratosphere

Troposphere

The Earth's outer structure

The Earth is surrounded by a layer of air roughly 2,000 km thick, called the atmosphere. It contains the air that we breathe, together with water vapour and tiny pieces of dust. Held by the pull of the Earth's gravity, the atmosphere protects us from the dangerous rays of the Sun, and the cold of outer space. The atmosphere is made up of layers. The layer closest to the Earth is the troposphere. It contains most of the gas in the atmosphere, and is the narrowest layer. Above the troposphere is the stratosphere. It extends from 11 km to 50 km above the Earth. The mesosphere lies between 50 km and 80 km above the Earth. If meteors fall into this layer, they burn up, causing shooting stars. A very thick layer of air called the thermosphere extends from about 80 km to 480 km above the ground. Above this is the exosphere, which has no definite upper limit.

The Earth's inner structure

At the centre of the Earth lies a solid core made of iron and a small amount of nickel. Its temperature is about 4,500°C. Around the core is the outer core, formed of liquid iron and nickel at a temperature of about 3,300°C. Outside the core is the mantle, a layer of rock about 2,900 km thick. The temperature reaches about 3,700°C at the bottom of the mantle, but high pressure there keeps the rock solid. There is less pressure on the top part of the mantle, which is relatively soft and can move. We live on the Earth's rocky outer layer, called the crust.

THE CHANGING EARTH

The Earth's crust, which covers the planet's surface, is made up of several sections, called tectonic plates. These plates interlock with each other, like the pieces of an enormous jigsaw puzzle. They are not fixed in position, however, but are moving slowly. As a result, the world's continents have shifted position over millions of years. More than 200 million years ago, the continents made up one single landmass, which gradually split up and moved apart to produce the continent shapes that we see today. The boundaries of the plates are places of huge stress. Sometimes, if plates are drifting apart, new crust is created as hot liquid rock from the mantle below fills the gap. If the plates are pushing towards each other, the land on one side can be pushed upwards, creating mountain ranges.

Earthquakes

Earthquakes occur when two tectonic plates slide past each other and friction is created along the line that lies between them. The friction causes violent vibrations, called tremors, that spread across the ground from the source. Sometimes the crust of the Earth cracks, or is faulted, and the land on one side of the fault line is raised, while on the other side it is lowered.

Sliding plates

The San Andreas Fault extends for over 1,000 km across California. This area is the site of frequent minor earthquakes.

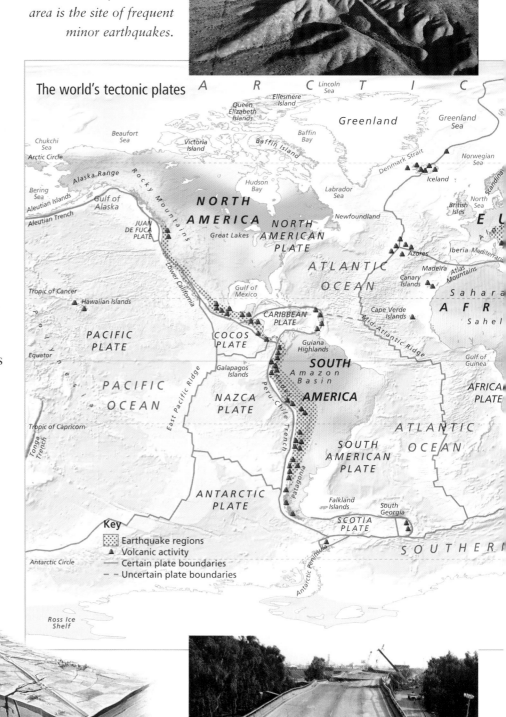

The world's tectonic plates

Key
- Earthquake regions
- ▲ Volcanic activity
- — Certain plate boundaries
- – – Uncertain plate boundaries

Fault line

Area of friction

Vibrations spreading
away from the source

The enormous power of an earthquake can pull down buildings and rip apart roads, sometimes causing death and injury in the process.

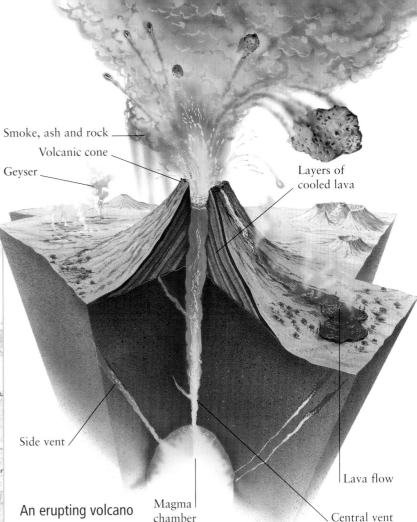

Lava flowing from volcanoes can reach temperatures of more than 1,000°C, and move at speeds of up to 60 km/h.

Smoke, ash and rock
Volcanic cone
Geyser
Layers of cooled lava
Side vent
Magma chamber
Lava flow
Central vent

An erupting volcano

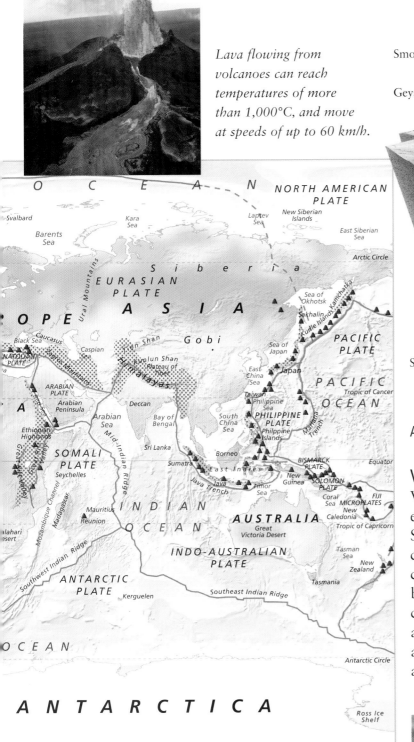

Volcanoes

When hot liquid rock, or magma, from the Earth's mantle escapes to the surface of the Earth, a volcano is created. Sometimes the magma collects in a huge underground chamber, before it rises through a channel called the central vent, or smaller side vents. Once the magma breaks the surface it is called lava. The lava gradually cools to form the shape of the volcano. Some volcanoes are cone-shaped, while others, called shield volcanoes, are more rounded. During a volcanic eruption, gases, ash and rock are often thrown high into the air.

Geysers

Geysers are found in the volcanic regions of New Zealand, Iceland, Chile, eastern Russian Federation and western USA. Pools of water, in underground caverns made of watertight volcanic rock such as rhyolite, are heated by scorching hot magma. The water boils, and some of it turns to steam. Eventually, the pressure in the cavern builds up, and the water and steam is forced upwards through a crevice to the Earth's surface. Here, the water and steam burst out of the ground, and spurt up into the air.

There are less than 1,000 geysers in the world. A number of them erupt very often and extremely regularly. Some geysers are known to reach heights of more than 100 metres.

CLIMATE AND WEATHER

Climate is the average sunshine, wind, rainfall and humidity that an area receives over a long period of time. The major influence on a region's climate is its latitude (the distance it lies north or south of the equator). The equator receives the most direct rays from the Sun, so the climates there are warm. Places near the poles receive less heat from the Sun, so they have colder climates. Other influences on an area's climate include its distance from an ocean, its height above sea level, ocean currents and wind patterns.

The Earth's climate zones

The Earth's climate varies from place to place. Polar and mountainous zones are freezing and dry all year round. Continental regions are cold in winter and warmer in summer. Steppe areas have cold winters and very hot summers, while temperate regions enjoy a milder climate without extremes of temperature. The tropics are mainly hot and wet all year round. Some subtropical zones have hot, dry summers and warm, wet winters. Arid areas are hot with very little rain at all. Savanna regions are hot throughout the year, but they have a rainy season that lasts about three months.

The greenhouse effect

Certain gases in the atmosphere, such as carbon dioxide, are called greenhouse gases because they act like the glass panes in a greenhouse. These gases let the Sun's rays pass through to the Earth, but they restrict the amount of energy that can pass back into space. The heat becomes trapped in the atmosphere, causing the Earth to warm up.

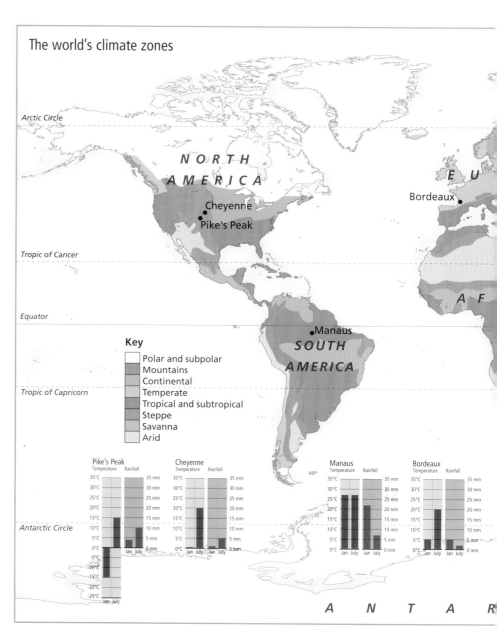

The world's climate zones

Key
- Polar and subpolar
- Mountains
- Continental
- Temperate
- Tropical and subtropical
- Steppe
- Savanna
- Arid

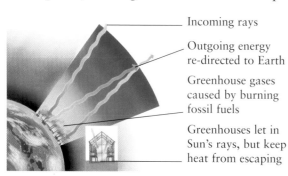

How the greenhouse effect works

Incoming rays

Outgoing energy re-directed to Earth

Greenhouse gases caused by burning fossil fuels

Greenhouses let in Sun's rays, but keep heat from escaping

Many deserts are so dry that virtually no plants can grow. The Namib Desert, in southern Africa, receives an average rainfall of only 25 mm per year.

Temperatures on Antarctica reach as low as −88.8°C. A few animals, such as penguins, have adapted to the freezing conditions and howling winds.

Tropical areas, such as the coast of Texas, USA, are wet and hot all year round. During storms, the rain falls in torrents and fierce winds lash trees and houses.

Archangel

Krasnoyarsk

OPE

ASIA

Tropic of Cancer

Massawa

CA

Equator

Dar es Salaam

AUSTRALASIA

Tropic of Capricorn

AND OCEANIA

Weather
Short-term events in the atmosphere, from showers to hurricanes, make up the world's daily weather. Changes in weather are mainly caused by the movements of large air masses. The temperature and moisture content of these air masses change as they pass over land and water. They also swirl around to produce depressions – bringing cooler, wetter weather – and anticyclones – tending to bring warmer, drier conditions.

The water vapour forms clouds that produce rain or snow

Rivers carry water to the sea

Massawa		Dar es Salaam		Archangel		Krasnoyarsk	
Temperature	Rainfall	Temperature	Rainfall	Temperature	Rainfall	Temperature	Rainfall

C T I C A

Moist air is blown towards the land

The Sun heats a body of water, and moisture from its surface evaporates

Water runs below the surface of the land to the sea

The water cycle
The continuous movement of water across the Earth and through its atmosphere is called the water cycle. Water in the oceans and the ground evaporates as the Sun heats the Earth. The water vapour rises into the sky where it begins to cool down, forming drops of water within clouds. Eventually, the drops of water become heavy enough to fall back to the Earth as rain or snow. The water soaks into the ground and feeds lakes and rivers. Then the cycle starts all over again.

Water falls back to the land and sea

How the water cycle works

THE NATURAL WORLD

All living things are connected with one another, and rely on each other for food, protection, or even shelter. It is possible to divide the world up into a number of broad zones, in which certain species of plants and animals live together within particular climate conditions. These ecological areas are called biomes.

The harshest habitats

The toughest of the world's biomes are those which have low rainfall, or experience bitterly cold or scorching hot temperatures. Polar regions are permanently covered in ice, so no plants can live in them. Animals, such as the walrus, have developed insulating fat and stocky limbs to survive in the freezing conditions here. With very little soil and large areas of frozen ground, tundra regions are treeless. A few plants, such as lichens and mosses, grow during the summer months. Needleleaf trees, including spruces and pines, are the only type of vegetation that can survive the long, snowy winters in the northern parts of Scandinavia, the Russian Federation and Canada. In mountainous regions, the lower slopes may be forested, but only ground-hugging shrubs can grow above the tree line. Deserts have very little rain. Certain plants and animals are adapted to the extreme temperatures and the lack of water in these regions.

For 50 to 60 days each year, the tundra regions, which are usually frozen, become carpeted with colourful, low-lying plants.

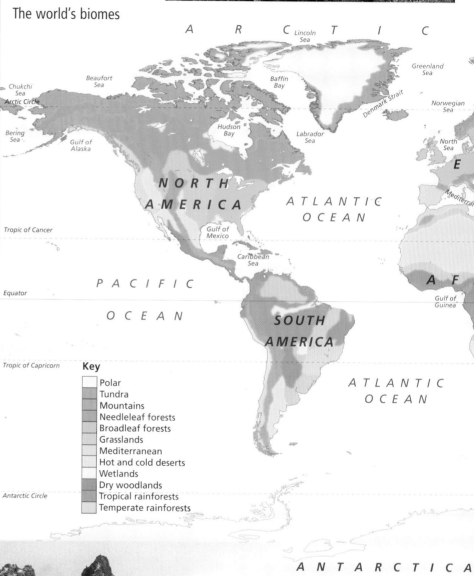

The world's biomes

A R C T I C

Lincoln Sea

Greenland Sea

Chukchi Sea

Beaufort Sea

Baffin Bay

Arctic Circle

Denmark Strait

Norwegian Sea

Bering Sea

Hudson Bay

Labrador Sea

Gulf of Alaska

North Sea

NORTH AMERICA

ATLANTIC OCEAN

E U

Mediterrane

Tropic of Cancer

Gulf of Mexico

Caribbean Sea

A F R

PACIFIC OCEAN

Gulf of Guinea

Equator

SOUTH AMERICA

Tropic of Capricorn

ATLANTIC OCEAN

Key
- Polar
- Tundra
- Mountains
- Needleleaf forests
- Broadleaf forests
- Grasslands
- Mediterranean
- Hot and cold deserts
- Wetlands
- Dry woodlands
- Tropical rainforests
- Temperate rainforests

Antarctic Circle

A N T A R C T I C A

Mountain peaks are hostile environments. The rocky terrain and thin air at high altitudes make it very difficult for plants and animals to survive.

A wealth of species of trees, ferns and creeping plants are found in tropical rainforests. These regions are also home to various animals, which range from snakes and monkeys to sloths, parrots and countless insects.

O C E A N

Kara Sea

Barents Sea

Laptev Sea

East Siberian Sea

Arctic Circle

O P E

Black Sea

Caspian Sea

A S I A

Yellow Sea

Sea of Okhotsk

Sea of Japan

East China Sea

PACIFIC

Tropic of Cancer

Philippine Sea

OCEAN

The Gulf

Red Sea

C A

Arabian Sea

Bay of Bengal

South China Sea

Equator

Mozambique Channel

I N D I A N

Timor Sea

Arafura Sea

Coral Sea

AUSTRALASIA

OCEAN

AND OCEANIA

Tropic of Capricorn

Tasman Sea

O U T H E R N   O C E A N

Antarctic Circle

Temperate and tropical zones

Much of the northern hemisphere was once covered in broadleaf, deciduous trees, but most of them have now been cleared for settlements. Trees and evergreen shrubs, adapted to dry summers, grow in Mediterranean regions and dry woodlands. The world's major grasslands are found in the centre of the larger continents. These regions are grazed by herbivores, such as bison and zebras. Wetlands are rich feeding grounds for fish and breeding grounds for birds. With plenty of rain and sunshine, the rainforests have the greatest variety of species on Earth.

Biodiversity

The number of plant and animal species, and the variety within each species, make up the Earth's biodiversity. Some plants and animals, such as the kangaroos in Australia, are endemic (found only in one region). Man-made environments, including cities and farms, ruin natural habitats and threaten plant and animal biodiversity. Increasing efforts are now being made to conserve the Earth's wild places.

The grasslands of Africa, with trees dotted here and there, are broad, open habitats where herds of grazing animals range free, while looking out for carnivores such as leopards and lions.

Isolated places have the greatest range of endemic species. Lemurs (above) are only found in Madagascar and Comoros.

The planet's oceans have a huge variety of different species, from enormous whales to the tiniest plankton.

THE HUMAN WORLD

There have been people on planet Earth for over 130,000 years. Humans first evolved in Africa, and they gradually spread across the world. They probably travelled in search of food, either following herds of animals, or looking for fruit. By about 10,000 years ago, people had reached most parts of the globe, and some had started to settle down. Today, there are about six billion people in the world, but they are not distributed evenly. Some areas, including China, India and Europe, are densely populated, while others are not.

Feeding the world

Humans have developed skills to help them survive, and these have had an impact on the Earth. One of the earliest skills was farming. In different parts of the world, people worked out how to raise animals. They also learned how to cultivate crops that grew well in the local environment – from rice in eastern Asia to wheat in North America. Today, almost two-fifths of the planet's land is farmed. Through fishing, we have also changed the oceans. A modern fishing ship can catch entire shoals of fish in one go and some species, such as cod, have suffered badly as a result. Agreements have now been made to reduce the numbers of fish caught, to allow stocks to recover.

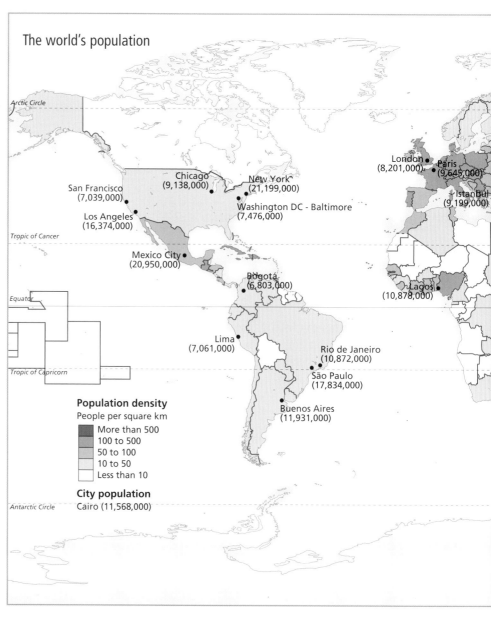

The world's population

London (8,201,000)
Paris (9,645,000)
Istanbul (9,199,000)
Chicago (9,138,000)
New York (21,199,000)
San Francisco (7,039,000)
Washington DC - Baltimore (7,476,000)
Los Angeles (16,374,000)
Mexico City (20,950,000)
Bogotá (6,803,000)
Lagos (10,878,000)
Lima (7,061,000)
Rio de Janeiro (10,872,000)
São Paulo (17,834,000)
Buenos Aires (11,931,000)

Arctic Circle
Tropic of Cancer
Equator
Tropic of Capricorn
Antarctic Circle

Population density
People per square km
More than 500
100 to 500
50 to 100
10 to 50
Less than 10

City population
Cairo (11,568,000)

The staple diet of half the world's people, rice has been cultivated for more than 5,000 years. Asia grows 91 per cent of the world's rice.

Traditional fishing methods, shown left, catch enough fish for the local market. But in some places, modern trawlers bring in vast quantities of fish. The catch is usually sold to factories, where it is processed for export.

In 1500, the world's population was about 425 million

In 1600, the world's population was about 545 million

In 1700, the world's population was about 610 million

1500
1600
1700

Cities, such as Tokyo (right), have many amenities, but some are also home to shanty towns (far right) where the very poor live with little or no services.

Moscow
(9,107,000)

Tehran
(8,650,000)

Beijing
(7,336,000)

Seoul
(14,250,000)

ire
(,568,000)

Delhi
(12,791,000)

Chongqing
(6,609,000)

Tokyo (29,950,000)

Osaka (14,190,000)

Karachi
(9,270,000)

Dhaka (11,726,000)

Shanghai
(9,537,000)

Tropic of Cancer

Kolkata (Calcutta)
(13,217,000)

Hong Kong
(6,930,000)

Mumbai
(Bombay)
(16,368,000)

Chennai
(Madras)
(6,425,000)

Bangkok
(7,642,000)

Manila
(10,492,000)

Equator

Jakarta
(12,435,000)

hannesburg
964,000)

Tropic of Capricorn

Antarctic Circle

Rushing to the cities

By 2007, half of the world's population will live in urban environments. This figure is expected to rise to 60 per cent of the total population by 2030. In many developing countries, cities are growing two or three times faster than the overall population. The world's cities are centres of government, education, industry and trade, but they also have problems, including crime, poverty and pollution.

World population growth

In 2000, the world's population was about 6.3 billion

In 1950, the world's population was about 2.5 billion

In 1900, the world's population was about 1.6 billion

8 billion

7 billion

6 billion

5 billion

4 billion

3 billion

2 billion

1 billion

The population explosion

In the second half of the 20th century, death rates in the developing countries of Africa, Asia and Latin America halved, particularly amongst children. This was due to improved public sanitation, better personal hygiene, and advances in medicine. Birth rates, however, did not decrease at the same rate, so there was a rapid rise in the population. By the year 2020, the number of people in the world is likely to reach about 8.6 billion.

In 1800, the world's population was about 900 million

1800

1900

2000

THE PHYSICAL WORLD

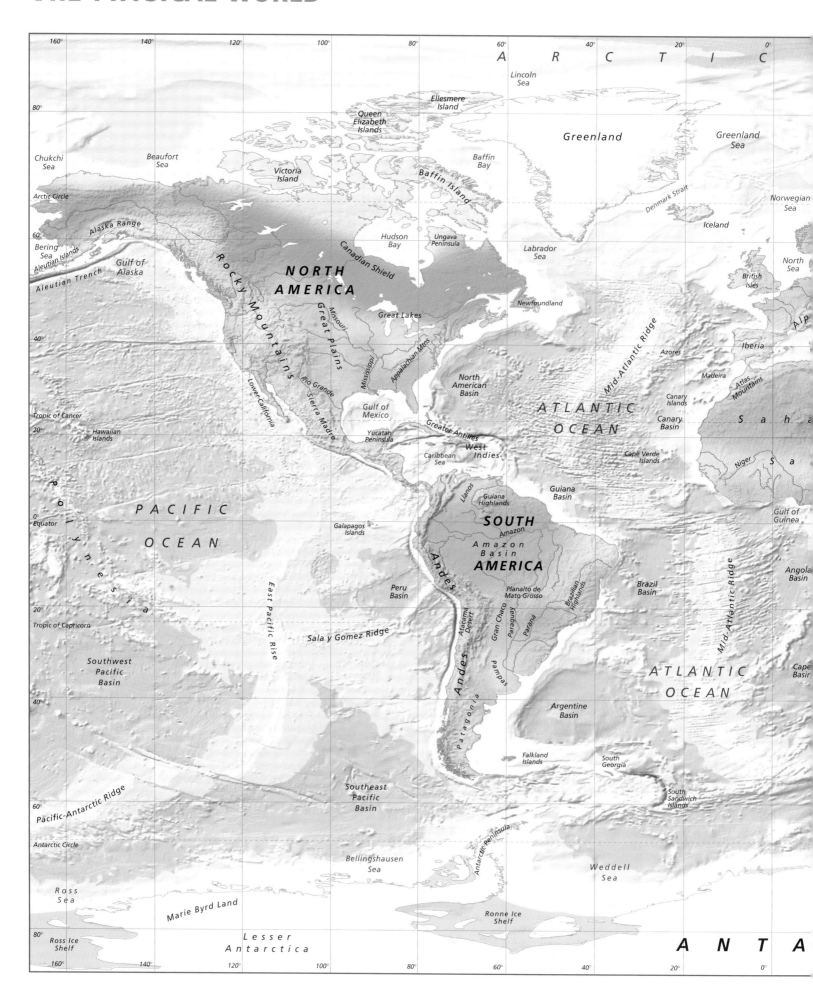

ARCTIC

Lincoln
Sea

Ellesmere
Island

Queen
Elizabeth
Islands

Greenland

Greenland
Sea

Chukchi
Sea

Beaufort
Sea

Baffin
Bay

Victoria
Island

Baffin Island

Arctic Circle

Denmark Strait

Norwegian
Sea

Iceland

Alaska Range

Hudson
Bay

Ungava
Peninsula

Labrador
Sea

North
Sea

Bering
Sea

Aleutian Islands

Gulf of
Alaska

Canadian Shield

British
Isles

Aleutian Trench

NORTH
AMERICA

Newfoundland

Alp

Rocky Mountains

Great Plains

Missouri

Great Lakes

Mississippi

Appalachian Mtns

North
American
Basin

Mid-Atlantic Ridge

Azores

Iberia

Madeira

Atlas
Mountains

Lower California

Rio Grande

Sierra Madre

North
American
Basin

ATLANTIC

OCEAN

Canary
Islands

S a h a

Tropic of Cancer

Gulf of
Mexico

Canary
Basin

Hawaiian
Islands

Yucatan
Peninsula

Greater Antilles

West
Indies

Cape Verde
Islands

Niger

S a

Caribbean
Sea

Galapagos
Islands

Llanos

Guiana
Highlands

Guiana
Basin

Gulf of
Guinea

PACIFIC

OCEAN

SOUTH

Amazon

AMERICA

A m a z o n

B a s i n

Andes

Peru
Basin

Planalto de
Mato Grosso

Brazilian
Highlands

Brazil
Basin

Angola
Basin

P o l y n e s i a

East Pacific Rise

Atacama
Desert

Gran Chaco

Paraguay

Paraná

Tropic of Capricorn

Sala y Gomez Ridge

Pampas

Mid-Atlantic Ridge

Southwest
Pacific
Basin

Andes

Argentine
Basin

ATLANTIC

OCEAN

Cape
Basin

Patagonia

Southeast
Pacific
Basin

Falkland
Islands

South
Georgia

South
Sandwich
Islands

Pacific-Antarctic Ridge

Antarctic Circle

Antarctic Peninsula

Bellingshausen
Sea

Weddell
Sea

Ross
Sea

Marie Byrd Land

Ronne Ice
Shelf

Ross Ice
Shelf

L e s s e r
A n t a r c t i c a

A N T A

160° 140° 120° 100° 80° 60° 40° 20° 0°

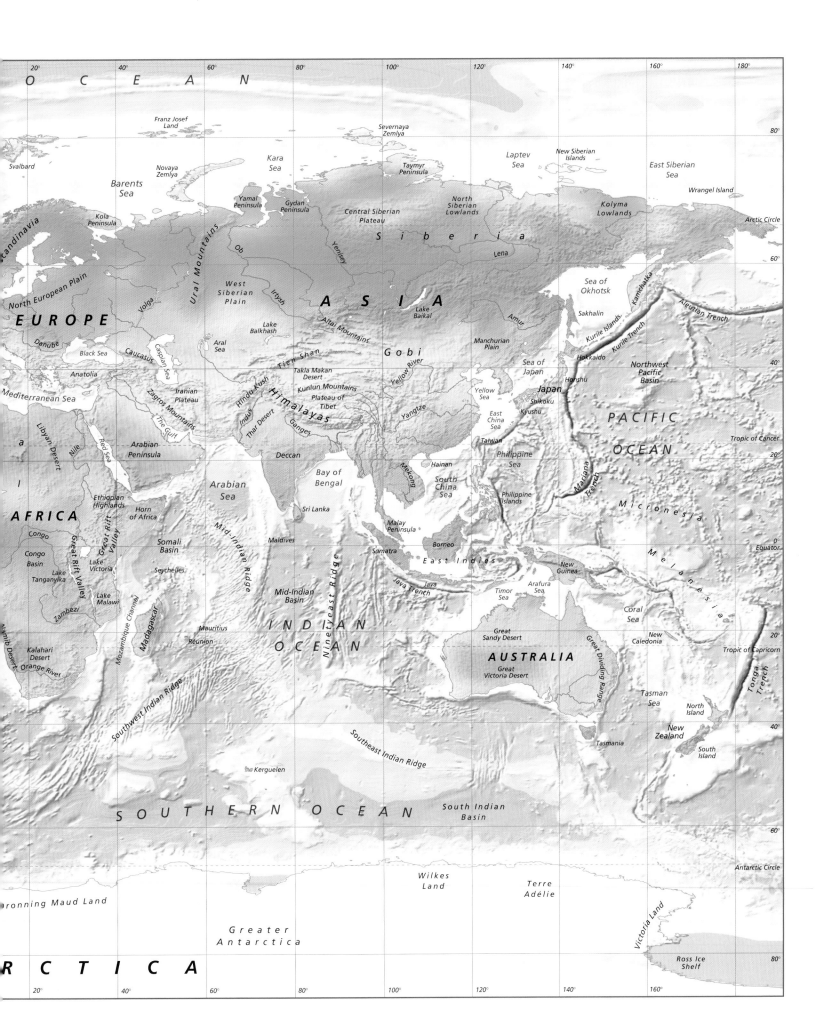

O C E A N

20° 40° 60° 80° 100° 120° 140° 160° 180°

80°

Svalbard

Franz Josef
Land

Kara
Sea

Severnaya
Zemlya

Taymyr
Peninsula

Laptev
Sea

New Siberian
Islands

East Siberian
Sea

Wrangel Island

Scandinavia

Barents
Sea

Novaya
Zemlya

Kola
Peninsula

Yamal
Peninsula

Gydan
Peninsula

Central Siberian
Plateau

North
Siberian
Lowlands

Kolyma
Lowlands

Arctic Circle

60°

North European Plain

Ural Mountains

Ob

Yenisey

S i b e r i a

Lena

Amur

Sea of
Okhotsk

Kamchatka

Aleutian Trench

EUROPE

Volga

West
Siberian
Plain

Irtysh

A S I A

Lake
Baikal

Sakhalin

Kurile Islands

Kurile Trench

Hokkaido

Northwest
Pacific
Basin

40°

Danube

Black Sea

Caucasus

Caspian Sea

Lake
Balkhash

Aral
Sea

Altai Mountains

Gobi

Yellow River

Sea of
Japan

Honshu

Japan

PACIFIC

Anatolia

Tien Shan

Yangtze

Shikoku

Kyushu

Mediterranean Sea

Iranian
Plateau

Hindu Kush

Takla Makan
Desert

Kunlun Mountains

Plateau of
Tibet

Yellow
Sea

East China
Sea

OCEAN

Zagros Mountains

Himalayas

Indus

Taiwan

Tropic of Cancer

20°

Libyan Desert

Red Sea

Nile

The Gulf

Arabian
Peninsula

Thar Desert

Ganges

Deccan

Bay of
Bengal

Mekong

Hainan

South
China
Sea

Philippine
Sea

Mariana Trench

M i c r o n e s i a

AFRICA

Ethiopian
Highlands

Horn
of Africa

Arabian
Sea

Sri Lanka

Philippine
Islands

Congo

Great Rift Valley

Somali
Basin

Maldives

Sumatra

Borneo

East Indies

M e l a n e s i a

0°
Equator

Congo
Basin

Lake
Victoria

Seychelles

Mid-Indian Ridge

Ninetyeast Ridge

Java Trench

Java

New
Guinea

Lake
Tanganyika

Malay
Peninsula

Timor
Sea

Arafura
Sea

Coral
Sea

Lake
Malawi

Mid-Indian
Basin

New
Caledonia

20°

Zambezi

Mozambique Channel

Madagascar

Mauritius

Réunion

I N D I A N
OCEAN

Great
Sandy Desert

Tropic of Capricorn

Namib Desert

Kalahari
Desert

Orange River

AUSTRALIA

Great
Victoria Desert

Great Dividing Range

Tasman
Sea

North
Island

New
Zealand

Tonga Trench

Southwest Indian Ridge

Southeast Indian Ridge

Tasmania

South
Island

40°

Kerguelen

S O U T H E R N   O C E A N

South Indian
Basin

60°

Antarctic Circle

Dronning Maud Land

Wilkes
Land

Terre
Adélie

Victoria Land

Greater
Antarctica

Ross Ice
Shelf

80°

R C T I C A

20° 40° 60° 80° 100° 120° 140° 160°

THE POLITICAL WORLD

Abbreviations
B&H   - BOSNIA & HERZEGOVINA
CRO.   - CROATIA
LIE.   - LIECHTENSTEIN
LUX.   - LUXEMBOURG
MAC.   - MACEDONIA
RUSS. FED. - RUSSIAN FEDERATION
SAN.   - SAN MARINO
SWITZ.   - SWITZERLAND
SERB. & MONT. - SERBIA & MONTENEGRO

A R C T I C

Greenland
(to Denmark)

Jan Mayen
(to Norway)

ICELAND

Faeroe Islands
(to Denmark)

Arctic Circle

UNITED STATES
OF AMERICA
(ALASKA)

C A N A D A

ATLANTIC

OCEAN

UNITED
KINGDOM   DENMARK

REPUBLIC OF   Isle
IRELAND   of Man   NETHERLANDS
            (to UK)   BELGIUM
Channel Islands   LUX.
(to UK)   LIE.
                        SWITZ.
FRANCE

MONACO

St Pierre &
Miquelon
(to France)

ANDORRA

PORTUGAL   SPAIN

Gibraltar
(to UK)

Azores
(to Portugal)   Madeira
                    (to Portugal)   MOROCCO

ALGERIA

UNITED STATES
OF AMERICA

Bermuda
(to UK)

Canary Islands
(to Spain)

WESTERN
SAHARA
(occupied by Morocco)

Tropic of Cancer

MEXICO

BAHAMAS

CUBA

Turks &
Caicos Is. (to UK)
Navassa
Island
(to US)
Cayman Is.
(to UK)

Virgin Is.
(to US)   British
Virgin Is. (to UK)

Anguilla (to UK)
Montserrat (to UK)
ANTIGUA & BARBUDA
Guadeloupe (to France)
DOMINICA

MAURITANIA   MALI

Hawaiian Islands
(to US)

Johnston Atoll
(to US)

DOMINICAN
REPUBLIC   Puerto Rico
           (to US)

HAITI

BELIZE

JAMAICA

CAPE VERDE

GUATEMALA   HONDURAS
EL SALVADOR

ST KITTS
& NEVIS
Netherlands
Antilles (to Neth.)
Aruba
(to Neth.)

ST LUCIA
Martinique (to France)

BARBADOS
ST VINCENT & THE GRENADINES
GRENADA
TRINIDAD & TOBAGO

SENEGAL

GAMBIA
GUINEA-BISSAU   GUINEA

SIERRA LEONE

BURKINA

IVORY
COAST   GHANA

BENIN

NIGERIA

TOGO

NICARAGUA

LIBERIA

EQUATORIAL GUINEA

Kingman Reef (to US)
Palmyra Atoll (to US)

Clipperton Island
(to France)

COSTA
RICA   PANAMA

VENEZUELA

French
Guiana
(to France)

SÃO TOMÉ
& PRÍNCIPE

P A C I F I C

Jarvis Island
(to US)

GUYANA

COLOMBIA

SURINAM

Equator

KIRIBATI

O C E A N

Galapagos Islands
(to Ecuador)

ECUADOR

Ascension
Island
(to St Helena)

American
Samoa
(to US)

Cook
Islands
(to NZ)

B R A Z I L

PERU

St Helena
(to UK)

Niue
(to NZ)

French Polynesia
(to France)

BOLIVIA

Tropic of Capricorn

Pitcairn Islands
(to UK)

PARAGUAY

ATLANTIC

Easter Island
(to Chile)

OCEAN

Juan
Fernández Islands
(to Chile)

URUGUAY

Tristan da Cunha
(to St Helena)

Gough Island
(to Tristan da Cunha)

Falkland Islands
(to UK)

South Georgia
(to UK)

Bouvet Island
(to Norway)

South Sandwich Islands
(to UK)

Antarctic Circle

S O U T H

Peter I
Island
(to Norway)

A N T A R C T I C A

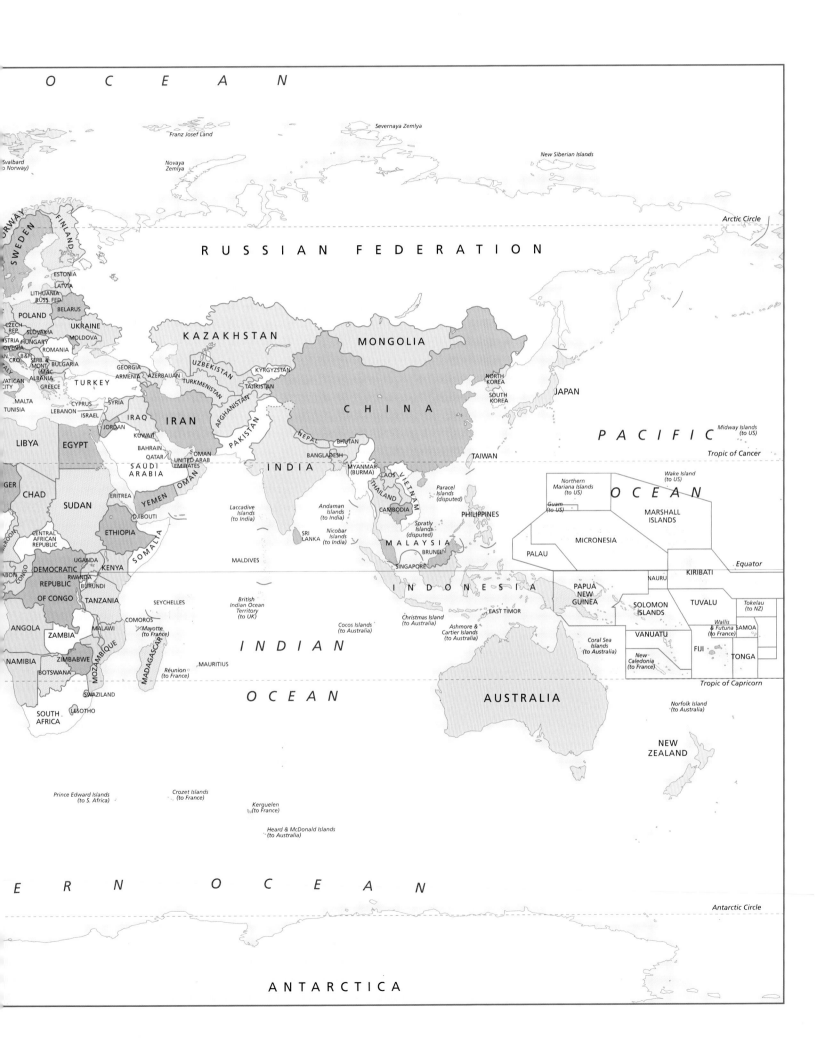

O C E A N

Franz Josef Land

Severnaya Zemlya

New Siberian Islands

Novaya Zemlya

Svalbard (to Norway)

Arctic Circle

R U S S I A N   F E D E R A T I O N

SWEDEN
FINLAND
NORWAY

ESTONIA
LATVIA
LITHUANIA
RUSS. FED.
BELARUS
POLAND
CZECH REP
SLOVAKIA
UKRAINE
MOLDOVA
AUSTRIA
HUNGARY
ROMANIA
SLOVENIA
CRO.
B&H.
SERB. & MONT.
MAC.
BULGARIA
ALBANIA
GREECE
ITALY
VATICAN CITY
MALTA
TUNISIA
CYPRUS
LEBANON
ISRAEL
SYRIA

GEORGIA
ARMENIA
AZERBAIJAN

KAZAKHSTAN

MONGOLIA

UZBEKISTAN
KYRGYZSTAN
TURKMENISTAN
TAJIKISTAN

NORTH KOREA
SOUTH KOREA

JAPAN

TURKEY
IRAQ
IRAN
AFGHANISTAN
PAKISTAN

JORDAN
KUWAIT
BAHRAIN
QATAR
UNITED ARAB EMIRATES
OMAN

SAUDI ARABIA

NEPAL
BHUTAN

BANGLADESH

CHINA

TAIWAN

P A C I F I C

Midway Islands (to US)

Tropic of Cancer

LIBYA
EGYPT

NIGER
CHAD
SUDAN

ERITREA
DJIBOUTI
YEMEN
OMAN

Wake Island (to US)

INDIA

MYANMAR (BURMA)
LAOS
VIETNAM
THAILAND

Paracel Islands (disputed)

O C E A N

Northern Mariana Islands (to US)

Guam (to US)

MARSHALL ISLANDS

CENTRAL AFRICAN REPUBLIC
ETHIOPIA
SOMALIA

CAMBODIA

Laccadive Islands (to India)

Andaman Islands (to India)

SRI LANKA

Nicobar Islands (to India)

Spratly Islands (disputed)

PHILIPPINES

MALAYSIA

BRUNEI

MICRONESIA

PALAU

CAMEROON
UGANDA
KENYA
RWANDA
BURUNDI
GABON
CONGO
DEMOCRATIC REPUBLIC OF CONGO
TANZANIA

MALDIVES

SINGAPORE

KIRIBATI

Equator

NAURU

SEYCHELLES

British Indian Ocean Territory (to UK)

I N D O N E S I A

PAPUA NEW GUINEA

SOLOMON ISLANDS

TUVALU

Tokelau (to NZ)

ANGOLA
ZAMBIA
MALAWI
COMOROS
Mayotte (to France)

EAST TIMOR

Christmas Island (to Australia)

Cocos Islands (to Australia)

Ashmore & Cartier Islands (to Australia)

Coral Sea Islands (to Australia)

VANUATU

New Caledonia (to France)

Wallis & Futuna (to France)

SAMOA

FIJI

TONGA

NAMIBIA
BOTSWANA
ZIMBABWE
MOZAMBIQUE
MADAGASCAR

Réunion (to France)

Mauritius

I N D I A N

SWAZILAND
LESOTHO
SOUTH AFRICA

O C E A N

A U S T R A L I A

Norfolk Island (to Australia)

NEW ZEALAND

Prince Edward Islands (to S. Africa)

Crozet Islands (to France)

Kerguelen (to France)

Heard & McDonald Islands (to Australia)

E R N   O C E A N

Antarctic Circle

A N T A R C T I C A

THE ARCTIC OCEAN

The Poles, at the Earth's northern and southern tips, are the planet's coldest places, where temperatures can fall as low as –80°C in winter. At the North Pole is the Arctic Ocean. With an area of 15,100,000 sq km, it is the smallest ocean on the planet. The Arctic is made up of two large basins divided by three underwater ridges, the greatest of which is the Lomonosov Ridge. Its waters are mainly covered with pack ice. When this ice breaks up, it forms enormous blocks of floating ice, called icebergs. The Arctic is fringed by the northernmost parts of North America, the Russian Federation and Europe.

Despite the region's harsh climate, it has been inhabited for thousands of years by people such as the European Lapps, the Russian Nenet and North American Inuit.

These peoples make their living from herding, hunting and fishing. There are stocks of cod, plaice and haddock in the unfrozen Arctic waters, but numbers have fallen over the years. Now there are restrictions on the amount of fish that people can take from the ocean. The peoples of the Arctic region must import foods, such as grains and vegetables, from elsewhere.

The Arctic is rich in oil, gas and coal, but because of the bitterly cold climate and severe landscape, extracting these resources is difficult and expensive. There are mines and wells in the coastal regions, but these cause pollution and threaten the area's unique wildlife. These industries have also damaged the traditional lifestyles of many of the Arctic region's native peoples.

ANTARCTICA

Antarctica, at the Earth's southern tip, is the planet's coldest and smallest continent. It is a frozen world where the land lies beneath a thick layer of ice. Nearly half of the Antarctic coastline is surrounded by ice shelves, which float on the sea. There are two distinct parts to Antarctica. Lesser Antarctica is a series of ice-covered, mountainous islands, which are joined together by ice. Greater Antarctica is a high plateau.

No people live permanently in Antarctica, but teams of scientists visit this region of environmental importance, and stay in research stations for months at a time. These scientists observe the region's wildlife and even study the ice itself. By analyzing chemicals in the ice they can find out how the Earth's atmosphere has changed over the years. Antarctica is governed by Argentina, Brazil, Chile, the United Kingdom, Norway, France, Australia and New Zealand. All these countries have agreed that the continent should only be used for peaceful work.

Colonies of penguins breed along the continent's coastal regions, and there are whales, seals and many fish species living in the surrounding waters. Antarctica has rich mineral reserves, such as gold, iron and coal, and there is natural gas in the seas. The harsh conditions in the region mean that the mining of these resources is too costly and difficult. Each year, between 2,000 and 3,000 tourists visit the Antarctic region. They come to view the unique wildlife and dramatic landscape from the decks of cruise liners.

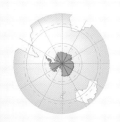

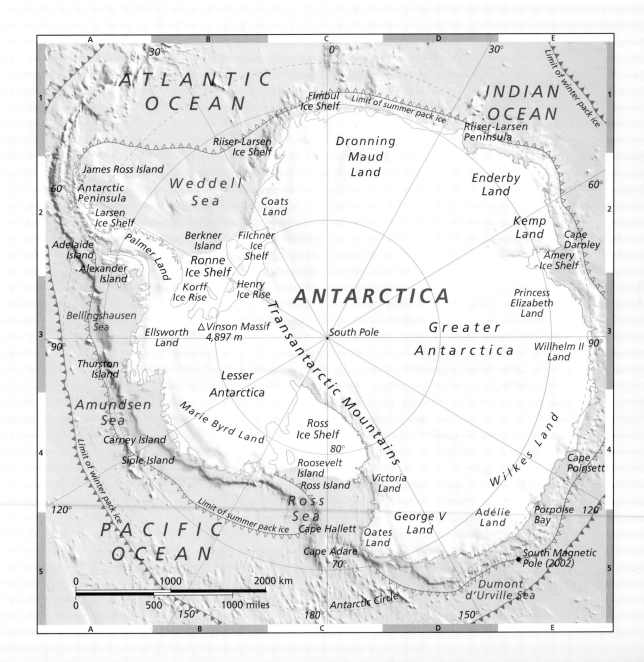

NORTH AMERICA

The continent of North America is shaped like a triangle, stretching from the frozen Arctic in the north to the tropics in the south. In the north, there are two huge countries, Canada and the USA. Smaller countries lie in the south and in the Caribbean Sea. The northern part of the continent has many different types of landscapes. The towering Rocky Mountains to the west give way to the Great Plains, where fertile soils help farmers to grow millions of hectares of crops. To the east are the vast Great Lakes, major rivers such as the Mississippi, and the lower mountains of

the Appalachians. Further south, the Rocky Mountains continue into Mexico and southern North America, where they are called the Sierra Madre. This region also contains high plateaux and low-lying tropical forests, lagoons and mangrove swamps.

North America has a variety of climates, from the frozen wastes and pine forests of northern Canada to the baking deserts of Arizona and Mexico. Areas like these can support few people, but the northeast and west coasts are more densely populated, and North America

is home to some of the world's biggest cities – New York, Los Angeles, Chicago and Mexico City.

Politically, there is a marked difference between northern and southern North America. The USA and Canada have stable administrations in which the central government shares power with the individual states and provinces. The nations of southern North America have been less peaceful, and dictators ruled some countries, such as Nicaragua and Haiti, for many years.

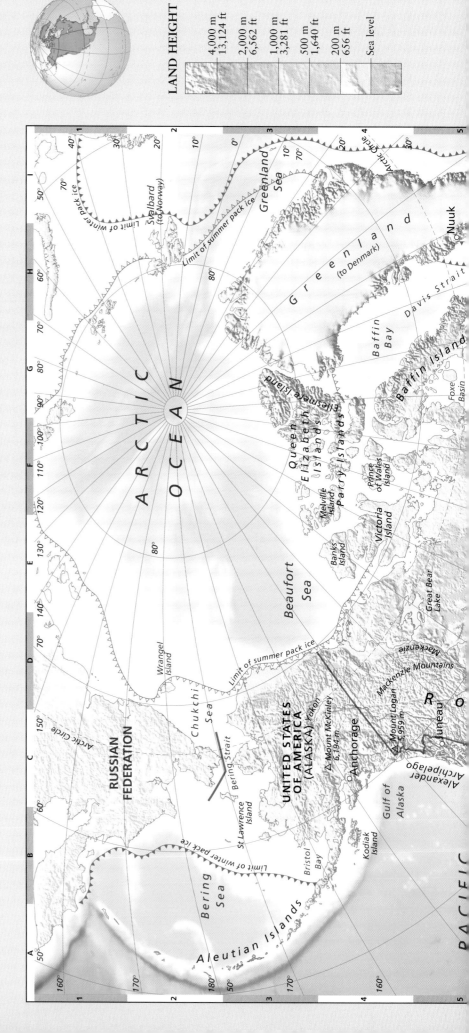

LAND HEIGHT

4,000 m	13,124 ft
2,000 m	6,562 ft
1,000 m	3,281 ft
500 m	1,640 ft
200 m	656 ft
	Sea level

PACIFIC OCEAN

ATLANTIC OCEAN

C A N A D A

UNITED STATES OF AMERICA

MEXICO

SOUTH AMERICA

Labrador Sea

Cape Farewell

Limit of winter pack ice

Labrador

Cape Chidley

Ungava Peninsula

Hudson Strait

Newfoundland

St Pierre & Miquelon (to France)

Cape Breton Island

Gulf of St Lawrence

Halifax

Boston
Cape Cod
Long Island
New York
Philadelphia
Baltimore
WASHINGTON D.C.

Montréal
Québec
OTTAWA
Toronto
Lake Ontario
Lake Erie
Cleveland

St Lawrence

Laurentian Highlands

Smallwood Reservoir

Belcher Islands

James Bay

Hudson Bay

Great Slave Lake

Reindeer Lake

Lake Athabasca

Lake Winnipeg

Lake Nipigon

Lake Superior

Lake Huron

Lake Michigan

Great Lakes

Appalachian Mountains

Charlotte
Columbia
Atlanta
Jacksonville

Cape Hatteras

Columbus
Detroit
Indianapolis
St Louis
Nashville
Memphis

Chicago
Milwaukee
St Paul
Minneapolis

Winnipeg
Saskatoon
Edmonton
Calgary

Great Plains

Missouri

Missouri

Arkansas

Kansas City
Oklahoma City
Fort Worth
Dallas
Austin
San Antonio
Houston

Baton Rouge
New Orleans
Jackson

Mississippi
Mississippi Delta

Gulf of Mexico

Tampa
Miami
The Everglades
Straits of Florida

BAHAMAS
NASSAU

Turks & Caicos Islands (to UK)

Bermuda (to UK)

West Indies

CUBA
HAVANA

Cayman Islands (to UK)

Caribbean Sea

HAITI
DOMINICAN REPUBLIC
PORT-AU-PRINCE
SANTO DOMINGO
Puerto Rico (to US)

JAMAICA
KINGSTON

Greater Antilles

Lesser Antilles

Netherlands Antilles (to Netherlands)
Aruba (to Netherlands)

TRINIDAD & TOBAGO

PANAMA CITY
PANAMA
COSTA RICA
SAN JOSE
NICARAGUA
MANAGUA
Lake Nicaragua
HONDURAS
TEGUCIGALPA
EL SALVADOR
SAN SALVADOR
GUATEMALA
GUATEMALA CITY
BELIZE
BELMOPAN

Yucatan Peninsula

MEXICO CITY
Popocatépetl 5,452 m
Pico de Orizaba 5,700 m

Acapulco
Leon
Guadalajara
Sierra Madre del Sur
Sierra Madre Oriental
Sierra Madre Occidental

Monterrey
Rio Grande
San Antonio

Hermosillo
Ciudad Juarez
El Paso
Phoenix
Las Vegas
Grand Canyon

Colorado Plateau
Colorado

Death Valley -86 m
Mount Whitney 4,418 m
Great Basin
Great Salt Lake

Denver

Rocky Mountains

Mount Rainier 4,392 m
Columbia

Seattle
Portland
Vancouver
Vancouver Island
Coast Mountains

San Francisco
San Jose
Los Angeles
San Diego
Coast Ranges

Gulf of California
Lower California

Saskatchewan
Saskatoon

Peace

Queen Charlotte Islands

Tropic of Cancer

Equator

1. ST KITTS & NEVIS
2. ANTIGUA & BARBUDA
3. DOMINICA
4. ST LUCIA
5. BARBADOS
6. ST VINCENT & THE GRENADINES
7. GRENADA

2000 km
1000 miles
1000
500
0

40°
50°
50°
40°
30°
20°

60°
70°
80°
90°
100°
110°
120°
130°
140°

10°

Tropic of Cancer

CANADA

The second-largest country in the world, Canada covers a vast area just north of the USA. This nation has quite a small population of just over 30 million, most of whom live in the south. Some of the people are Native Americans, members of tribes such as the Inuit, Algonquin and Cree. Others are descendants of the Europeans who settled here from the 16th century onwards, especially the French and British.

The landscape of Canada varies greatly. There are mountains in the west and east, and between these two regions is the Canadian Shield. This is a vast area of ancient rocks, low hills, thousands of lakes and huge tracts of forest. In the north, the Arctic regions are cold all year round, and the areas of tundra experience only a slight rise in temperature during summer. Further south, where most of the cities lie, the climate is a little warmer, although winter in many places is long, cold and snowy.

Canadians work in all sorts of businesses, from mining and farming to high-tech industries. The country is rich in minerals such as zinc and iron ore, and it has huge reserves of oil, coal and natural gas. There are good fishing waters off the east and west coasts, and large areas of forest make Canada the world's biggest exporter of timber products. Wheat, which grows well on fertile plains just west of the Canadian Shield, is exported to many countries.

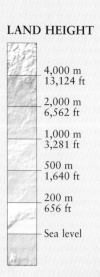

LAND HEIGHT

4,000 m	13,124 ft
2,000 m	6,562 ft
1,000 m	3,281 ft
500 m	1,640 ft
200 m	656 ft
Sea level	

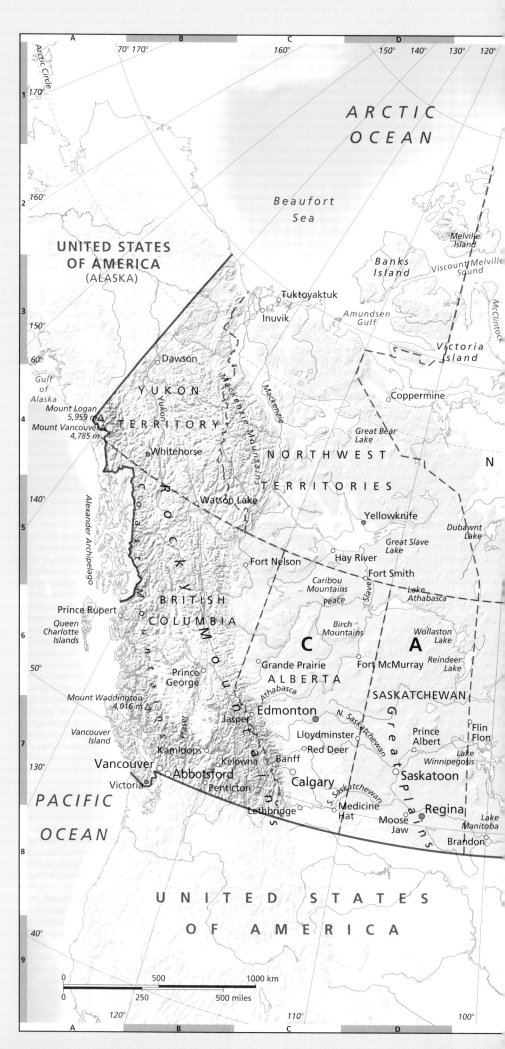

Canada

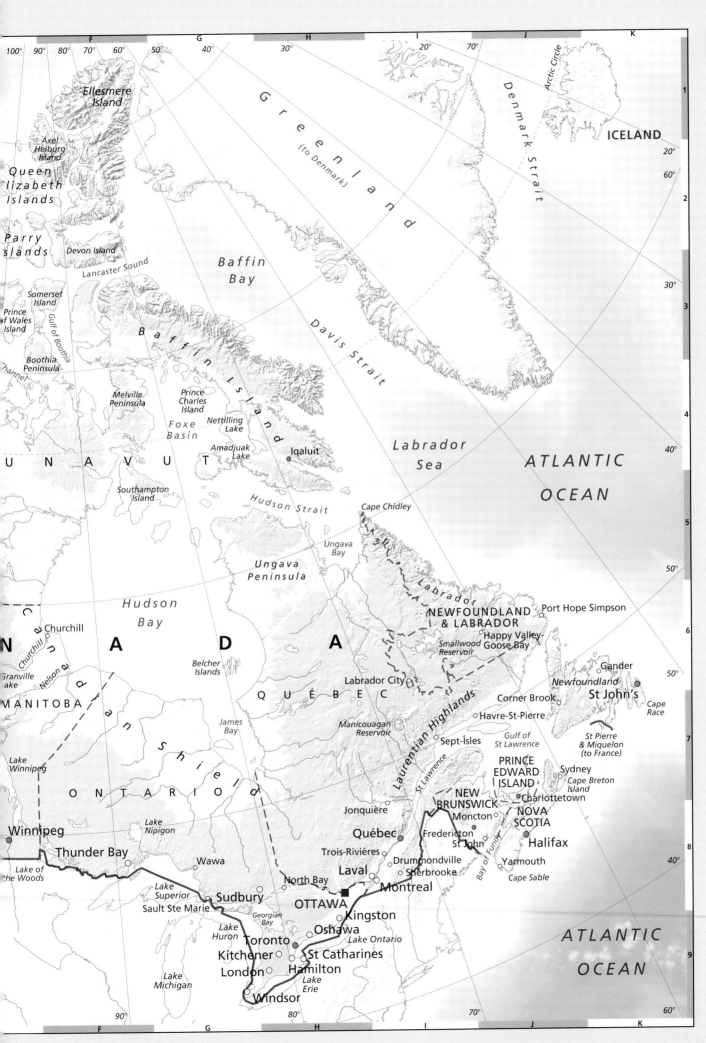

F 100° 90° 80° 70° 60° G 50° 40° H 30° I 20° 70° J K

1

Ellesmere
Island

*Axel
Heiburg
Island*

*Queen
Elizabeth
Islands*

Arctic Circle

Denmark Strait

ICELAND

20°

60°

2

*Parry
Islands*

Devon Island

Lancaster Sound

G r e e n l a n d

(to Denmark)

30°

*Somerset
Island*

*Prince
f Wales
Island*

Gulf of Boothia

*Baffin
Bay*

3

*Boothia
Peninsula*

Channel

B a f f i n   I s l a n d

Davis Strait

*Melville
Peninsula*

*Prince
Charles
Island*

*Foxe
Basin*

*Nettilling
Lake*

40°

4

N   U   N   A   V   U   T

*Amadjuak
Lake*

Iqaluit

*Labrador
Sea*

ATLANTIC

40°

*Southampton
Island*

Hudson Strait

Cape Chidley

OCEAN

5

*Ungava
Bay*

50°

*Ungava
Peninsula*

*Hudson
Bay*

Labrador

Port Hope Simpson

6

Churchill

Churchill

Nelson

*Belcher
Islands*

**NEWFOUNDLAND
& LABRADOR**

Happy Valley-
Goose Bay

*Smallwood
Reservoir*

*Granville
ake*

MANITOBA

C   a   n   a   d   i   a   n   S   h   i   e   l   d

Q   U   É   B   E   C

Labrador City

Gander

Newfoundland

St John's

50°

*James
Bay*

*Manicouagan
Reservoir*

Corner Brook

*Cape
Race*

7

*Lake
Winnipeg*

O   N   T   A   R   I   O

Laurentian Highlands

Havre-St-Pierre

Sept-Îles

*Gulf of
St Lawrence*

*St Pierre
& Miquelon
(to France)*

St Lawrence

**PRINCE
EDWARD
ISLAND**

Sydney

*Cape Breton
Island*

Winnipeg

*Lake
Nipigon*

Jonquière

**NEW
BRUNSWICK**

Moncton

Charlottetown

**NOVA
SCOTIA**

40°

8

Thunder Bay

Québec

Fredericton

St John

Halifax

*Lake of
the Woods*

Lake Superior

Wawa

Trois-Rivières

Drummondville

Bay of Fundy

Yarmouth

North Bay

Laval

Sherbrooke

Cape Sable

Sudbury

Montreal

ATLANTIC

Sault Ste Marie

OTTAWA

Kingston

*Georgian
Bay*

*Lake
Huron*

Oshawa

OCEAN

9

Toronto

Lake Ontario

Kitchener

St Catharines

London

Hamilton

*Lake
Michigan*

*Lake
Erie*

Windsor

60°

90°

80°

70°

F G 80° H I J K

WESTERN UNITED STATES

The western states have some of the most dramatic scenery in the USA. All of these states are partly mountainous, and much of the region is arid. In the west, the Central Valley separates the Sierra Nevada mountains from California's Coast Ranges. The area east of the Sierra Nevada contains mountain ranges, river basins, deserts and salt lakes. Off the southwest coast is a chain of volcanoes that emerge from the Pacific Ocean as the Hawaiian islands.

A break in the Earth's crust, known as the San Andreas Fault, runs through California. It is the site of frequent earthquakes. Most of the west has dry, hot summers and to the south of the region, the Sonoran Desert and California's Death Valley are two of the hottest places on Earth. In winter, while the Pacific coast is wet and warm, the temperature inland, in states such as Utah and Idaho, drops dramatically.

With large areas of forest, Oregon and Washington are the USA's major timber-producing states. Alaska is rich in oil and natural gas. In other areas farming is important. There are cattle ranches in Nevada, and the heavily irrigated land of California produces half of the USA's fruit and vegetables.

Manufacturing industries, from aircraft building to clothing, employ many people in this region. The western states' best-known products are the computers and other electronic goods that are made in the famous 'Silicon Valley', just south of San Francisco, California. Tourism is another major industry. Some people come to visit the spectacular physical features, such as the Grand Canyon, while others are lured by the sunny beaches of Hawaii and California.

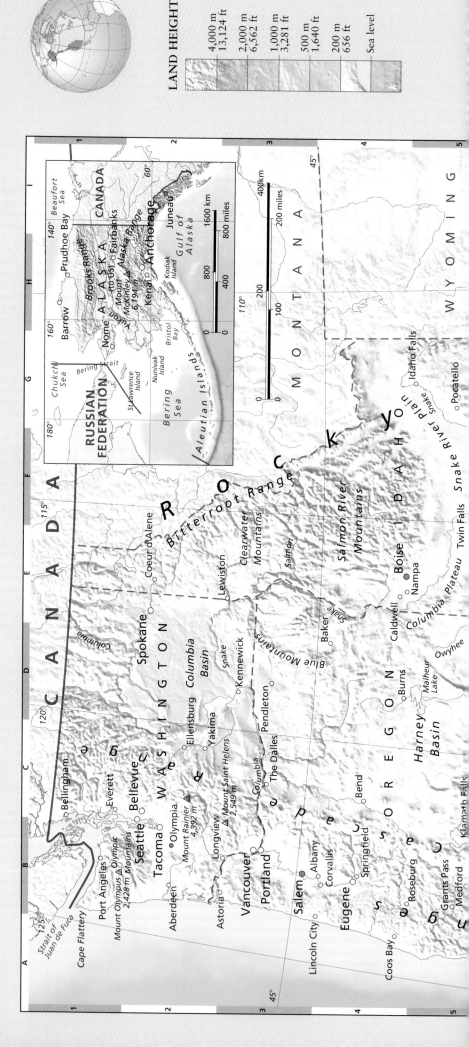

LAND HEIGHT

| 4,000 m / 13,124 ft | 2,000 m / 6,562 ft | 1,000 m / 3,281 ft | 500 m / 1,640 ft | 200 m / 656 ft | Sea level |

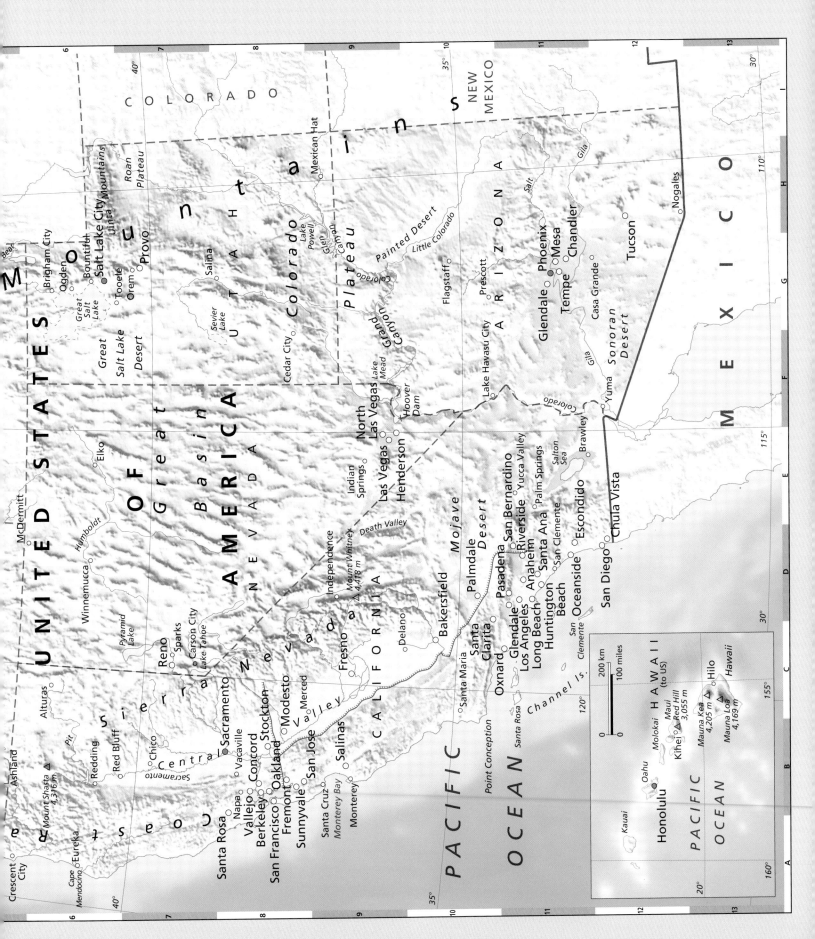

United States
of America

COLORADO

NEW
MEXICO

M O U N T A I N S

U N I T E D   S T A T E S   O F   A M E R I C A

M E X I C O

Mexican Hat

Roan
Plateau

Brigham City
Ogden
Bountiful
Salt Lake City
Tooele
Orem
Provo

Uinta Mountains

Bear

Great
Salt
Lake

Sevier
Lake

U T A H

Great
Salt Lake
Desert

Salina

Cedar City

Colorado

Lake
Powell

Glen
Canyon

Painted Desert

Little Colorado

Colorado

A R I Z O N A

Salt

Gila

Flagstaff

Prescott

Glendale
Phoenix
Mesa
Tempe
Chandler

Casa Grande

Tucson

Nogales

Sonoran
Desert

Gila

Yuma

Colorado

G R E A T   B A S I N

N E V A D A

Elko

Humboldt

McDermitt

Ashland

Alturas

Pit

Redding
Red Bluff

Chico

Winnemucca

Pyramid
Lake

Reno
Sparks
Carson City
Lake Tahoe

S i e r r a   N e v a d a

Independence

Mount Whitney
△ 4,418 m

Death Valley

North
Las Vegas
Las Vegas
Henderson

Lake
Mead

Hoover
Dam

Indian
Springs

Grand
Canyon

C o l o r a d o   P l a t e a u

Mojave
Desert

Salton
Sea

Brawley

Palm Springs
Yucca Valley

Lake Havasu City

San Bernardino
Riverside

Palmdale
Desert

Pasadena
Glendale
Los Angeles
Long Beach
Huntington
Beach

Santa Ana
Anaheim

Escondido
Oceanside

San Clemente

San
Clemente Is.

San Diego
Chula Vista

C A L I F O R N I A

Bakersfield

Delano

Fresno
Merced
Modesto
Stockton

San Jose
Sunnyvale
Fremont
Oakland
Berkeley
San Francisco
Concord
Vallejo
Napa

Sacramento
Vacaville

Santa Rosa

Santa Cruz
Monterey Bay
Monterey

Salinas

Santa
Clarita

Santa Maria

Oxnard

Point Conception

Santa Rosa

Channel Is.

Central
Valley

Sacramento

Crescent
City

Cape
Mendocino
Eureka

Mount Shasta △
4,316 m

C o a s t   R a n g e s

P A C I F I C

O C E A N

P A C I F I C

O C E A N

200 km

100 miles

H A W A I I
(to US)

Kauai

Oahu

Honolulu

Molokai

Maui

Kihei

Red Hill
3,055 m

Mauna Kea
4,205 m △

Mauna Loa
4,169 m △

Hilo

Hawaii

MIDWESTERN UNITED STATES

In the heart of the USA is a large area of land known as the Midwest. To the west, it is bordered by the Rocky Mountains, a huge chain of peaks running all the way from Alaska to New Mexico. Few people live in this rugged landscape, but many of those who do are involved in the mining industry, because the Rockies are rich in coal, natural gas and many metals.

To the east of the Rocky Mountains, much of the Midwest is covered by the Great Plains. These plains were once natural grasslands, where native peoples such as the Crow and Cheyenne hunted buffalo. Today, the plains contain many large cattle ranches and cereal farms. Food processing is a major industry in the cities. Far inland, the plains have quite low rainfall and are hot in summer, so the USA's second-longest river, the Missouri, is a vital source of water for farming. This river is also used to generate electricity and for transporting heavy goods.

Not all of the plains are covered with rich grasslands. In the north are the Badlands. The land here is dry, and few plants and animals can survive in the arid conditions. Storms have washed away the soil to reveal a harsh, stony landscape covered with multi-coloured rocks, such as shales and limestones. This striking terrain makes parts of the Badlands popular with tourists.

LAND HEIGHT

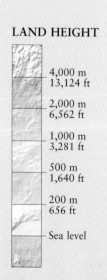

4,000 m
13,124 ft

2,000 m
6,562 ft

1,000 m
3,281 ft

500 m
1,640 ft

200 m
656 ft

Sea level

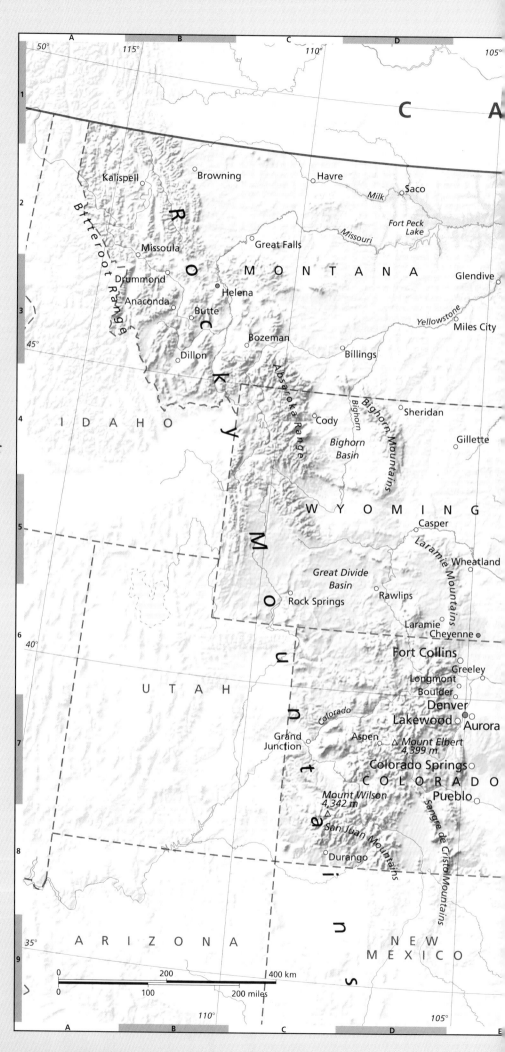

United States
of America

C A N A D A

Williston
Lake Sakakawea
Minot
Sheyenne
Red River
Lake of the Woods
Grand Forks
Bemidji
Hibbing

Dickinson
Missouri
Jamestown
Fargo
Moorhead
MINNESOTA
Duluth

Little Missouri
Badlands
Bismarck
Fergus Falls
Brainerd
Mississippi
Saint Cloud

NORTH DAKOTA

Lake Superior

Grand River
Lake Oahe
Aberdeen
Willmar
Stillwater

SOUTH DAKOTA
Watertown
Minnesota
Minneapolis
Saint Paul
Bloomington
WISCONSIN

Rapid City
Cheyenne
Pierre
New Ulm
Faribault
Winona

UNITED STATES
Mitchell
Fairmont
Rochester
Austin
Mississippi

Pine Ridge
OF
Sioux Falls
Albert Lea

Niobrara
Valentine
Spencer
Mason City
Dubuque

AMERICA
Sioux City
Cedar Falls
Waterloo

Fort Dodge
Des Moines
IOWA
Cedar
Cedar Rapids

Scottsbluff
NEBRASKA
Norfolk
Missouri
Ames
Iowa City
Davenport

North Platte
Columbus
Council Bluffs
Des Moines

North Platte
Omaha
Burlington

Big Springs
Platte
Grand Island
Lincoln
ILLINOIS

South Platte
Sterling
Hastings
Maryville
Kirksville

Republican
Saint Joseph
Mississippi

Colby
Manhattan
Kansas City
Kansas City
Columbia
Saint Charles

Burlington
Hays
Topeka
Independence
Missouri

Cheyenne Wells
Smoky Hill
KANSAS
Overland Park
Jefferson City
Saint Louis

Great Bend
Ottawa
Saint Louis

Garden City
Arkansas
Emporia
MISSOURI

Dodge City
Hutchinson
Wichita
Pittsburg
Springfield
Poplar Bluff

Springfield
Liberal
Arkansas City
Joplin
Ozark Plateau

TEXAS
OKLAHOMA
ARKANSAS
TENNESSEE

MISSISSIPPI

SOUTHERN UNITED STATES

This region of the USA is home to many Native American peoples, such as the Cherokee, Creek and Choctaw. To the south of the area is the large Gulf Coastal Plain. It is drained by many rivers, including the Mississippi, which flows south to a huge swampy delta on the coast of Louisiana. Elsewhere, the landscape ranges from the deserts and mountains of New Mexico to the Everglades, which are southern Florida's swamplands. Further north are uplands, including the Appalachian and Ouachita Mountains. The southern states have a warm climate with mild winters. Summer is generally hot, and the southeastern part of the region can be very humid.

Crops such as peanuts and citrus fruit grow well in the south, while the west contains large cattle ranches and wheat farms. Another typical crop is cotton, which was grown on plantations worked mainly by slaves until the mid-19th century. Many of this region's cities are industrialized, and the states of Texas and Oklahoma are major sources of oil and natural gas. As well as manufacturing and engineering, this area has high-tech computer and aerospace industries. Florida's unique scenery and warm climate make it a favourite tourist destination. People from all over the world come to visit its attractions, including the Everglades National Park.

LAND HEIGHT

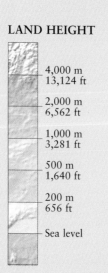

4,000 m
13,124 ft

2,000 m
6,562 ft

1,000 m
3,281 ft

500 m
1,640 ft

200 m
656 ft

Sea level

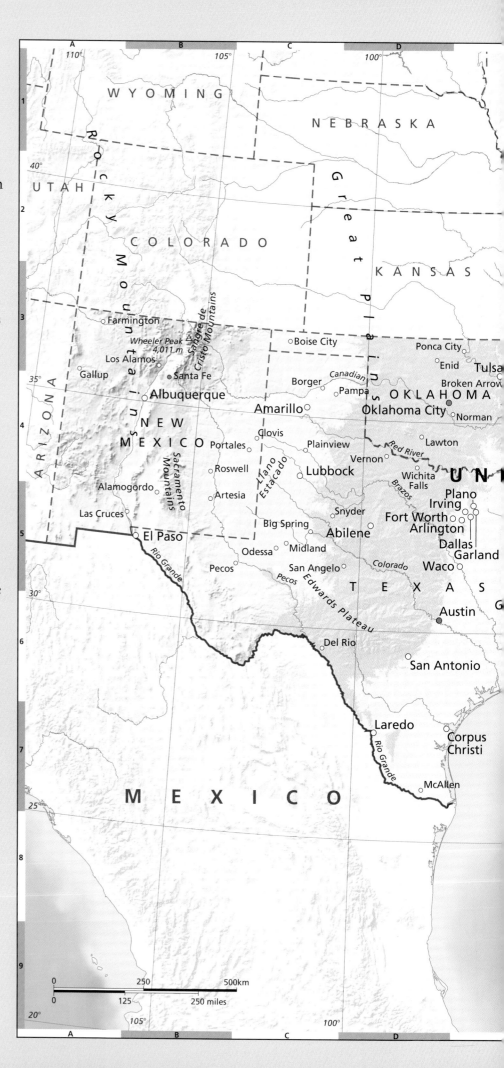

United States
of America

WISCONSIN

MICHIGAN

CANADA

PENNSYLVANIA

IOWA

OHIO

NEW JERSEY

ILLINOIS

INDIANA

WEST VIRGINIA

DELAWARE

MARYLAND

MISSOURI

KENTUCKY

VIRGINIA

Appalachian Mountains

Greensboro Durham NORTH CAROLINA

Clarksville Morristown Winston-Salem Raleigh Wilson Cape Hatteras

Oak Ridge

Nashville Knoxville Asheville Charlotte Fayetteville Jacksonville

Murfreesboro Gastonia

Fayetteville Pocohontas TENNESSEE Greenville SOUTH CAROLINA Wilmington

uskogee ARKANSAS Memphis Chattanooga Anderson Cape Fear

Arkansas Florence Huntsville Columbia

Fort Smith Decatur Athens Orangeburg

achita Mountains North Little Rock Little Rock Anniston Atlanta Augusta North Charleston

Hot Springs Birmingham Macon Charleston

Pine Bluff Columbus Tuscaloosa

ED STATES Greenville MISSISSIPPI ALABAMA Columbus Savannah ATLANTIC

OF Selma Montgomery GEORGIA

Sabine Monroe Meridian Albany Brunswick OCEAN

Tyler AMERICA Jackson Valdosta

Shreveport Dothan Jacksonville

Alexandria Hattiesburg Gainesville

l f Coastal Plain Mobile Tallahassee

LOUISIANA Baton Rouge Biloxi Pensacola Panama City Daytona Beach

Lake Charles Gulfport Cape San Blas Deltona

ouston Beaumont Metairie New Orleans Orlando Cape Canaveral

Pasadena Lafayette FLORIDA Melbourne

Galveston Mississippi Delta Clearwater Lakeland

reeport Saint Petersburg Tampa

Bradenton West Palm Beach

Sarasota Lake Okeechobee

Cape Coral Hialeah Fort Lauderdale

Naples The Everglades Hollywood

Miami

Key Largo

Gulf

of

Mexico

Cape Sable Florida Keys Straits of Florida BAHAMAS

CUBA

MEXICO

NORTHEASTERN UNITED STATES

Along the eastern coast of this area are rocky headlands and sandy beaches, with flooded river valleys that make ideal harbours. Inland, beyond the coastal plain, are the Appalachians, an ancient chain of mountains covered in woods. Still further to the west is part of the huge Mississippi basin, with the Great Lakes to the north.

For thousands of years the region was home to native peoples, such as the Iroquois and Delaware. They were expert farmers and fishers. In the 17th century, some of North America's first European settlers arrived here and the native peoples showed the settlers how to grow local crops. In the 19th century, millions of immigrants passed through New York before settling in the region, and today it is still densely populated. The northeast contains major cities such as New York, the country's financial centre, Chicago and Washington D.C., the capital of the USA.

Many farmers in the northeast grow maize or fruit, or raise livestock. Some areas, such as Detroit and the state of Pennsylvania, have for many years been centres of heavy industry, from mining and steel production to manufacturing. Although these are still important, newer, high-tech industries, producing electronic goods, have developed in Massachusetts and New Jersey.

LAND HEIGHT

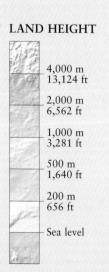

	4,000 m 13,124 ft
	2,000 m 6,562 ft
	1,000 m 3,281 ft
	500 m 1,640 ft
	200 m 656 ft
	Sea level

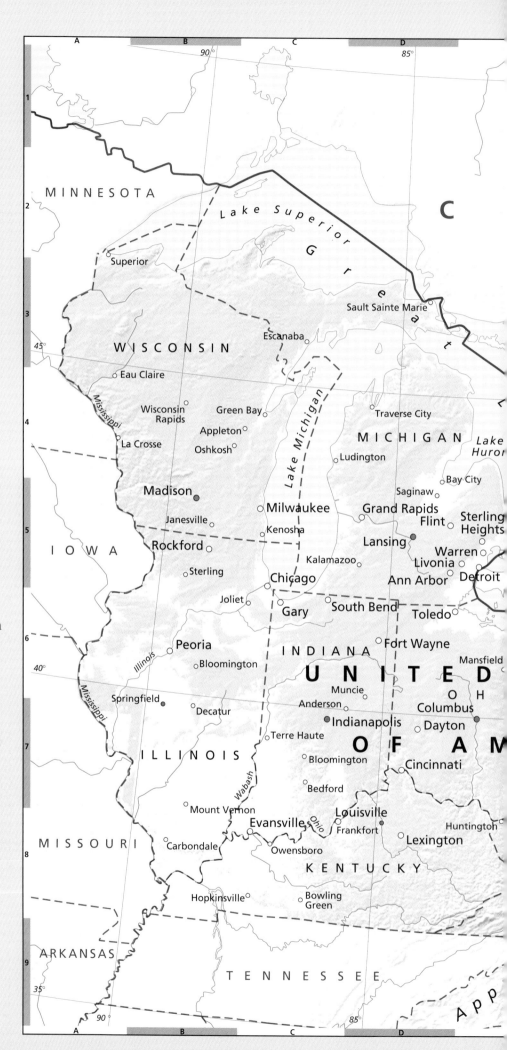

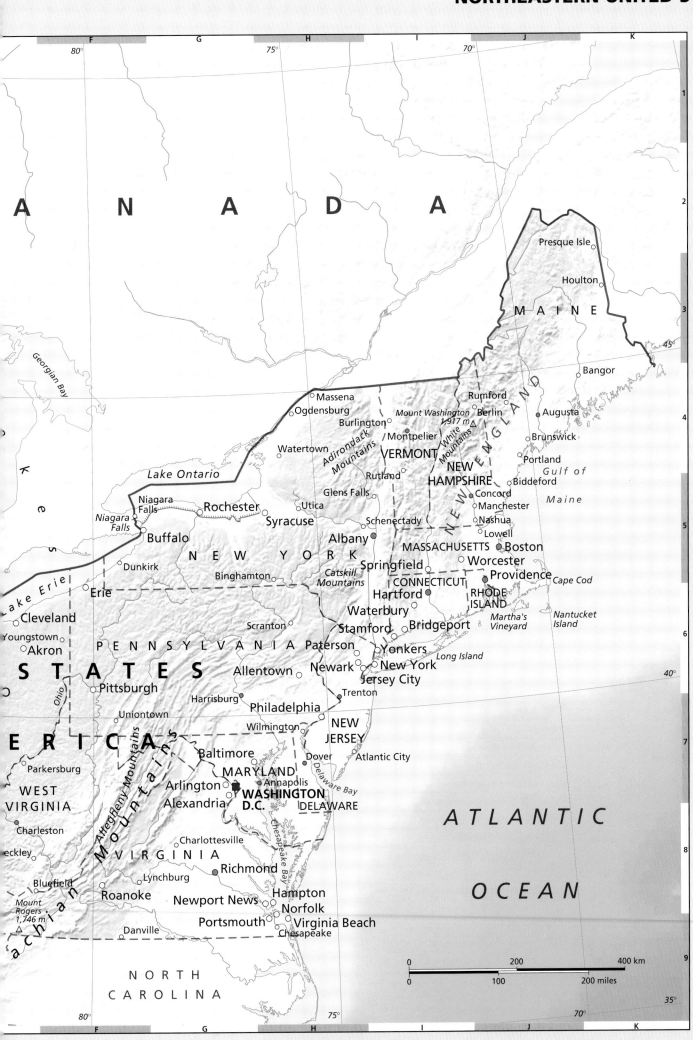

United States
of America

C A N A D A

Presque Isle

Houlton

M A I N E

45

Bangor

Massena
Ogdensburg   Rumford
Burlington   Mount Washington   Berlin
                    1,917 m
Watertown   Montpelier   Brunswick
        Adirondack   VERMONT   White
        Mountains   Mountains
                    Rutland   NEW   Portland
Lake Ontario   HAMPSHIRE   Biddeford
                    Glens Falls   Concord   Gulf of
Niagara   Rochester   Manchester Maine
Falls   Utica   Schenectady Nashua
Niagara   Syracuse   Lowell
Falls   Albany
Buffalo   N E W   Y O R K   MASSACHUSETTS Boston
                                     Springfield   Worcester
        Dunkirk   Providence Cape Cod
                    Binghamton   Catskill   CONNECTICUT
Erie   Mountains Hartford RHODE
                                     Waterbury   ISLAND
Cleveland   Stamford Bridgeport Martha's Nantucket
                    Scranton   Vineyard Island
Youngstown   P E N N S Y L V A N I A Paterson Yonkers
Akron   Long Island
S T A T E S   Allentown   Newark   New York
        Pittsburgh   Jersey City
                    Harrisburg   Trenton
        Uniontown   Philadelphia   40
                         Wilmington NEW
E R I C A's   JERSEY
        Baltimore   Dover   Atlantic City
Parkersburg   MARYLAND Annapolis
WEST   Arlington   Delaware Bay
VIRGINIA Alexandria WASHINGTON DELAWARE
                    D.C.
Charleston   A T L A N T I C
        Charlottesville   Chesapeake Bay
eckley   V I R G I N I A
        Lynchburg Richmond   O C E A N
Bluefield
Mount   Roanoke   Newport News Hampton
Rogers   Norfolk
1,746 m Danville Portsmouth Virginia Beach
                    Chesapeake

N O R T H
C A R O L I N A

Lake Erie
Georgian Bay
Ohio
Allegheny Mountains
achian Mountains

0   200   400 km
0   100   200 miles

80°   75°   70°   35°

MEXICO AND CENTRAL AMERICA

A chain of mountains, broken by fertile river valleys, forms the backbone of Mexico and Central America. Lowlands run along the east coast, widening to form Mexico's Yucatan Peninsula and Nicaragua's Mosquito Coast. In the south, Costa Rica and Panama form a narrow neck of land that measures less than 100 km across in some places. The Panama Canal, which was completed in 1914, provides a shipping link between the Atlantic and Pacific Oceans.

Most of the inhabitants of this area are descended from native peoples – such as the Maya and Aztec – and Europeans, especially the Spanish, who conquered the region in the 15th and 16th centuries. They are mainly farmers, either producing corn and beans for local use, or growing crops such as coffee, cotton and bananas for export. The area's major industries include mining, manufacturing and construction.

The population of Mexico and Central America is rising rapidly. Millions of people, unable to make a living from farming, have moved to the towns. Some cities have grown very quickly, and have poor housing, health and education services. The air quality in these urban areas is often low due to pollution from cars and factories. As the cities grow, large areas of tropical forest are being cut down to clear land for building.

LAND HEIGHT

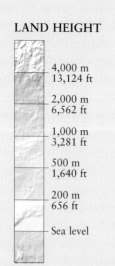

4,000 m
13,124 ft

2,000 m
6,562 ft

1,000 m
3,281 ft

500 m
1,640 ft

200 m
656 ft

Sea level

Mexico

Belize

Guatemala

Honduras

El Salvador

Nicaragua

Costa Rica

Panama

STATES

RICA

ATLANTIC

OCEAN

Reynosa
Matamoros
Laguna Madre

*G u l f
o f
M e x i c o*

30°

Straits of Florida

BAHAMAS

25°

Tropic of Cancer

CUBA

Ciudad Madero
Tampico
*Laguna de
Tamiahua*

Poza Rica
Pachuca

Mérida

Cancún
Isla Cozumel

Yucatan Channel

20°

*Cayman Islands
(to UK)*

Tlaxcala Xalapa
Puebla Veracruz
△ *Pico de Orizaba 5,700 m*
Orizaba San Andrés
Tuxtla
Tehuacán
Coatzacoalcos
Villahermosa
*Istmo de
Tehuantepec*
Oaxaca Tuxtla
Sierra Madre

Campeche *Yucatan*
Peninsula

Carmen *Laguna de
Términos*
Frontera

Petén

Chetumal

BELIZE
Belize City
BELMOPAN

*Gulf of
Honduras*

JAMAICA

*Swan Island
(to Honduras)*

C a r i b b e a n

S e a

15°

Flores

*Gulf of
Tehuantepec*

*Presa de
la Angostura*
Usumacinta

GUATEMALA
Cobán

Puerto
Barrios
La Ceiba
San Pedro Sula

Trujillo

*Laguna de
Caratasca*

Tapachula
Volcán
△ *Tajumulco 4,220 m*
GUATEMALA CITY
Santa Ana
SAN SALVADOR
EL SALVADOR San Miguel
Chinandega
León
MANAGUA

HONDURAS
TEGUCIGALPA

Coco

Somoto
Matagalpa

Mosquito Coast

Granada
Lake Nicaragua

NICARAGUA

San Juan
La Cruz

10°

COSTA RICA
Puntarenas

Limón

*Mosquito
Gulf*

Colón

SAN JOSÉ

*Panama
Canal*

San
Miguelito
PANAMA CITY

*Gulf of
Darien*

PANAMA
David

*Gulf of
Chiriquí*
Isla de Coiba

Las Tablas

*Gulf of
Panama*

COLOMBIA

*Bay of
Campeche*

95° F   90° G   85° H   80° I   75° J   K

1
2
3
4
5
6
7
8
9

THE CARIBBEAN

In the Caribbean Sea there are two mountain ranges, called the Greater and Lesser Antilles, which run from Florida to Trinidad. For part of their length, these mountains are hidden underwater, but where they break the surface they form the islands of the Caribbean. Many of these islands are small and mountainous, but two larger ones, Cuba and Hispaniola (which is divided into Haiti and the Dominican Republic), have a more varied landscape. On Cuba, the mountains are broken up by plains, while on Hispaniola, valleys divide the uplands.

The Caribbean is well known for its warm, sunny climate, but during the hottest months between July and October, violent storms and hurricanes blow in from the Atlantic Ocean and lash the islands. These winds reach up to 250 km/h and they can flatten everything in their path.

The people of the Caribbean are mostly descendants of Africans, Europeans and Asians who settled here over the years, or were brought to the area as slaves. In the past, nearly everyone lived by farming, and these islands still produce large amounts of crops, such as sugar cane and bananas. Today, the Caribbean's warm weather and sandy beaches attract millions of visitors from North America and further afield. Tourism has had a damaging effect on the environment, but it has also brought much-needed money into the region.

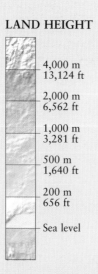

LAND HEIGHT

	4,000 m
	13,124 ft
	2,000 m
	6,562 ft
	1,000 m
	3,281 ft
	500 m
	1,640 ft
	200 m
	656 ft
	Sea level

UNITED STATES
OF AMERICA
(FLORIDA)

Gulf of
Mexico

Grand
Bahama Island Freeport
Great
Abaco

NASSAU
New
Providence
Eleuthera
Island

Andros
Island
Cat
Island

BAHAMAS

Long
Island

Straits of Florida

HAVANA Matanzas

Pinar del Río
Santa Clara

Cienfuegos CUBA
Sancti Spíritus Ciego de Ávila

Isla de la
Juventud Camagüey

Las Tunas Holguín

Manzanillo Bayamo
Guantánamo

Cayman
Islands
(to UK) Santiago
de Cuba

Grand
Cayman

Jérémie
Montego Bay Navassa Island
(to US)

JAMAICA May Pen
Spanish Town KINGSTON

Caribbean

Sea

NICARAGUA

COSTA
RICA

PANAMA

COLOM

ATLANTIC

OCEAN

250 km
0   125   250 miles

West Indies

Turks & Caicos Islands
(to UK)

Great
Inagua

Acklins
Island

Windward Passage

Port-de-Paix
Cap-Haïten
Gonaïves
Santiago
St Marc
La Vega
HAITI
Hispaniola
Pico Duarte
3,175 m
Jacmel
PORT-AU-PRINCE
SANTO
DOMINGO

DOMINICAN REPUBLIC

San Francisco
de Macorís
La Romana
San
Pedros de
Macorís

Mona Passage

Puerto Rico
(to US)
Bayamón
San Juan
Mayagüez
Caguas
Ponce

British
Virgin Islands
(to UK)

Anguilla
(to UK)

St Martin
(to France & Netherlands)
St Barthélémy (to France)

Barbuda

Leeward Islands

Netherlands
Antilles
(to Netherlands)

Virgin Islands
(to US)

St Kitts
BASSETERRE
Nevis

**ST KITTS
& NEVIS**

Montserrat
(to UK)

ANTIGUA & BARBUDA
■ST JOHN'S
Antigua

Guadeloupe Passage

Basse Terre
Grande Terre

Guadeloupe
(to France)
■Basse Terre

DOMINICA ROSEAU
■

Martinique Passage

Martinique
(to France)
Fort-de-France

ST LUCIA ■
CASTRIES

St Vincent Passage

KINGSTOWN
St Vincent

**ST VINCENT &
THE GRENADINES**

The Grenadines

BARBADOS
BRIDGETOWN■

St George's
GRENADA

Windward Islands

Lesser Antilles

Aruba
(to Netherlands)
Oranjestad

Netherlands Antilles
(to Netherlands)
Willemstad
Curaçao
Bonaire

Antilles

Tobago

PORT-OF-SPAIN
■
Arima
Point Fortin
Trinidad

**TRINIDAD
& TOBAGO**

V E N E Z U E L A

BIA

Bahamas

Cuba

Haiti

Dominican Republic

Jamaica

Antigua & Barbuda

St Kitts & Nevis

Dominica

St Lucia

**St Vincent & the
Grenadines**

Barbados

Grenada

Trinidad & Tobago

SOUTH AMERICA

The continent of South America is shaped like a triangle. It tapers from the warm Caribbean coasts of Colombia and Venezuela to the cold waters of the Southern and Pacific Oceans at the southern tips of Argentina and Chile. Three very different types of landscape dominate the continent. In the west, the Andes stretch for 7,250 km along the entire Pacific coast. These towering mountains reach more than 6,900 m in height. In the hot and humid regions of the northeast, the world's largest rainforest, the Amazon, covers an area of 6.5 million sq km. The mighty Amazon river

flows through this region. Further south, there are great open plains of grass and scrub.

Hundreds of years ago, the native peoples of South America built up powerful civilizations, but later, between the 16th and 19th centuries, much of the continent was ruled by the Spanish and Portuguese. As a result, the official language in Brazil is Portuguese, while Spanish is spoken in most of the other countries. The Spanish and Portuguese also developed South America's cities, building on the Atlantic coast for easy access to Europe. Today, most South

Americans still live on the coast, in places such as Rio de Janeiro, Montevideo and São Paulo, which is one of the world's largest cities.

South America has rich mineral deposits and fertile farming lands, and most of the countries export goods, including oil and foodstuffs. The wealth is not divided equally. Many people are desperately poor, and large sections of the population cannot read or write. A number of South America's countries have borrowed money from wealthier nations and are struggling to repay their debts.

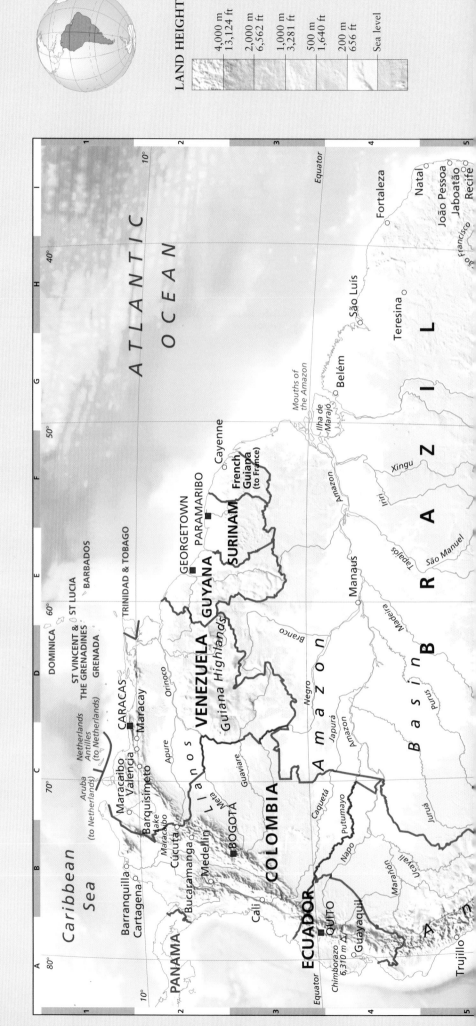

LAND HEIGHT

4,000 m 13,124 ft
2,000 m 6,562 ft
1,000 m 3,281 ft
500 m 1,640 ft
200 m 656 ft
Sea level

ATLANTIC

OCEAN

PACIFIC

OCEAN

1000 km

500 miles

500

250

South Georgia
(to UK)

Maceió

Salvador

Represa de
Sobradinho

Tocantins

Araguaia

Brazilian

Highlands

Belo Horizonte

Ribeirão Prêto

Nova
Iguaçu

São Gonçalo
Rio de Janeiro

BRASÍLIA

Goiânia

Uberlândia

Rio Grande

Campinas

São Paulo Guarulhos

Curitiba

Planalto de
Mato Grosso

Campo Grande

Paraná

Serra Geral

Porto Alegre

Lagoa
dos Patos

Lagoa
Mirim

Pantanal

PARAGUAY

Paraguay

ASUNCIÓN

Gran Chaco

Pilcomayo

Mesopotamia (Uruguay)

Uruguay

URUGUAY

MONTEVIDEO

Río de la Plata

La
Plata

Mar del Plata

Falkland Islands
(to UK)

Stanley
East
Falkland

BOLIVIA

Santa Cruz

Cochabamba

SUCRE

Salado

Córdoba

Rosario

BUENOS AIRES

Lomas de Zamora

West
Falkland

LA PAZ

Lake
Titicaca

Altiplano

Laguna
Mar Chiquito

San Miguel
de Tucumán

ARGENTINA

Pampas

Bahía
Blanca

Punta Rasa

Gulf of
San Matías

Bahía
Grande

Strait of Magellan

Nevado
Sajama
6,542 m

Atacama Desert

Ojos del Salado
6,880 m

Aconcagua
6,960 m

Río Negro

Gulf of
San Jorge

Patagonia

Guaporé

Beni

Madre de Dios

Juruena

Purus

PERU

Callao

LIMA

Arequipa

A N D E S

Salado

SANTIAGO

Patagonia

Isla de
Chiloé

Archipiélago
de los Chonos

Isla
Wellington

Archipiélago
Reina Adelaida

Terra
del Fuego

Cape Horn

Islas de los
Desventurados

Juan Fernández
Islands

Tropic of Capricorn

Tropic of Capricorn

NORTHERN SOUTH AMERICA

The northern part of South America is fringed by uplands – the Guiana Highlands in the north, the Andes in the west and the Brazilian Highlands in the south. This region has many amazing physical features. Lake Titicaca, on the border between Peru and Bolivia, is South America's largest lake. It is also the highest navigable lake in the world. The Angel Falls in Venezuela is the world's highest waterfall. Across the middle of this region is the basin of the Amazon, a river so vast that it carries about one-fifth of the world's fresh water.

Few people live in the interior areas. Most of this region's huge population lives in coastal cities, working in the industries that have grown up around them. These include oil production and metal refining in Venezuela, and chemical and textile industries in Brazil. Mining occurs in most countries. The Amazon region has a thriving timber industry, but loggers are steadily cutting away the rainforest. Large areas of trees have been cleared by farmers for cropland and cattle ranches. Plans to build new oil pipelines and roads across the region will also lead to deforestation. Every year, about eight million hectares of forest disappear from the Amazon, and as about half of the world's known plant and animal species live here, environmentalists are fighting to preserve this important area.

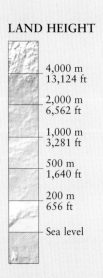

LAND HEIGHT

4,000 m
13,124 ft

2,000 m
6,562 ft

1,000 m
3,281 ft

500 m
1,640 ft

200 m
656 ft

Sea level

BOLIVIA'S TWO CAPITALS
LA PAZ – legislative and administrative capital
SUCRE – legal captial

ATLANTIC OCEAN

GRENADA

Isla de Margarita

TRINIDAD & TOBAGO

Maturín

Ciudad Guayana

Ciudad Bolívar

Embalse de Guri

Angel Falls

Highlands

Boa Vista

GEORGETOWN

GUYANA

Essequibo

Branco

PARAMARIBO

SURINAM

Cayenne

French Guiana (to France)

Negro

Amazon

Manaus

Represa de Balbina

Macapá

Mouths of the Amazon

Isla de Marajó

Baía de Marajó

Santarém

Amazon

Tapajós

Iriri

Belém

Baía de São Marcos

São Luís

Parnaíba

Madeira

Pôrto Velho

São Manuel

Xingu

Represa Tucuruí

Imperatriz

Sobral

Teresina

Fortaleza

Cabo de São Roque

Mossoró

Natal

BRAZIL

Parnaíba

Juazeiro do Norte

Campina Grande

João Pessoa

Jaboatão

Olinda

Recife

Caruarú

Juàzeiro

Maceió

Guaporé

Juruena

Araguaia

Rio das Mortes

Tocantins

Represa de Sobradinho

Arapiraca

Aracaju

Taguatinga

Feira de Santana

Alagoinhas

VIA

Santa Cruz

Planalto de Mato Grosso

Cuiabá

São Francisco

Salvador

Jequié

Corumba

Pantanal

BRASÍLIA

Goiânia

Anápolis

Vitória da Conquista

Ilhéus

Montes Claros

Brazilian

Teófilo Otoni

Campo Grande

Paranaíba

Uberlândia

Highlands

Uberaba

Divinópolis

Linhares

PARAGUAY

Dourados

Marília

Franca

Rio Grande

Belo Horizonte

Vitória

Ribeirão Prêto

Juiz de Fora

Campos

Paraná

Campinas

Guarulhos

São Gonçalo

Londrina

Nova

Rio de Janeiro

Maringá

São Paulo

Iguaçu

Cascavel

Santos

ENTINA

Ponta Grossa

Curitiba

Uruguay

Serra Geral

Joinville

Lages

Florianópolis

ATLANTIC OCEAN

Passo Fundo

Santa Maria

Porto Alegre

Bagé

Lagoa dos Patos

Rio Grande

Lagoa Mirim

URUGUAY

AMÉRICA

ATLANTIC OCEAN

0 500 1000 km

0 250 500 miles

Equator

Tropic of Capricorn

60° 50° 40° 30°

10° 20° 30°

Colombia

Venezuela

Guyana

Surinam

Brazil

Ecuador

Peru

Bolivia

SOUTHERN SOUTH AMERICA

The southern part of South America is made up of Paraguay, Uruguay, Argentina and Chile. The Andes Mountains run from the north to the south, forming the backbone of the region. The Atacama Desert, the driest place on Earth, lies in the northwest. To the east are the forests and grasslands of Gran Chaco, the grasslands of the Pampas, and Patagonia, a high, cold plateau in southern Argentina. The southwest has a dramatic landscape of icy fjords, jagged mountain peaks, U-shaped valleys and frozen glaciers. Further south are the windy islands of Tierra del Fuego.

Most of the people in southern South America live in cities, particularly in the capitals. Buenos Aires, for example, is home to over one-third of Argentina's population. The majority of those who live in this region speak Spanish, the language of the people who ruled the area until the 19th century. In some places, small groups of people still speak the native languages.

The big cities of Chile, Argentina and Uruguay are centres for heavy industries, and some of these have polluted the larger rivers, such as the Paraná and its tributaries. Argentina is famous

for raising cattle on its rich grasslands, and beef from its ranches is exported worldwide. Some of this meat is processed into products such as corned beef in factories in Córdoba and Buenos Aires. Paraguay grows wheat and other crops for its own use, while cotton, coffee, tobacco and oilseeds such as soya, are the country's major export crops. Uruguay's main export is wool. The Chilean Andes, with their deposits of copper, are mined heavily. A wide range of fruits and more specialized crops such as walnuts, and grapes for wine, are grown in Chile's fertile Central Valley.

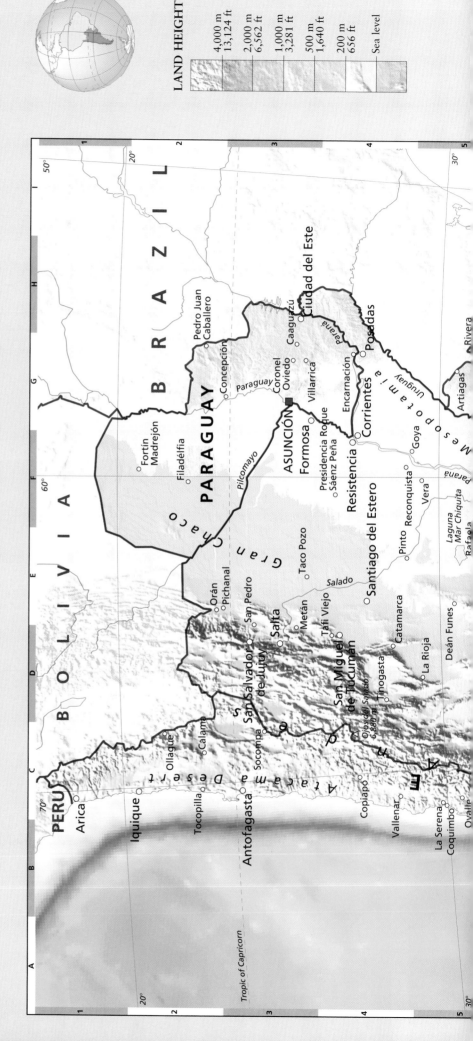

LAND HEIGHT

| 4,000 m 13,124 ft | 2,000 m 6,562 ft | 1,000 m 3,281 ft | 500 m 1,640 ft | 200 m 656 ft | Sea level |

Chile
Paraguay
Argentina
Uruguay

PACIFIC
OCEAN

ATLANTIC
OCEAN

URUGUAY

ARGENTINA

CHILE

Lagoa
Mirim

Tacuarembó
Melo
Paysandú
Durazno
Mercedes
MONTEVIDEO
San José de Mayo
Florida
Las Piedras
Minas
San Nicolás de Los Arroyos
Fray Bentos
Gualeguaychú
San José de Los Arroyos
La
Plata
Río de la Plata
Punta Norte

Santa
Fé
Paraná
Concordia
Mar del Plata
Rosario
Pergamino
Necochea
BUENOS AIRES
Lomas de Zamora
Junín
Azul
Tres
Arroyos
Olavarría
Punta Alta
Coronel
Pringles
Bahía
Blanca
Punta Rasa
Bahía Blanca
Viedma
Río Colorado
Punta Alta

Francisco Santa
Venado Tuerto
Rufino
Córdoba
Villa María
Río Cuarto
San Luis
Mercedes
San Rafael
Salado
Colorado
Chos Malal
Neuquén
Zapala
General Roca
Río Negro
San Antonio Oeste

San Juan
Mendoza
Godoy Cruz
San Bernado
Malargüe
Gulf of
San Matías
Peninsula
Valdés

Viña del Mar
Valparaíso
Rancagua
SANTIAGO
Los
Andes
Aconcagua
6,960m
Central
Valley
Talca
Constitución
Pichilemu
Chillán
Talcahuano
Concepción
Lebu
Temuco
Valdivia
Los Ángeles
Osorno
Puerto Montt
San Carlos
de Bariloche
Esquel
Corcovado
Gulf of
Corcovado
Isla de
Chiloé
Archipiélago
de los Chonos
Puerto Aisén
Coihaique
Taitao
Peninsula
Gulf of
Penas
Nueva
Lubecka
Sarmiento
Deseado
Comodoro Rivadavia
Gulf of
San Jorge
Fitz Roy
Cabo Tres Puntas
Puerto Deseado
Rawson
Chubut
Chico
Puerto San Julián
Gobernador
Gregores
Chico
Santa Cruz
Puerto Santa Cruz
Bahía
Grande
El Calafate
Río Gallegos
Strait of Magellan
San Sebastián
Río Grande
Tierra del Fuego
Ushuaia
Cape Horn
Isla de los
Estados
Punta Arenas
Puerto Natales
Isla
Wellington
Archipiélago
Reina Adelaida

Falkland Islands
(to UK)
West
Falkland
East
Falkland
Stanley

40°
40°
50°
50°
60°
70°
80°
80°

600 km
300 miles
300
150
0
0

THE ATLANTIC OCEAN

Covering about one-fifth of the planet's surface, the Atlantic is the world's second-largest ocean. To the west are the Americas, and Europe and Africa lie to the east. The Earth's longest mountain chain, the Mid-Atlantic Ridge, dominates the ocean's underwater landscape. In places, the ridge rises above the water as volcanic islands, such as Iceland and the Azores. The deepest part of the Atlantic, the Puerto Rico Trench, plunges to −8,605 m.

Since Portuguese and Spanish explorers began to cross the ocean from Europe to America in the 15th century, the Atlantic has been one of the world's major transport routes. Today, ships carry bulk goods, such as oil, grain and iron, between the ocean's many international ports.

The Atlantic is rich in natural resources. The shallow areas along the coasts have deposits of oil and gas, and in recent years, offshore oil and gas reserves have been exploited in the Gulf of Mexico, the Niger Delta and the North Sea. Sand, gravel and shell deposits are mined by the USA and the United Kingdom for use in the construction industry. The ocean is also a vital source of food. Most of the Atlantic's coastal countries fish in its waters, but in the north Atlantic, stocks of cod, herring and haddock have been reduced by overfishing. The ocean's environment is also threatened by pollution. Oil is discharged into the water by ships and drilling rigs. Industrial waste, fertilizers and sewage enter the Atlantic at the coasts, particularly in the Mediterranean, Baltic and North Sea regions, and off the USA, southern Brazil and eastern Argentina. A number of countries are trying to reach agreements to tackle some forms of pollution.

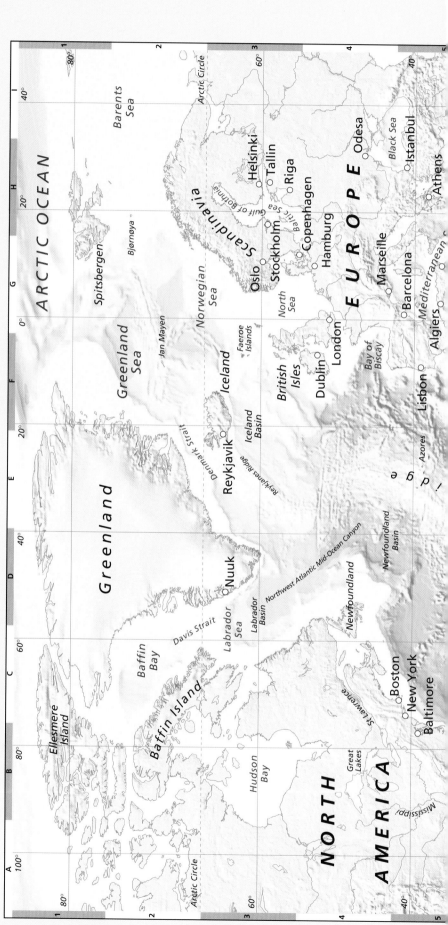

THE ATLANTIC OCEAN . 45

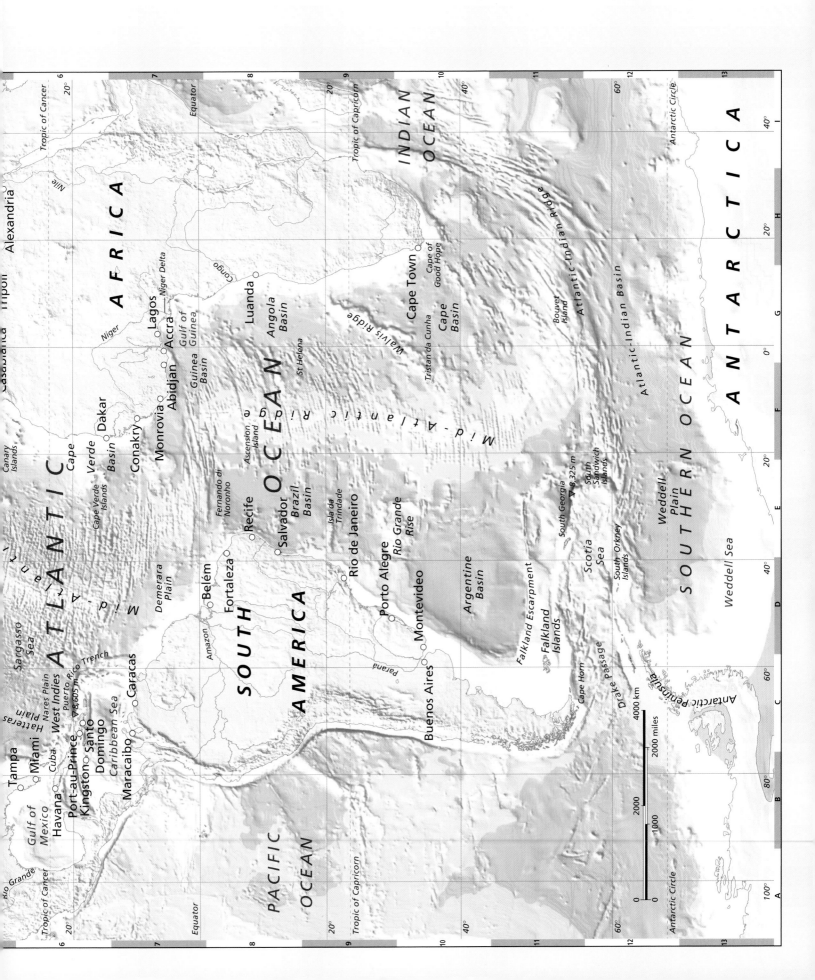

AFRICA

INDIAN OCEAN

ANTARCTICA

SOUTHERN OCEAN

Cape Town
Cape of Good Hope
Cape Basin
Angola Basin
Luanda
Congo
Niger Delta
Lagos
Accra
Abidjan
Gulf of Guinea
Guinea Basin
Monrovia
Conakry
Dakar
Cape Verde
Cape Verde Islands
Canary Islands
Casablanca
Tripoli
Alexandria
Nile
Tropic of Cancer
Equator
Tropic of Capricorn

Walvis Ridge
St Helena
Ascension Island
Tristan da Cunha
Bouvet Island
Atlantic-Indian Ridge
Atlantic-Indian Basin

Mid-Atlantic Ridge

SOUTH OCEAN

SOUTH AMERICA

Fernando di Noronho
Recife
Salvador
Brazil Basin
Isla da Trindade
Rio de Janeiro
Rio Grande Rise
Porto Alegre
Montevideo
Buenos Aires
Paraná
Argentine Basin
Falkland Escarpment
Falkland Islands
Cape Horn
Drake Passage
South Georgia
South Sandwich Islands
Scotia Sea
South Orkney Islands
Weddell Plain
Weddell Sea
Antarctic Peninsula
Antarctic Circle

Belém
Fortaleza
Amazon
Demerara Plain
Caracas
Maracaibo
Domingo
Santo
Kingston
Port-au-Prince
Havana
Miami
Tampa
Gulf of Mexico
Rio Grande
Cuba
West Indies
Caribbean Sea
Puerto Rico Trench
Nares Plain
Hatteras Plain
Sargasso Sea
ATLANTIC

PACIFIC OCEAN

∇ 8,325 m
∇ 8,605 m

4000 km
2000 miles
2000
1000
2000
1000
0
0

Tropic of Cancer
Equator
Tropic of Capricorn
Antarctic Circle

EUROPE

The continent of Europe extends from the Ural Mountains in the east to the Atlantic Ocean in the west, north to the Arctic Ocean and south to the Mediterranean Sea. There are a number of mountain ranges, including the Alps, which rise to more than 4,800 m, and lesser ranges, such as the Carpathians, Pyrenees and Apennines. Most of the continent's population lives between these uplands on the North European Plain. The plain's rich, fertile soil and temperate climate help farmers to grow a variety of crops, such as wheat, fruit and vegetables, and raise both dairy and beef cattle.

During the Industrial Revolution of the 18th and 19th centuries, Europe developed heavy industries, such as iron and steel-making. Today, in western Europe, these businesses are being replaced by high-tech industries and financial services. In the east, however, many old-fashioned factories remain. These cause terrible environmental pollution in some places.

Many of Europe's countries have existed for hundreds of years and some, such as the United Kingdom and France, had large empires. Although these empires no longer exist, the countries that ran them still play a major role in world affairs. In the 20th century, many of western Europe's countries came together to form the European Union. The union is working towards bringing its members closer politically and economically.

LAND HEIGHT

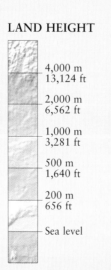

4,000 m
13,124 ft

2,000 m
6,562 ft

1,000 m
3,281 ft

500 m
1,640 ft

200 m
656 ft

Sea level

Barents
Sea

Novaya
Zemlya

North Cape

Vesterålen
ofoten

Murmansk

Kola
Peninsula

ASIA

Arctic Circle

Ural Mountains

Pechora

White
Sea

SWEDEN

FINLAND

Oulu

Archangel

Northern Dvina

Perm

Tampere

Lake
Onega

RUSSIAN

Kirov

Izhevsk

Ufa

Kama

Turku
(Åbo)

HELSINKI

Lake
Ladoga

FEDERATION

Naberezhnyye Chelny

Kazan

St Petersburg

Yaroslavl

TOCKHOLM

ESTONIA

TALLINN

Gulf of Finland

Tver

Ivanovo

Nizhniy Novgorod

Tolyatti

Gotland

LATVIA

RIGA

Volga

MOSCOW

Simbirsk

Samara

Orenburg

Öland

Western Dvina

Ryazan

Penza

Ural

Baltic
Sea

LITHUANIA

Vitsyebsk

Tula

Saratov

Volga

dansk

RUSS. FED.

VILNIUS

Smolensk

Kaliningrad

Bryansk

Lipetsk

North

MINSK

Kursk

Voronezh

Poznan

Vistula

BELARUS

WARSAW

Lodz

Homyel

Don

Volgograd

Wroclaw

Oder

POLAND

Rivne

KIEV

Kharkiv

Astrakhan

Caspian Sea

Krakow

Lviv

UKRAINE

Dnipropetrovsk

Rostov-na-Donu

SLOVAKIA

Carpathian Mountains

Dniester

Donetsk

BRATISLAVA

Krivyy Rih

Stavropol

Tisza

Cluj-
Napoca

Iasi

MOLDOVA

Dnieper

Sea of
Azov

BUDAPEST

CHISINAU

Krasnodar

Grozny

HUNGARY

Timisoara

Odesa

Crimean
Peninsula

Elbrus
5,642 m

ROATIA

ROMANIA

Caucasus

OSNIA &
ERZEGOVINA

BELGRADE

BUCHAREST

Constanta

Sevastopol

Danube

Black Sea

SARAJEVO

SERBIA &
MONTENEGRO

BULGARIA

Pristina

SOFIA

Burgas

ASIA

SKOPJE

Plovdiv

MACEDONIA

Istanbul

TIRANA

Thessaloniki

ALBANIA

GREECE

Aegean
Sea

onian
Sea

Patra

ATHENS

Mediterranean
Sea

Rhodes

Irakleio

Crete

European Plain

0   500   1000 km

0   250   500 miles

NORTHWESTERN EUROPE

Denmark, Norway and Sweden, in the far northwest of Europe, are together known as Scandinavia. These countries have similar languages and for part of their history shared the same rulers. Out at sea to the west lies Iceland. Finland is in the east. Until 1917, Finland was a province of the Russian Empire, so it has a very different language and culture to Scandinavia. All of these countries are highly industrialized and have a high standard of living.

Iceland has a unique landscape. Icy and rocky, it is dotted with volcanoes and dramatic hot springs, some of which are tapped to heat buildings. Much of the rest of northwestern Europe is rugged, mountainous and wooded. The landscape is harsh, and most of the population live in the flatter southern areas, where lakes were scraped out by glaciers thousands of years ago. The soil in the south is more fertile than in the north, allowing farmers to grow crops and lush grass for dairy farming. The western coasts have been eroded by the sea and ice into deep inlets known as fjords. The climate in this part of the region is wet, but mild, and many of the people who live here

work in fishing and fish-processing. Further east, the climate is much colder and drier. A great number of those who live inland are employed in the timber industry.

The countries of northwestern Europe produce very little pollution. Most of the region's power is generated from clean hydro-electric stations that harness the fast-flowing mountain streams to produce electricity. However, pollution from elsewhere in Europe blows north and falls as acid rain. This rain poisons forests and lakes, killing the plants and animals living in them.

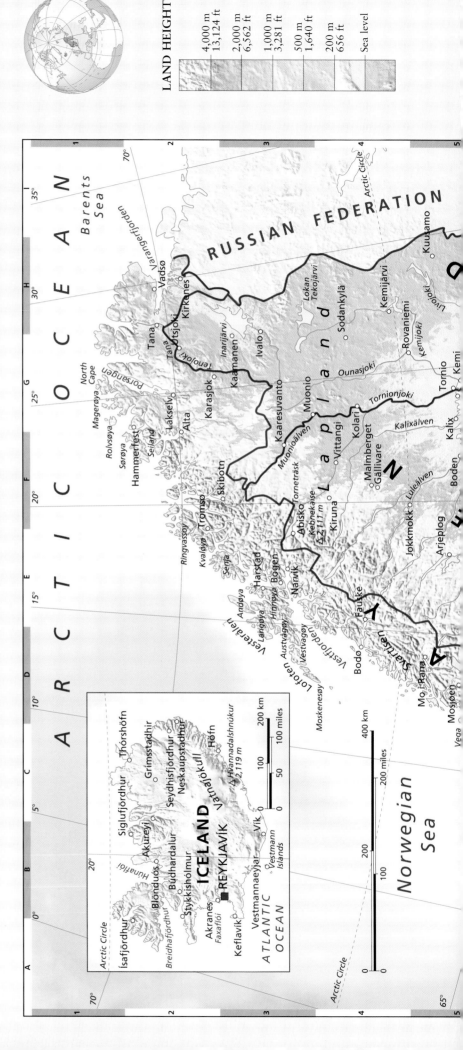

LAND HEIGHT

| 4,000 m 13,124 ft | 2,000 m 6,562 ft | 1,000 m 3,281 ft | 500 m 1,640 ft | 200 m 656 ft | Sea level |

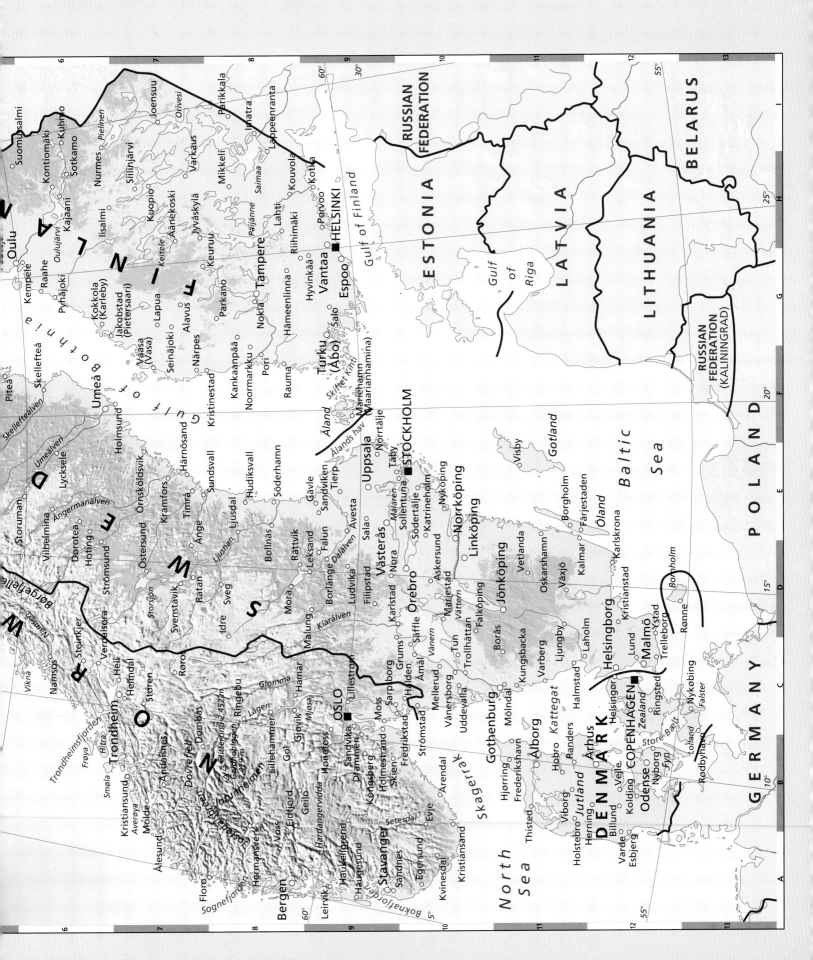

THE BRITISH ISLES

Located in the northwest of Europe, this group of islands contains two countries: the United Kingdom and the Republic of Ireland. The United Kingdom includes the national regions of England, Wales and Scotland, and the province of Northern Ireland. Britain and Ireland are the British Isles' largest islands.

In the north and west of Britain are uplands, fringed by rocky, jagged coasts. To the south and east of the island are lowlands. They range from the flat fens of the east to the rolling hills of the southeast. Ireland has a low-lying plain

in its centre, which is covered by numerous lakes, peat bogs and grassy hills. The plain is surrounded by low coastal mountains.

Sheep and cattle are raised in Britain's uplands, and cereal crops are grown in the east. The flatter areas of the island, such as central England, produce fruit and vegetables. Dairy products and beef are important sources of income for the Republic of Ireland.

In the late 18th century, the United Kingdom began to develop heavy industries, and by the

early 20th century, the country was a world leader in mining, steel production and textiles. Recently, many of these heavy industries have been replaced by high-tech businesses and financial services. Computer hardware and software companies employ a great number of people in Ireland, Scotland and southern England, while tourism is an important industry throughout the islands. The move away from heavy industry has helped to reduce pollution in the area, but the British Isles is a small, densely populated region with high numbers of cars, so poor air quality is a big problem in large cities.

LAND HEIGHT

4,000 m	13,124 ft
2,000 m	6,562 ft
1,000 m	3,281 ft
500 m	1,640 ft
200 m	656 ft
Sea level	

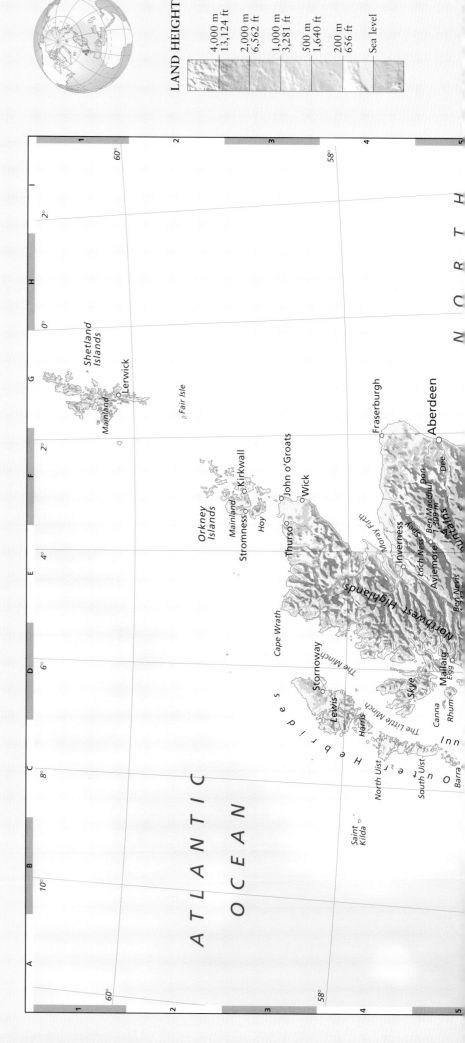

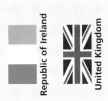

Republic of Ireland

United Kingdom

FRANCE

NORTH SEA

ATLANTIC OCEAN

SCOTLAND

Hebrides

Tiree
Mull
Oban
Colonsay
Jura
Islay
Arran
Kintyre

Grampian Mountains

Dundee
Perth
Stirling
Loch Lomond
Greenock
Paisley
Glasgow
Kilmarnock
East Kilbride
Ayr
Firth of Forth
Dunfermline
Edinburgh
Berwick-upon-Tweed

UNITED KINGDOM

Southern Uplands
Dumfries
Stranraer
Solway Firth

NORTHERN IRELAND

Londonderry (Derry)
Coleraine
Omagh
Donegal
Strabane
Lough Neagh
Portadown
Enniskillen
ULSTER
Lower Lough Erne
Upper Lough Erne
Newtownabbey
Bangor
Belfast
Lisburn
Newry
Dundalk
Drogheda

REPUBLIC OF IRELAND

Donegal Bay
Sligo
Lough Ree
Lough Corrib
Lough Mask
CONNAUGHT
Cavan
Athlone
Port Laoise
LEINSTER
DUBLIN
Dun Laoghaire
Wicklow Mountains
Liffey
Barrow
Kilkenny
Wexford
Waterford

Galway
Galway Bay

Ennis
Limerick
Shannon
Tipperary
Clonmel
MUNSTER
Tralee
Killarney
Blackwater
Cork

Dingle Bay
Bantry Bay

Isle of Man (to UK)
Douglas
Irish Sea

Newcastle-upon-Tyne
Sunderland
Durham
Middlesbrough
Scarborough
North York Moors
Flamborough Head
Kingston-upon-Hull
Grimsby
Humber
The Wolds
York
Leeds
Bradford
Huddersfield
Doncaster
Sheffield
Mansfield
Peak District
Derby
Nottingham
Blackpool
Preston
Blackburn
Morecambe
Lake District
Carlisle
Tyne
Tees
Pennines
Ouse

Manchester
Liverpool
Chester
Stoke-on-Trent
Wrexham
Bangor
Holyhead
Anglesey
Caernarfon
Snowdon 1,085 m
Cader Idris 892 m
Cardigan Bay
Aberystwyth
WALES
Cambrian Mountains
Shrewsbury
Telford
Wolverhampton
Birmingham
Coventry
Leicester
Trent
Severn
Worcester
Brecon Beacons
Carmarthen
Llanelli
Swansea
Cardiff
Barry
Newport
Gloucester
Bristol
Bath
Avon
Bristol Channel

ENGLAND

Mansfield
Peterborough
Cambridge
King's Lynn
The Fens
The Wash
Norwich
Ipswich
Colchester
Great Ouse
Northampton
Banbury
Oxford
Luton
Watford
Basildon
Southend-on-Sea
LONDON
Slough
Reading
Swindon
Thames
Chiltern Hills
Newbury
Basingstoke
Crawley
North Downs
The Weald
Canterbury
Dover
Strait of Dover
Dungeness
Hastings
Brighton
Beachy Head
South Downs
Portsmouth
Isle of Wight
Southampton
Salisbury Plain
Bournemouth
Weymouth
Portland Bill
Lyme Bay
Taunton
Exmoor
Barnstaple
Exe
Exeter
Dartmoor
Dart
Bodmin Moor
Plymouth
Truro
Newquay
Penzance
Land's End
Isles of Scilly

English Channel
Channel Islands (to UK)
Alderney
Guernsey
St Peter Port
Sark
Jersey
St Helier

Celtic Sea
St George's Channel
Fishguard

Firth of Clyde
Loch

North York Moors

200 km
100 miles

0   100
0   50   100

THE LOW COUNTRIES

Luxembourg, Belgium and the Netherlands are known as the Low Countries because most of their land is flat and low-lying. Nearly one-third of the Netherlands lies below sea level. The Dutch reclaimed this land from the sea by building dykes to enclose areas of shallow water, which were then drained into canals by pumps. Regions such as these are called polders, and they need constant care to stop them from flooding. Rising to heights of 500 m, the forested hills of the Ardennes, in southern Belgium and Luxembourg, are the Low Countries' only uplands. Two major rivers –

the Meuse and the Rhine – flow through the region on their way to the North Sea.

The reclaimed areas, plus flat plains such as Flanders in northern Belgium, have fertile soils, and provide good conditions for agriculture. Barley, potatoes and flax are the main crops. The Netherlands also produces cut flowers and bulbs, which are exported all over the world. Beef, dairy and pig farming take place in the higher inland parts of this region. Luxembourg is a major centre for banking, and Belgium has a great number of factories. Brussels, which is

the capital of Belgium, is also the administrative capital of the European Union.

Many people work in chemical companies, engineering, the textile industry, and in the new high-tech businesses that are springing up in this region. The majority of people live in towns or cities and the largest urban area is known as *Randstad Holland.* This is a densely-populated, built-up region between Amsterdam and Rotterdam. Most people have a comfortable lifestyle in the cities, but large numbers of cars and factories cause serious air pollution.

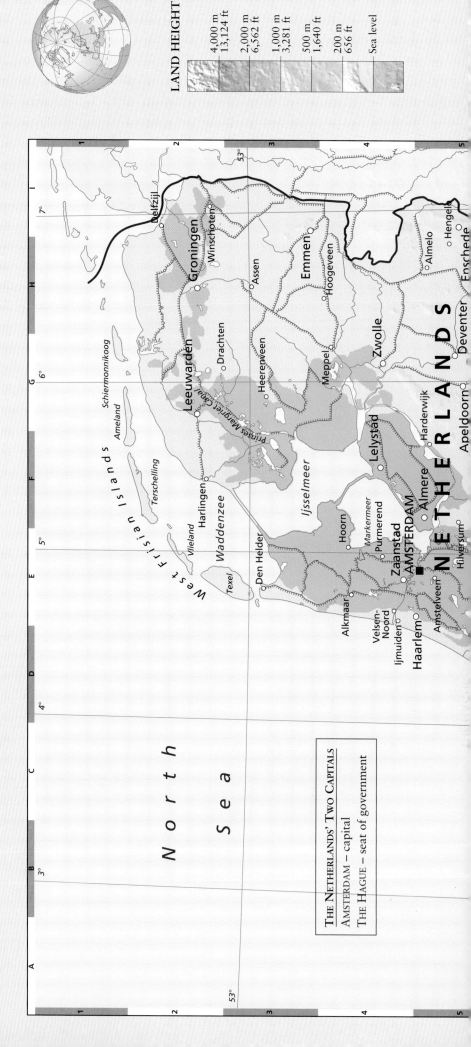

LAND HEIGHT

4,000 m / 13,124 ft
2,000 m / 6,562 ft
1,000 m / 3,281 ft
500 m / 1,640 ft
200 m / 656 ft
Sea level

THE NETHERLANDS' TWO CAPITALS
AMSTERDAM – capital
THE HAGUE – seat of government

Netherlands Belgium Luxembourg

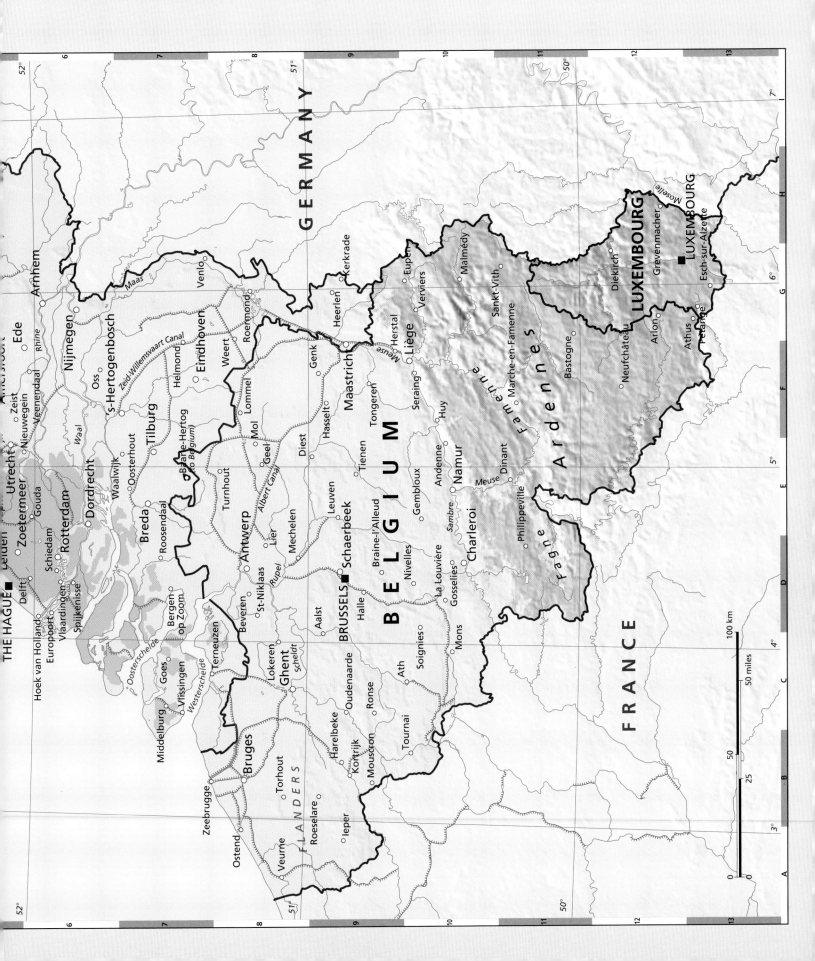

GERMANY

Arnhem
Ede
Zeist
Nijmegen
Nieuwegein
Veenendaal
Rhine
Oss
's-Hertogenbosch
Waal
Eindhoven
Venlo
Maas
Roermond
Weert
Kerkrade
Heerlen
Helmond
Lommel
Heerlen
Eupen
Malmédy
Zeid Willemsvaart Canal
Tilburg
Braine-Hertog
(to Belgium)
Mol
Geel
Diest
Hasselt
Genk
Maastricht
Herstal
Verviers
Sankt-Vith
Dordrecht
Oosterhout
Waalwijk
Breda
Turnhout
Albert Canal
Tienen
Tongeren
Meuse
Liège
Seraing
Famenne
Bastogne
Rotterdam
Roosendaal
Lier
Mechelen
Leuven
Huy
Marche-en-Famenne
Schiedam
Antwerp
Andenne
Dinant
Neufchâteau
Gouda
Bergen op Zoom
St-Niklaas
Rupel
Schaerbeek
Braine-l'Alleud
Gembloux
Namur
Meuse
Zoetermeer
Beveren
Aalst
BRUSSELS
Halle
Nivelles
Charleroi
Philippeville
Fagne
Ardennes
Delft
Terneuzen
Lokeren
Ghent
Scheldt
Oudenaarde
Soignies
Mons
Sambre
Gosselies
La Louvière
THE HAGUE
Hoek van Holland
Europoort
Vlaardingen
Spijkenisse
Goes
Vlissingen
Westerschelde
Middelburg
Oosterschelde
Bruges
Torhout
Harelbeke
Ronse
Ath
Tournai
Zeebrugge
FLANDERS
Veurne
Roeselare
Ieper
Kortrijk
Mouscron
Ostend

BELGIUM

FRANCE

LUXEMBOURG
Moselle
Diekirch
Grevenmacher
LUXEMBOURG
Arlon
Athus
Esch-sur-Alzette
Pétange

100 km
50 miles
50
25

FRANCE

One of the largest countries in western Europe, France has a variety of landscape types, which fall into two main areas. In the north and west are flat plains and low hills. The plains are drained by three great rivers, the Seine, the Loire and the Garonne. These rivers form basins with rich soils. To the south and east are the uplands – the high plateau of the Massif Central and two mountain ranges, the Pyrenees and the Alps. The Pyrenees form a natural border with Spain. The Alps are crossed by high passes that lead into Italy and Switzerland.

Fertile soils and a temperate climate make France a successful food producer. Wheat and vegetables are grown in the north, and corn and fruit are produced in the south. The lowlands make good dairy pasture and grapes for wine are grown in many areas. France is also highly industrialized. It exports a vast range of products, from cars to clothing. Both the northern and southern coasts suffer from industrial pollution, but because France generates about 75 per cent of its electricity in nuclear power stations, the country is less polluted by the use of fossil fuels than other industrialized nations.

From the 18th–20th centuries, France was a colonial power, with an empire in Africa, Asia and North America. Almost all of its colonies are now independent. Today, France plays a leading role in the European Union.

LAND HEIGHT

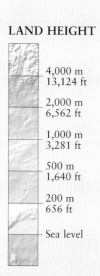

4,000 m
13,124 ft

2,000 m
6,562 ft

1,000 m
3,281 ft

500 m
1,640 ft

200 m
656 ft

Sea level

France

Monaco

Strait of Dover
2° Dunkerque
Calais
Boulogne-sur-Mer
Béthune Lens
Abbeville Arras
Lille Roubaix
Tourcoing
Valenciennes

BELGIUM

LUXEMBOURG

GERMANY

50°

Dieppe
Rouen
Amiens
St-Quentin
Beauvais
Laon
Compiègne
Creil
Pontoise
Évreux
Argenteuil PARIS
Versailles Créteil
Chartres
Melun

Somme
Oise
Charleville-Mézières
Reims
Thionville
Metz Forbach
Haguenau
Nancy
Strasbourg
St-Dié
Épinal Colmar

Meuse
Moselle
Rhine

Vosges

2°

Seine
Seine
Yonne
Sens
Troyes
Chaumont
Châlons-en-Champagne
Bar-le-Duc
Marne

CHAMPAGNE

Orléans
Olivet
Blois
Tours
Auxerre
Clamecy
Langres
Dijon
Mulhouse
Belfort
Vesoul
Besançon
Montbéliard

48°

AUSTRIA

LIECHTENSTEIN

SWITZERLAND

Cher
Bourges
Nevers
Loire
Morvan
BURGUNDY
Saône
Chalon-sur-Saône
Châteauroux
Creuse
Montceau-les-Mines
Moulins
Mâcon
Vichy
Bourg-en-Bresse
Roanne
Lyon Villeurbanne
Annemasse
Lake Geneva
Thonon-les-Bains
Chamonix
Mont Blanc 4,810 m
Annecy
Chambéry

J u r a

A l p s

46°

FRANCE

Vienne

Clermont-Ferrand
Limoges
Puy de Sancy 1,885 m
St-Étienne St-Chamond

Massif

Central

ITALY

Périgueux
Brive-la-Gaillarde
Dordogne
Le Puy
Isère
Grenoble
Les Ecrins 4,102 m
Valence
Gap

A

44°

Cahors
Lot
Mende
Rodez
Tarn
Montauban
Albi
Cévennes
Rhône
Montélimar
Orange
Avignon
Nîmes
Tarascon
Durance
Digne

Maritime Alps

MONACO
MONACO
Nice
Antibes

Toulouse
Castres
Montpellier
Béziers
Sète
Arles
Camargue
Marseille

PROVENCE

Aix-en-Provence
Cannes
Fréjus
St-Tropez
Côte d'Azur

Cap Corse

Carcassonne
Canal du Midi
Narbonne
Foix
Perpignan

Toulon
La Seyne-sur-Mer
Îles d'Hyères

Gulf of Lion

Bastia

ANDORRA

Pyrenees

Mediterranean Sea

Corsica

42°

Ajaccio
Sartène
Bonifacio
Strait of Bonifacio

Aléria

2° 4° 6° 8° 10°

THE IBERIAN PENINSULA

The Iberian Peninsula is separated from the rest of Europe by the Pyrenees mountains. To the west is the Atlantic Ocean, while the Mediterranean Sea lies in the east. Spain and Portugal occupy most of this large landmass, together with the tiny mountainous state of Andorra, and Gibraltar, a small British territory. The centre of the peninsula is dominated by a vast plateau, which is enclosed by the Cordillera Cantábrica to the north, and the Sierra Morena to the south.

Wheat and barley are Iberia's main crops, but in the south, farmers irrigate the dry land to grow citrus fruits, especially oranges and lemons. Both Spain and Portugal make wines and these two countries also produce two-thirds of the world's cork.

Spain's industries, which are concentrated in the north of the country, make cars, machinery, steel and chemicals. Portugal exports textiles, clothing, shoes and processed fish, and tourism is an important source of income for this entire region.

Soil erosion, which is caused when forests are cleared for farmland, has affected much of the peninsula. High-rise hotels along the Mediterranean coast have spoilt the character of this area, and popular beaches here are extremely overcrowded.

LAND HEIGHT

4,000 m
13,124 ft

2,000 m
6,562 ft

1,000 m
3,281 ft

500 m
1,640 ft

200 m
656 ft

Sea level

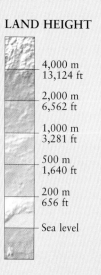

Spain

Andorra

Portugal

FRANCE

Gulf of
Gascony

Gulf
of Lion

antander
San Vicente
de Barakaldo
Bilbao   Donostia-   Irún
                San Sebastián   Pyrenees   ANDORRA
PAIS VASCO   Aneto 3,404 m △   Llívia (to Spain)
                Pamplona   ANDORRA LA VELLA
Vitoria-Gasteiz   Figueres
              NAVARRA   Jaca   Segre   Roses
Burgos   Logroño   Ripoll
          LA RIOJA   Huesca   Girona
IEJA   Costa Brava
Aranda   Monzón   Manresa
de Duero   Soria   Ebro   CATALONIA   Mataró
                      Zaragoza   Lleida   Terrassa
                                                    Sabadell   Badalona
        Calatayud   ARAGÓN   L'Hospitalet de   Barcelona
                Daroca   Embalse   Llobregat
                              de Mequinenza   Reus
                      Alcañiz   Tarragona
Guadalajara   Tortosa
Alcobendas   Amposta
Alcalá de Henares   Vinaròs
MADRID   Teruel   Balearic Islands   Ciutadella
Getafe   de Menorca
            Cuenca   Castelló   Mahón
Aranjuez   de la Plana   Alcúdia   Menorca
A   I   N   Costa del Azahar   (Minorca)
                                                          Palma de Mallorca
            NUEVA   Sagunto   Andratx   Manacor
Alcázar de   Utiel   Paterna   Mallorca   Santanyí
San Juan   Torrente   Valencia   (Majorca)
Villarrobledo   Júcar   Alzira
La Roda   Gulf of
LA MANCHA   Valencia
Manzanares   Albacete   Gandía   San Antonio   Eivissa
Valdepeñas   Denia   Cabo de   Abad   (Ibiza)
                Alcoy   la Nao   Eivissa (Ibiza)
        Hellín   Elda   Benidorm   Formentera
Linares   Elche   Alicante
            (Elx)   Costa Blanca
Jaén   Orihuela   Mediterranean
Murcia   Torrevieja   Sea
        Huéscar
            Cabo de Palos
Lorca   Cartagena
Baza
Granada Huércal-Overa   Aguilas
Nevada
Sierra Mulhacén
3,478 m Almería
Motril Adra   Cabo
            de Gata
el Sol

ALGERIA

Melilla
(to Spain)

GERMANY

Germany lies in the very heart of Europe. There are flat plains in the northern part of the country, and in the south are forests and the Alps. Two of Europe's greatest rivers flow through Germany. The Rhine runs from the south, where it forms a natural border with France, to the north. It is an important transport link between many industrial centres. To the south, the Danube rises in the Black Forest and flows east on its course to the Black Sea.

Germany's northern plains make good farmland – cattle and pigs are raised here, and cereal crops are grown. Livestock farms are located in the south, but the uplands here are often more suited to growing vegetables. Grapes for Germany's successful wine industry also grow well in the mountainous regions, and vineyards cover the slopes surrounding the Rhine and its tributaries. The chemicals industry, car manufacturing and engineering employ many people in and around major cities, especially in Berlin, and in the Ruhr, Rhine and Main valleys. Germany also has strong high-tech industries, producing goods such as computers and telecommunications equipment.

In 1945, Germany was defeated in World War II and the country was divided. East Germany became part of communist Europe. Many people worked in old-fashioned heavy industries, and salaries and working conditions were poor for most people. West Germany made a rapid recovery following the war, and became one of Europe's richest and most powerful countries. In 1990, the two states joined again, and since then, the German goverment has been trying to unite the country economically and politically. Germany is also an important member of the European Union.

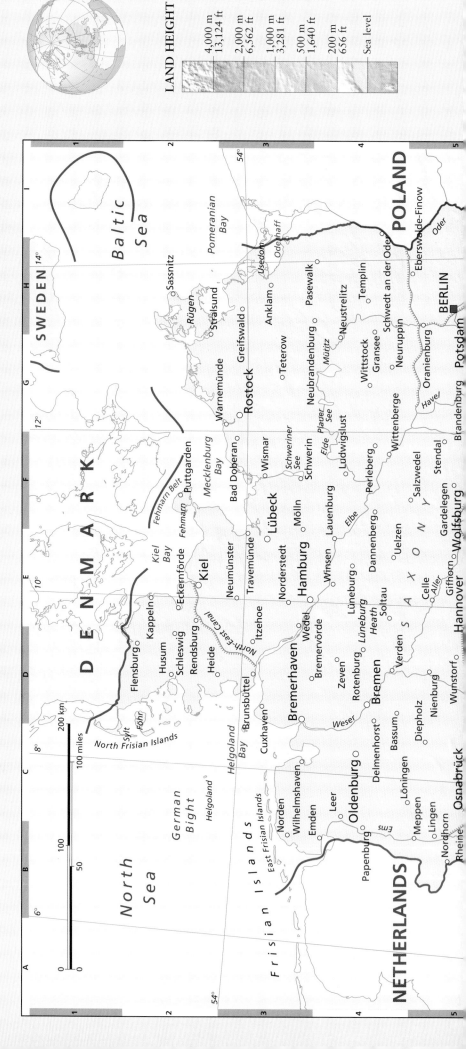

LAND HEIGHT

| 4,000 m | 2,000 m | 1,000 m | 500 m | 200 m | Sea level |
| 13,124 ft | 6,562 ft | 3,281 ft | 1,640 ft | 656 ft | |

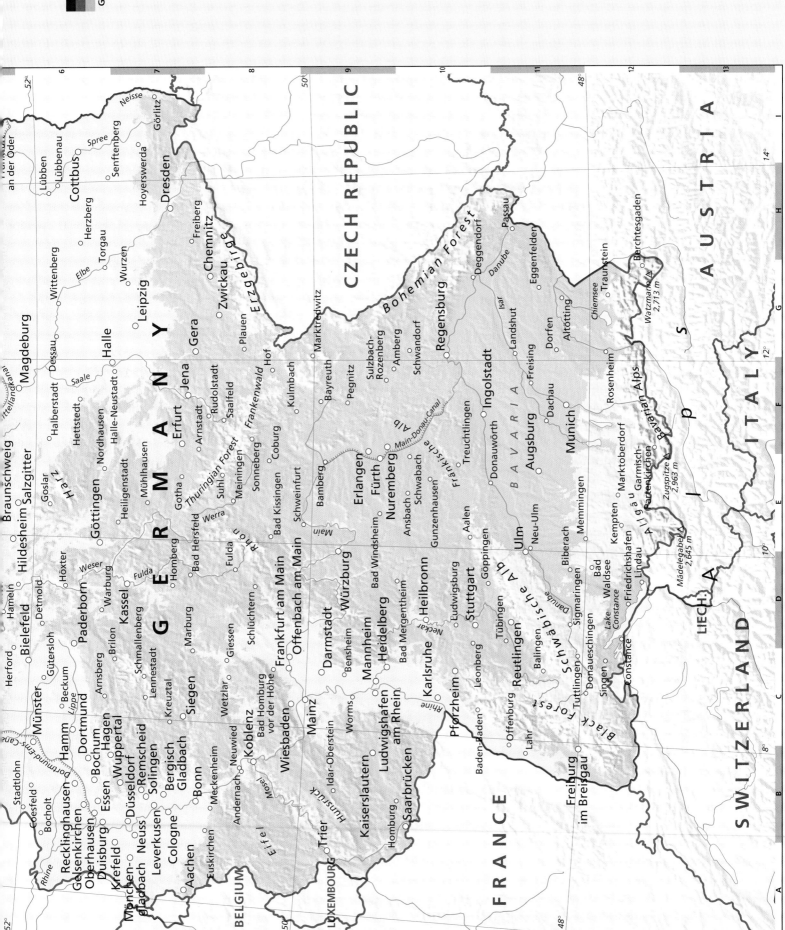

Germany

FRANCE

BELGIUM

LUXEMBOURG

CZECH REPUBLIC

AUSTRIA

ITALY

SWITZERLAND

LIECH.

G E R M A N Y

B A V A R I A

A l p s

Bavarian Alps

Black Forest

Schwäbische Alb

Fränkische Alb

Bohemian Forest

Thuringian Forest

Frankenwald

Erzgebirge

Eifel

Hunsrück

Harz

Rhön

Alb

an der Oder
Lübben
Lübbenau
Cottbus
Senftenberg
Spree
Neisse
Görlitz
Herzberg
Hoyerswerda
Dresden
Freiberg
Torgau
Wittenberg
Elbe
Wurzen
Chemnitz
Leipzig
Zwickau
Dessau
Halle
Saale
Gera
Plauen
Hof
Marktredwitz
Magdeburg
Mittellandkanal
Halberstadt
Halle-Neustadt
Jena
Rudolstadt
Saalfeld
Bayreuth
Pegnitz
Sulzbach-Rozenberg
Amberg
Schwandorf
Regensburg
Danube
Deggendorf
Passau
Braunschweig
Salzgitter
Hildesheim
Goslar
Nordhausen
Heiligenstadt
Mühlhausen
Erfurt
Arnstadt
Gotha
Meiningen
Suhl
Sonneberg
Coburg
Kulmbach
Bamberg
Erlangen
Fürth
Nuremberg
Schwabach
Ansbach
Main-Donau-Canal
Aalen
Treuchtlingen
Donauwörth
Ingolstadt
Neuburg
Isar
Landshut
Dorfen
Altötting
Eggenfelden
Chiemsee
Traunstein
Watzmann 2,713 m
Berchtesgaden
Hameln
Hildesheim
Göttingen
Heiligenstadt
Homberg
Bad Hersfeld
Werra
Fulda
Bad Kissingen
Schweinfurt
Bad Windsheim
Bad Mergentheim
Würzburg
Main
Gunzenhausen
Schwabach
Neu-Ulm
Ulm
Biberach
Memmingen
Kempten
Marktoberdorf
Bad Waldsee
Friedrichshafen
Lindau
Lake Constance
Mädelegabel 2,645 m
Zugspitze 2,963 m
Garmisch-Partenkirchen
Rosenheim
Dachau
Freising
Munich
Augsburg
Herford
Bielefeld
Detmold
Gütersloh
Höxter
Paderborn
Warburg
Kassel
Brilon
Arnsberg
Schmallenberg
Lennestadt
Siegen
Kreuztal
Marburg
Giessen
Wetzlar
Schlüchtern
Frankfurt am Main
Offenbach am Main
Darmstadt
Bensheim
Mannheim
Heidelberg
Bad Homburg vor der Höhe
Wiesbaden
Mainz
Worms
Ludwigshafen am Rhein
Neckar
Heilbronn
Ludwigsburg
Stuttgart
Göppingen
Tübingen
Reutlingen
Balingen
Sigmaringen
Donaueschingen
Singen
Tuttlingen
Constance
Danube
Leonberg
Pforzheim
Karlsruhe
Baden-Baden
Offenburg
Lahr
Freiburg im Breisgau
Stadtlohn
Coesfeld
Bocholt
Recklinghausen
Gelsenkirchen
Oberhausen
Duisburg
Krefeld
Mönchengladbach
Neuss
Essen
Bochum
Dortmund
Hamm
Beckum
Lippe
Hagen
Wuppertal
Remscheid
Solingen
Düsseldorf
Leverkusen
Bergisch Gladbach
Cologne
Bonn
Euskirchen
Aachen
Meckenheim
Neuwied
Andernach
Koblenz
Mosel
Idar-Oberstein
Trier
Kaiserslautern
Homburg
Saarbrücken
Rhine
Dortmund-Ems-Canal
Münster
Rhine
52°
50°
48°
6°
8°
10°
12°
14°

THE ALPINE STATES

The Alps, Europe's tallest range of mountains, stretch across the Alpine states – Austria, Liechtenstein, Switzerland and Slovenia. This region in central Europe has a landscape of jagged snow-topped peaks, deep valleys and lakes that were scooped out by glaciers over 20,000 years ago. The mountainous terrain of the Alpine states limits the amount of land that can be cultivated by farmers, although the rich pastures of the lower slopes are used to graze both beef and dairy cattle.

Switzerland and Liechtenstein have few raw materials, so these countries concentrate on producing high-quality goods, including pharmaceuticals and watches. They also act as international centres for banking. Austria is heavily industrialized, and all four countries have strong tourist industries. People from many parts of the world come to the Alpine states to ski and to admire the mountain scenery. The vast numbers of visitors, and the buildings needed to house them, put a strain on the environment. This region lies on the main trading routes across the Alps, so air pollution caused by passing lorries is another environmental problem.

Switzerland takes a neutral position in wars and other conflicts. This policy makes the country an ideal base for a number of important international organizations, including the Red Cross and various agencies of the United Nations.

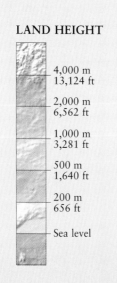

LAND HEIGHT

4,000 m
13,124 ft

2,000 m
6,562 ft

1,000 m
3,281 ft

500 m
1,640 ft

200 m
656 ft

Sea level

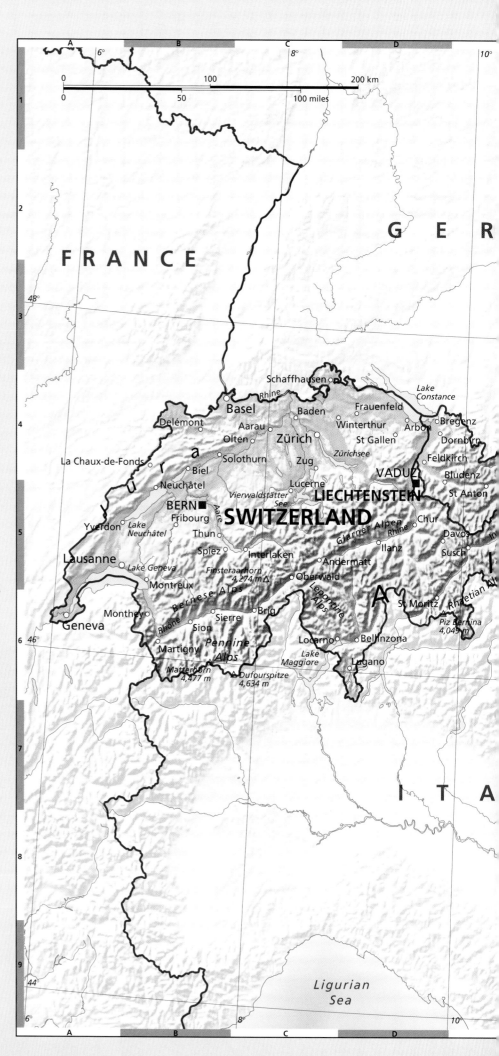

Austria

Switzerland

Liechtenstein

Slovenia

CZECH REPUBLIC

SLOVAKIA

M A N Y

Gmünd

Mistelbach

Hollabrunn

Krems an der Donau

Danube

Tulln

Linz

VIENNA

Wels

Amstetten

Mödling

Vocklabruck

Steyr

Baden

Neusiedler See

Attersee

Gmunden

Waidhofen an der Ybbs

Wiener Neustadt

Eisenstadt

Traunsee

Salzburg

A U S T R I A

Hallein

Bad Ischl

Neunkirchen

Enns

Mürzzuschlag

Zugspitze 2,963 m

Kufstein

Liezen

Rottenmann

Bavarian Alps

Wörgl

Bruck an der Mur

Bischofshofen

Kitzbühel

Schwaz

Radstadt

Knittelfeld

T I R O L

Telfs

Niedere Tauern

Judenburg

Graz

Innsbruck

Mittersill

Mur

Wildspitze 3,774 m

Hohe Tauern

St Michael im Langau

Köflach

HUNGARY

Grossglockner 3,797 m

Raab

Ötztaler Alpen

S

Lienz

Wolfsberg

Wildon

p

Spittal an der Drau

St Veit an der Glan

Leibnitz

Mur

Drau

Völkermarkt

Murska Sobota

Karnische Alpen

Villach

Klagenfurt

Maribor

Karawanken

Ptuj

Drava

Triglav 2,864 m

Jesenice

Celje

Julian Alps

Kranj

Tolmin

Sava

Trbovlje

Krsko

LJUBLJANA

SLOVENIA

Nova Gorica

Postojna

Novo Mesto

Ribnica

Kocevje

Koper

Kozina

C R O A T I A

L Y

Adriatic Sea

BOSNIA & HERZEGOVINA

ITALY AND MALTA

This region stretches from the Alps in the north to the Mediterranean islands of Malta in the south. Much of the Italian peninsula is mountainous, with the Apennines extending along almost the whole length of Italy, and the Dolomites in the northeast. In the south are volcanoes, such as Etna and Vesuvius. This area also experiences earthquakes.

The northern and southern halves of the region are different from each other in several ways. The north, which has a milder climate than the south, is more developed. Big cities, including

Turin, Milan and Genoa, are centres of industry. Here, manufacturing companies make cars, engines and other products. There are also high-tech businesses, and design studios specializing in everything from clothing to furniture. The north is a popular tourist destination, luring many people with its stunning scenery, fine food and historical cities including Venice, Florence and Rome. Lake Garda and Lake Como also attract many visitors. In the north are two tiny countries. The Vatican City, a small area of Rome, is the headquarters of the Catholic

Church. The ancient independent state of San Marino is located near the Adriatic coast.

In the south, the climate is hotter, the towns are generally smaller, and industry is less well developed. The dry soils often have to be irrigated, but some crops, such as olives, citrus fruits, grapes and tomatoes, grow well in the baking sun. Still further south are Sicily and Malta, which have an even hotter climate. Sicily is part of Italy, while the islands of Malta form a separate nation. Tourism and shipping are Malta's major sources of income.

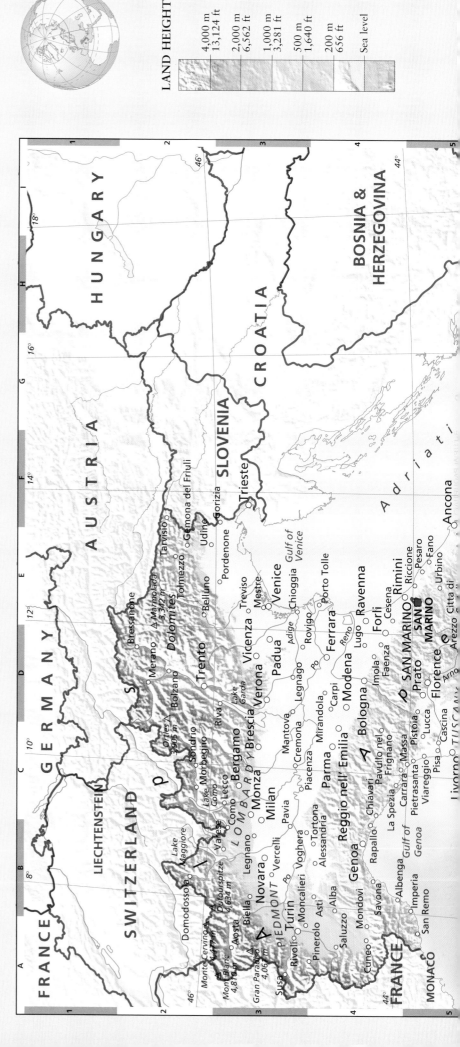

LAND HEIGHT

4,000 m	2,000 m	1,000 m	500 m	200 m	
13,124 ft	6,562 ft	3,281 ft	1,640 ft	656 ft	Sea level

Italy
San Marino
Vatican City
Malta

Ligurian Sea

Corsica (to France)

Strait of Bonifacio

Sardinia

Porto Torres
Alghero
Sassari
Ozieri
Macomer
Oristano
Guspini
Iglesias
Carbonia
San Antioco
Nuoro
Siniscola
Olbia
Tortoli
Villaputzu
Quartu Sant'Elena
Cagliari
Punta La Marmora △1,834 m
Terralba
Tirso
Capo Carbonara
Capo Spartivento

Cecina
Piombino
Elba
Follonica
Grosseto
Orbetello
Siena
Lake Trasimeno
Cortona
Perugia
Assisi
Gubbio
Spoleto
Orvieto
Lake Bolsena
Viterbo
Civitavecchia
Terni
Rieti
L'Aquila
Corno Grande △2,912 m
Avezzano
Sora
Tivoli
ROME
VATICAN CITY
Lido di Ostia
Anzio
Latina
Terracina
Gaeta
Tiber

ITALY

Civitanova Marche
Fermo
Ascoli Piceno
San Benedetto del Tronto
Teramo
Pescara
Chieti
Lanciano
Vasto
Termoli
Sulmona
Isernia
Cassino
Formia
Gulf of Gaeta

Lake Varano
Lake Lesina
Gargano Peninsula
Gulf of Manfredonia
Manfredonia
San Severo
Foggia
Campobasso
Benevento
Caserta
Avellino
Naples
Salerno
Cerignola
Andria
Barletta
Molfetta
Bari
Bitonto
Gioia del Colle
Altamura
Rionero in Vulture
△Vesuvius 1,279 m
Eboli
Battipaglia
Gulf of Salerno
Capri
Ischia
Potenza
Matera
Taranto
Gulf of Taranto
Appennino Lucano
Basento
Agropoli
Lauria
Maratea
Castrovillari
Ostuni
Nardo
Brindisi
Lecce
Otranto
Gallipoli
Capo Santa Maria di Leuca

Tyrrhenian Sea

Ponziane Islands
Ustica

Mediterranean Sea

Corigliano Calabro
Rossano
Ciro Marina
Cosenza
Crotone
Capo Colonna
Cetraro
Lamezia
Catanzaro
Gulf of Squillace
Vibo Valentia
Rosarno
CALABRIA
Reggio di Calabria
Capo Spartivento

Ionian Sea

Stromboli
Aeolian Islands
Milazzo
Messina
Strait of Messina
Taormina
△Mount Etna 3,350 m
Paterno
Adrano
Catania
Siracusa
Avola
Pachino
Capo Passero
Palermo
Cefalù
Bagheria
Partinico
Capo San Vito
Trapani
Marsala
Castelvetrano
Mazara del Vallo
Sciacca
Agrigento
Canicattì
Caltanissetta
Enna
Licata
Gela
Vittoria
Ragusa
Modica
Sicily
Adrano

Pantelleria
Strait of Sicily
Malta Channel

Linosa
Pelagic Islands
Lampedusa

Gozo
MALTA ■VALLETTA
Malta

TUNISIA

ALGERIA

200 km
100 miles
100
50
0

42°
40°
38°
36°

42°
40°
38°
36°

6 7 8 9 10 11 12 13
8° 10° 12° 14° 16° 18°

EASTERN EUROPE

The countries of eastern Europe have a varied landscape which extends from the cliffs and sandy beaches of the Baltic coast, through the vast Pripet Marshes in southern Belarus, to the great open steppes that cover almost three-quarters of the Ukraine.

Most of the countries in this region have spent long periods of their history under Russian rule. For much of the 20th century, they all formed part of the Soviet Union. The Soviets encouraged the growth of heavy industry and manufacturing, turning these

states into industrial nations. When the Soviet Union broke up in 1991, the countries of this area became independent and their old-fashioned factories had to compete with the modern, high-tech businesses of the rest of Europe. For a number of years there were price rises and food shortages. Recently, however, this region has developed new high-tech industries, and the countries have also formed trade links with western Europe.

Farming is the main source of employment for much of the population. The rich black soils of

the Ukraine are ideal for growing cereal crops and sugar beet. The smaller countries of the Baltic coast have many cattle and pig farms. The Baltic states have few natural resources, and they have to import goods and services from their larger, richer neighbours.

In 1986, the world's worst nuclear accident took place at the power station at Chernobyl, in the Ukraine near the border with Belarus. Thirty-one people were killed immediately, and radioactive particles spread over a huge area, contaminating farmland and making thousands of people ill.

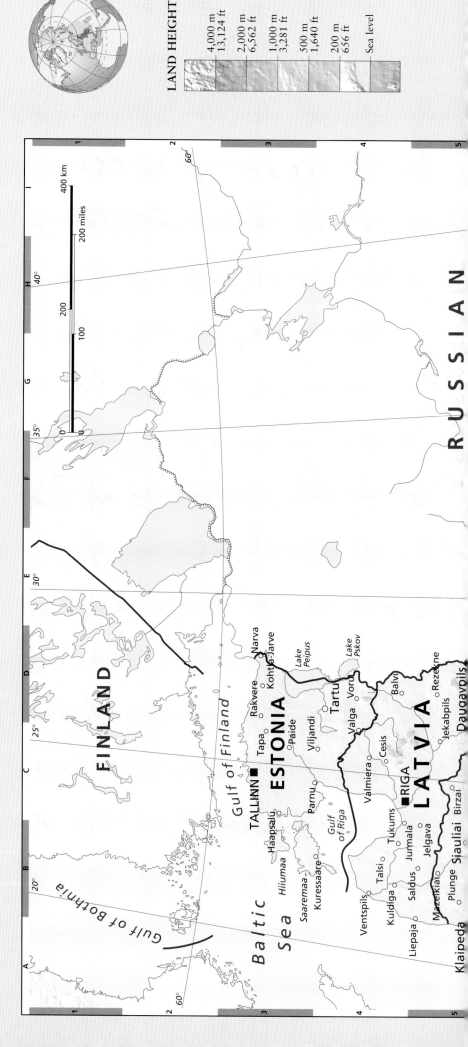

LAND HEIGHT

4,000 m	13,124 ft
2,000 m	6,562 ft
1,000 m	3,281 ft
500 m	1,640 ft
200 m	656 ft
	Sea level

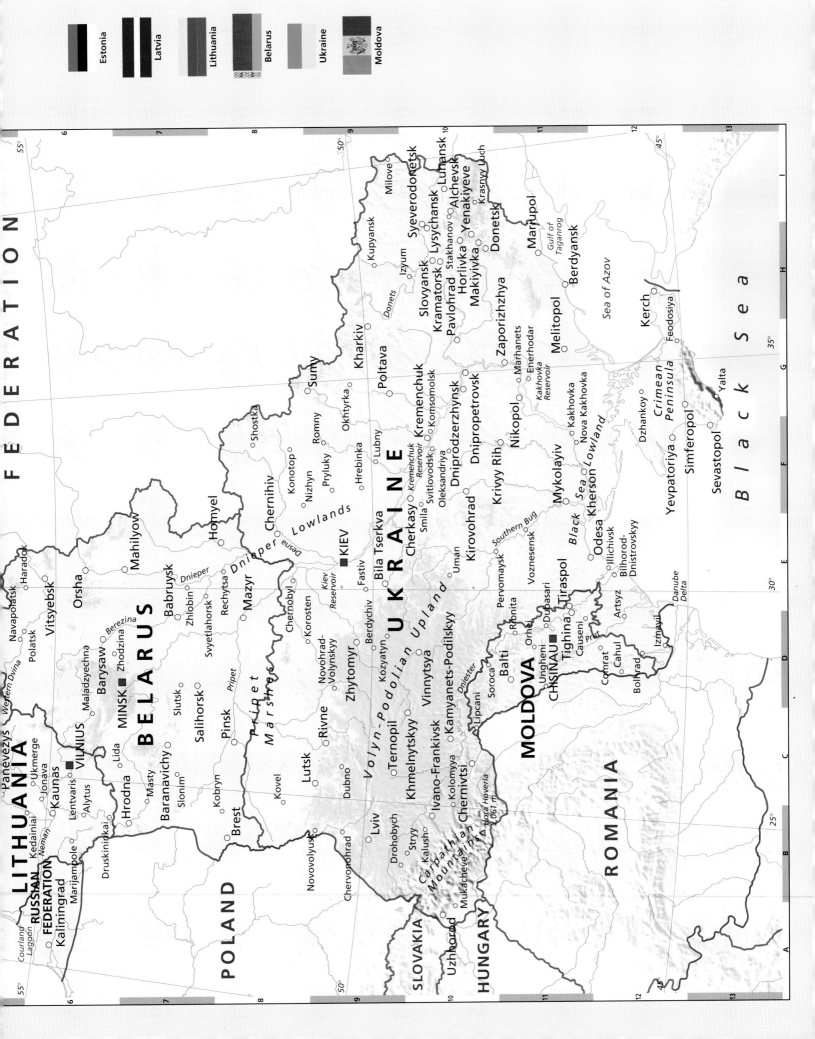

Estonia
Latvia
Lithuania
Belarus
Ukraine
Moldova

RUSSIAN FEDERATION

LITHUANIA

RUSSIAN FEDERATION
Kaliningrad

Courland Lagoon

Panevezys
Ukmerge
Kedainiai
Jonava
Kaunas
Lentvaris ■ **VILNIUS**
Marijampole
Druskininkai
Alytus
Lida
Masty
Hrodna

POLAND

Neman

Navapolatsk
Polatsk
Vitsyebsk
Orsha
Harad
Maladzyechna
MINSK ■ Zhodzina
Barysaw
Babruysk
Zhlobin
Slutsk
Slonim
Baranavichy
Salihorsk
Pinsk
Kobryn
Brest

BELARUS

Western Dvina
Berezina
Dnieper
Svyetlahorsk
Rechytsa
Mazyr

Pripet Marshes

Pripet

Mahilyow
Homyel

Novovolynsk
Chervonohrad

Chernobyl
Korosten
Novohrad-Volynskyy
Zhytomyr
Berdychiv

Lutsk
Dubno
Rivne
Kovel

Kiev Reservoir
Fastiv
Bila Tserkva
Kozyatyn

KIEV ■

Chernihiv

Dnieper Lowlands

Desna

Shostka
Konotop
Nizhyn
Pryluky
Romny
Hrebinka
Lubny

Volyn-Podolian Upland

Ternopil
Khmelnytskyy
Vinnytsya
Kamyanets-Podilskyy
Chernivtsi

Lviv
Drohobych
Stryy
Kalusho
Ivano-Frankivsk
Kolomyya
Mukacheveo
Uzhhorod

Carpathian Mountains

△ Hora Hoverla
2,061 m

SLOVAKIA

HUNGARY

Sumy
Okhtyrka
Kharkiv
Poltava

Kupyansk
Izyum
Milove
Donets

UKRAINE

Cherkasy
Smila
Svitlovodsk
Oleksandriya
Dniprodzerzhynsk
Kremenchuk Reservoir
Kremenchuk
Komsomolsk

Kirovohrad
Uman

Dnipropetrovsk
Dniprodzerzhynsk

Southern Bug

Syeverodonetsk
Lysychansk
Luhansk
Slovyansk
Kramatorsk
Pavlohrad
Stakhanov
Alchevsk
Horlivka
Yenakiyeve
Makiyivka
Donetsk
Krasnyy Luch

Zaporizhzhya
Marhanets
Enerhodar
Nikopol
Kakhovka Reservoir
Kakhovka
Nova Kakhovka
Krivyy Rih

Mariupol

Berdyansk

Gulf of Taganrog

Sea of Azov

Black Sea Lowland

Kherson Lowland

Mykolayiv
Pervomaysk
Voznesensk

Odesa
Illichivsk
Bilhorod-Dnistrovskyy

Melitopol

Kerch
Feodosiya
Crimean Peninsula
Simferopol
Yevpatoriya
Sevastopol
Yalta
Dzhankoy

Black Sea

MOLDOVA

Balti
Soroca
Lipcani
Ribnita
Orhei
CHIŞINĂU ■
Ungheni
Dubasari
Tighina
Tiraspol
Causeni
Comrat
Cahul
Bolhrad
Artsyz
Izmayil

Danube Delta

ROMANIA

Dniester
Prut

55°
55°
50°
50°
45°
45°
35°
30°
25°

6 7 8 9 10 11 12 13
A B C D E F G H I

CENTRAL EUROPE

Central Europe is made up of two plains, which are divided by a chain of mountains. To the north, in Poland, is the North European Plain. The Great Hungarian Plain, with its farmlands and grasslands, lies in the south. Much of the land area of the Czech Republic and Slovakia falls in the mountainous region in the centre. For most of the 20th century, these countries were united as Czechoslovakia, but in 1993, they split into two separate nations.

Central Europe's farmers grow cereal crops such as barley, oats, wheat and rye, as well as large quantities of potatoes and sugar beet. They also raise livestock, especially pigs. In Hungary, where the climate is warmer, farmers grow grapes for wine and sweet peppers for paprika, a hot spice that is used in Hungarian cooking. Much of Slovakia is covered with forest and the country has a large timber industry.

Poland has enormous reserves of a brown coal, called lignite, which is exported. A variety of minerals are mined in the mountains of the Czech Republic and Slovakia. Hungary has a wide range of industries, producing vehicles, metals, chemicals, textiles and electrical goods, while the Czech Republic is famous for its breweries and fine glassware.

For much of the 20th century, the countries of central Europe were ruled by communist governments, which were dominated by the powerful, Russian-led Soviet Union. The old-fashioned heavy industries that were developed under communist rule have caused terrible pollution in some places. However, the countries of central Europe are now moving towards more modern, high-tech industries.

LAND HEIGHT					
4,000 m 13,124 ft	2,000 m 6,562 ft	1,000 m 3,281 ft	500 m 1,640 ft	200 m 656 ft	Sea level

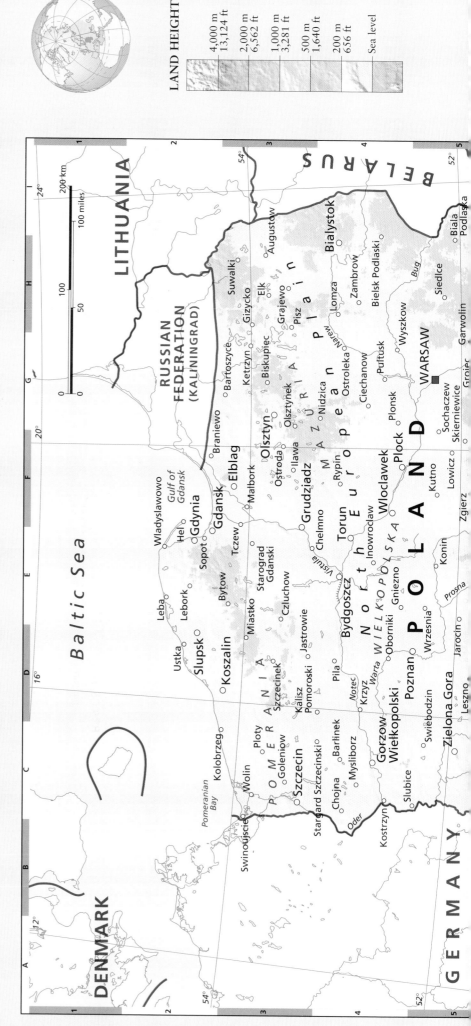

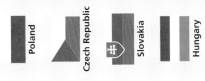

Poland · Czech Republic · Slovakia · Hungary

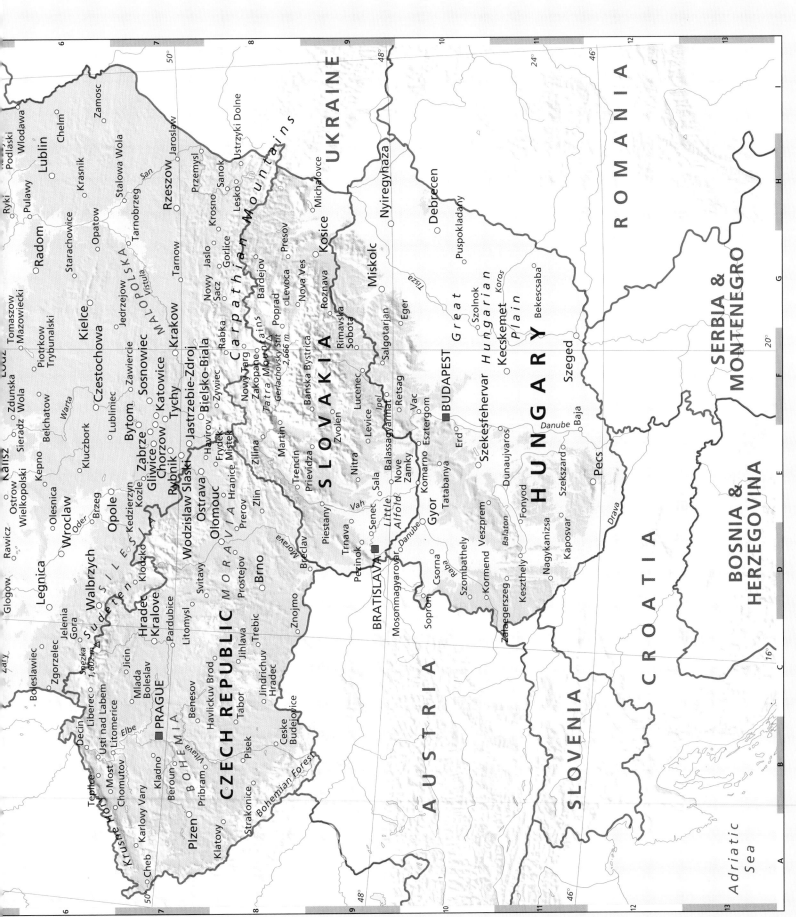

UKRAINE

ROMANIA

SERBIA & MONTENEGRO

BOSNIA & HERZEGOVINA

CROATIA

SLOVENIA

AUSTRIA

HUNGARY

SLOVAKIA

CZECH REPUBLIC

Adriatic Sea

Lublin · Chelm · Wlodawa · Podlaski · Ryki · Pulawy · Radom · Krasnik · Stalowa Wola · Zamosc · Opatow · Tarnobrzeg · Starachowice · Rzeszow · Jaroslaw · Przemysl · Sanok · Ustrzyki Dolne · Lesko · Krosno · Gorlice · Jaslo · Nowy Sacz · Bardejov · Presov · Michalovce · Kosice · Roznava · Rimavska Sobota · Miskolc · Nyiregyhaza · Debrecen · Puspokladany · Bekescsaba · Szolnok · Kecskemet · Szeged · Baja · Pecs · Kaposvar · Szekszard · Nagykanizsa · Keszthely · Fonyod · Balaton · Zalaegerszeg · Szombathely · Kormend · Veszprem · Szekesfehervar · Dunaujvaros · Erd · BUDAPEST · Vac · Esztergom · Komarno · Tatabanya · Gyor · Sopron · Mosonmagyarovar · BRATISLAVA

Warta · Oder · Vistula · MALOPOLSKA · Tatra Mountains · Carpathian Mountains · Gerlachovsky Stit 2,666 m · Banska Bystrica · Zvolen · Lucenec · Salgotarjan · Eger · Great Hungarian Plain · Koros · Tisza · Little Alfold · Danube · Drava · Raba · BOHEMIA · MORAVIA · SILESIA · Sudeten Mtns · Bohemian Forest · Krusne Hory · Snezka 1,602 m · PRAGUE · Plzen · Elbe · Vltava

SOUTHEASTERN EUROPE

Southeastern Europe extends east from the Adriatic Sea to the Black Sea, south to the Mediterranean Sea and north to the Carpathian Mountains. The ancient country of Greece lies in the far south. It has been an independent nation since 1829. Albania, Romania and Bulgaria were ruled by communist governments for almost 50 years, until the 1990s. The rest of this region was part of a communist union of states called Yugoslavia. In 1991, a civil war led to the break-up of this union, and after the war, five separate countries were created.

Southeastern Europe is mainly mountainous, but the northern part of the region has good soils where cereals, vegetables and fruits are grown. The upland areas are used for grazing sheep and goats. Further south, and in the coastal areas, grapes and olives are the main crops. Southeastern Europe has some textile, engineering and manufacturing businesses, and these are concentrated around major cities, such as Zagreb and Bucharest. Fumes from motor vehicles and factories combine to pollute the atmosphere in the urban areas. The Greek government controls the number of vehicles that come into Athens, but despite this, the air quality here is still bad. Mainland Greece and the islands in the Aegean Sea are centres of a thriving tourist trade, while tourism on the Black Sea coast is growing steadily.

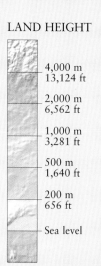

LAND HEIGHT

	4,000 m 13,124 ft
	2,000 m 6,562 ft
	1,000 m 3,281 ft
	500 m 1,640 ft
	200 m 656 ft
	Sea level

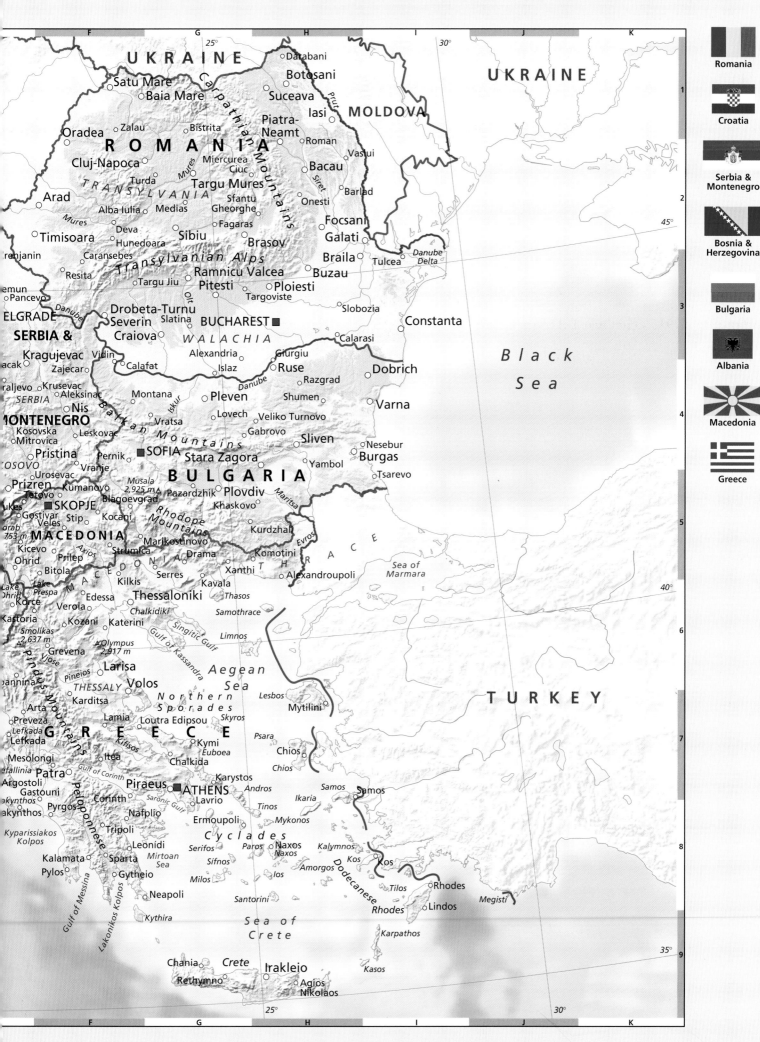

Romania

Croatia

Serbia & Montenegro

Bosnia & Herzegovina

Bulgaria

Albania

Macedonia

Greece

UKRAINE

UKRAINE

Satu Mare
Baia Mare

Darabani

Botosani

Suceava

Iasi

MOLDOVA

Oradea Zalau Bistrita

ROMANIA

Piatra-Neamt

Roman

Cluj-Napoca

Miercurea Ciuc

Bacau

TRANSYLVANIA

Turda Targu Mures

Vaslui

Arad

Sfantu Gheorghe

Barlad

Alba Iulia Medias

Fagaras

Focsani

Deva

Sibiu

Galati

Timisoara Hunedoara

Brasov

Braila

renjanin Caransebes

Transylvanian Alps

Ramnicu Valcea

Tulcea Danube Delta

Resita

Targu Jiu

Pitesti

Buzau

emun Pancevo

Drobeta-Turnu Severin Slatina BUCHAREST

Slobozia

ELGRADE

Craiova

WALACHIA

Constanta

SERBIA &

Targoviste

Kragujevac Vidin Alexandria Giurgiu Calarasi

acak Zajecar Calafat Islaz Ruse Dobrich

raljevo Krusevac Montana Razgrad

SERBIA Aleksinac

Pleven Shumen Varna

Nis Vratsa Lovech Veliko Turnovo

MONTENEGRO

Kosovska Mitrovica Leskovac Gabrovo Sliven Nesebur

Pristina Pernik SOFIA Stara Zagora Burgas

KOSOVO Urosevac Vranje Yambol Tsarevo

Prizren Kumanovo Musala 2,925 m Pazardzhik Plovdiv

Tetovo Blagoevgrad BULGARIA

ukes SKOPJE Khaskovo

Gostivar Veles Stip Kocani Rhodope Mountains

orab Kurdzhali

753 m MACEDONIA Marikostinovo

Kicevo Prilep Strumica Drama Komotini T R A C E

Ohrid Bitola Serres Xanthi Evros

Lake Ohrid Kilkis Kavala Alexandroupoli

Korce Edessa Thessaloniki Thasos Sea of Marmara

Kastoria Veroia Chalkidiki Samothrace

Smolikas 2,637 m Kozani Katerini Singitic Gulf Limnos

Grevena Olympus 2,917 m Gulf of Kassandra

Vjose

Pindus Mountains Larisa Aegean Sea

annina THESSALY Volos Lesbos

Arta Karditsa Northern Sporades Mytilini

Preveza Lamia Skyros

Lefkada Loutra Edipsou

Lefkada GREECE Psara Chios

Mesolongi Itea Kymi Chios

efallinia Patra Gulf of Corinth Chalkida Euboea

Argostoli Piraeus Karystos Samos

Gastouni Corinth ATHENS Andros Samos

akynthos Pyrgos Nafplio Lavrio Tinos Ikaria

akynthos Tripoli Ermoupoli Mykonos

Kyparissiakos Kolpos Leonidi Cyclades Naxos Kalymnos

Sparta Serifos Paros Naxos Kos

Kalamata Gytheio Sifnos Ios Amorgos Kos

Pylos Milos Dodecanese Tilos Rhodes

Neapoli Santorini Rhodes Lindos

Gulf of Messina Megisti

Lakonikos Kolpos Kythira Karpathos

Sea of Crete

Chania Crete Irakleio Kasos

Rethymno Agios Nikolaos

Black Sea

TURKEY

AFRICA

Africa, the world's second-largest continent, is separated from Asia by the Red Sea and from Europe by the Mediterranean Sea. A major feature of this huge landmass is the Sahara, the planet's biggest desert. It divides Africa's northern coast from the rest of the continent. South of the Sahara, the landscape consists mainly of broad plateaux, broken by the basins of major rivers, such as the Congo and the Zambezi. The Great Rift Valley cuts through the uplands of east Africa. Some of the rivers have dramatic waterfalls, such as the Victoria Falls, where the Zambezi plunges into a chasm more than 120 m deep. Africa also has high mountains, such as the Atlas range in the northwest and the Drakensberg in the south.

Most experts believe that the human race first evolved in Africa, but the continent's long history has been a troubled one. In the 19th century, European powers such as Britain, France and Belgium took over much of the continent. Most areas won independence from their foreign rulers in the 1960s, to create 53 separate African nations. These contain many different peoples, and have a rich variety of languages. A number of countries, however, have struggled to develop as modern states.

Some African countries rely on income from a single 'cash crop', such as oranges, olives or sugar cane. This means that their economies suffer badly if prices for the crop decrease or the harvests fail. The continent's rapidly rising population is often hit hard by famine, and some countries have suffered war. Africa also has lots of advantages, from its plentiful natural resources to some of the planet's most spectacular scenery and fascinating wildlife.

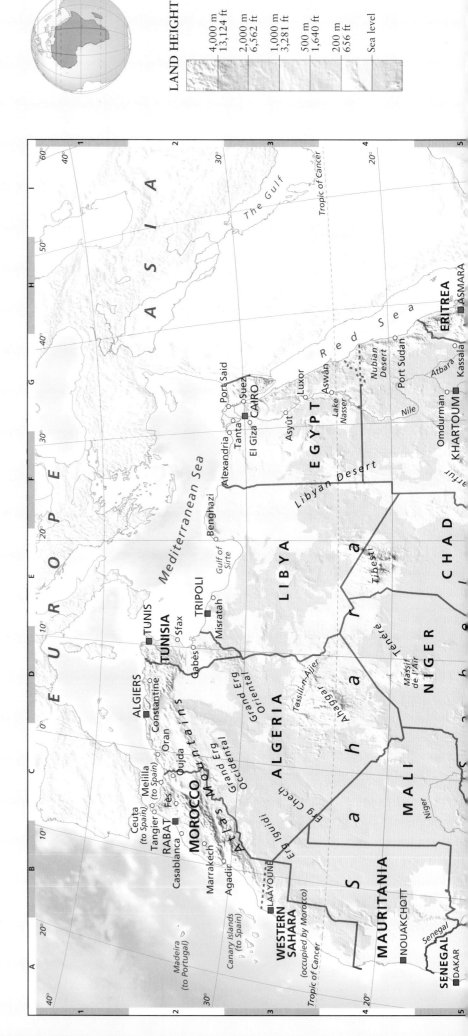

LAND HEIGHT

4,000 m	13,124 ft
2,000 m	6,562 ft
1,000 m	3,281 ft
500 m	1,640 ft
200 m	656 ft
Sea level	

ATLANTIC OCEAN

INDIAN OCEAN

Gulf of Aden

DJIBOUTI DJIBOUTI

Hargeysa

Horn of Africa

SOMALIA

MOGADISHU

Dire Dawa

Ras Dashen 4,620 m

ETHIOPIA

Ethiopian Highlands

ADDIS ABABA

Ogaden

Shebeli

Blue Nile

White Nile

Equator

Kismaayo

SUDAN

Sudd

El Obeid

Juba

CENTRAL AFRICAN REPUBLIC

NDJAMENA

Lake Chad

Maiduguri

NIGERIA

Kano

Zaria

Kaduna

ABUJA

Ilorin

Ibadan

Lagos

Niger

Benue

Jos

Benin City

PORTO-NOVO

BENIN

TOGO

LOMÉ

ACCRA

GHANA

OUAGADOUGOU

BURKINA

NIAMEY

BAMAKO

GUINEA

GUINEA-BISSAU

BISSAU

CONAKRY

SIERRA LEONE

FREETOWN

MONROVIA

LIBERIA

IVORY COAST

YAMOUSSOUKRO

Abidjan

Lake Volta

Gulf of Guinea

Abuja

Douala

Port Harcourt

Aba

CAMEROON

YAOUNDÉ

MALABO

EQUATORIAL GUINEA

SÃO TOMÉ & PRÍNCIPE

SÃO TOMÉ

Adamawa Highlands

Port-Gentil

GABON

LIBREVILLE

BANGUI

BRAZZAVILLE

CONGO

Pointe-Noire

Congo

Uele

Kisangani

Lualaba

Mbandaka

DEMOCRATIC REPUBLIC OF CONGO

Congo Basin

KINSHASA

ANGOLA (CABINDA)

LUANDA

Kasai

Kananga

Mbuji-Mayi

Cuango

Kolwezi

Lubumbashi

Kasama

Kitwe Ndola

Lubumbashi

ZAMBIA

LUSAKA

Zambezi

Livingstone

Victoria Falls

ANGOLA

Benguela

Namibe

Huambo

Bié Plateau

Cuando

Cubango

Okavango Delta

Francistown

BOTSWANA

GABORONE

Kalahari Desert

Johannesburg

PRETORIA

MBABANE

SWAZILAND

MAPUTO

NAMIBIA

WINDHOEK

Namib Desert

Walvis Bay

Skeleton Coast

SOUTH AFRICA

BLOEMFONTEIN

MASERU

LESOTHO

Orange River

Vaal

Pietermaritzburg

Durban

East London

Port Elizabeth

CAPE TOWN

Cape of Good Hope

Cape Agulhas

Tropic of Capricorn

UGANDA

KAMPALA

Lake Victoria

Kisumu

KENYA

NAIROBI

Kirinyaga 5,199 m

Mwanza

Kilimanjaro 5,895 m

Arusha

Mombasa

Tanga

Zanzibar

Dar es Salaam

RWANDA

KIGALI

BURUNDI

BUJUMBURA

Lake Tanganyika

TANZANIA

DODOMA

Masai Steppe

Great Rift Valley

Lake Nyasa

MALAWI

LILONGWE

Blantyre

MOZAMBIQUE

Nampula

Quelimane

Beira

Zambezi

Limpopo

Inhambane

ZIMBABWE

HARARE

Mutare

Gweru

Bulawayo

Victoria Falls

Lake Turkana

Great Rift Valley

COMOROS

MORONI

Mayotte (to France)

Mozambique Channel

Aldabra Group (to Seychelles)

MADAGASCAR

ANTANANARIVO

Toamasina

Mahajanga

Fianarantsoa

Tropic of Capricorn

Ascension Island (to St Helena)

St Helena (to UK)

Equator

2000 km

1000 miles

1000

500

0

NORTHWEST AFRICA

Morocco, Algeria, Tunisia and Libya occupy the coast of northwestern Africa and part of the northern Sahara Desert. The region's uplands, including the Atlas Mountains, stretch from the north of Tunisia to the Atlantic coast of Morocco. Most of the people live in towns and villages on a fertile strip of land along the north coast, although Western Sahara and the southern parts of Algeria and Libya are thinly populated by Tuareg nomads.

On the coast, farmers grow grapes and olives, or raise sheep and goats. The bark of the cork tree is harvested in Morocco and Algeria, and dates are grown at oases in the desert. This region has a thriving textile industry, producing colourful rugs and fabrics, and in the past few decades, oil and natural gas have brought wealth to Libya. Tourism is also a strong industry in the area, with ancient cities and hot weather attracting many overseas visitors.

The main environmental problem in northwest Africa is the northward spread of the Sahara Desert due to droughts and the cutting down of trees and plants for fuel and animal food. As a result, farmers are losing land, and they are forced to overgraze the existing pastures. This puts more stress on the land, and leads to the further expansion of the desert.

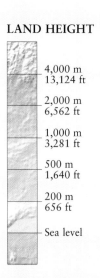

LAND HEIGHT

4,000 m	13,124 ft
2,000 m	6,562 ft
1,000 m	3,281 ft
500 m	1,640 ft
200 m	656 ft
Sea level	

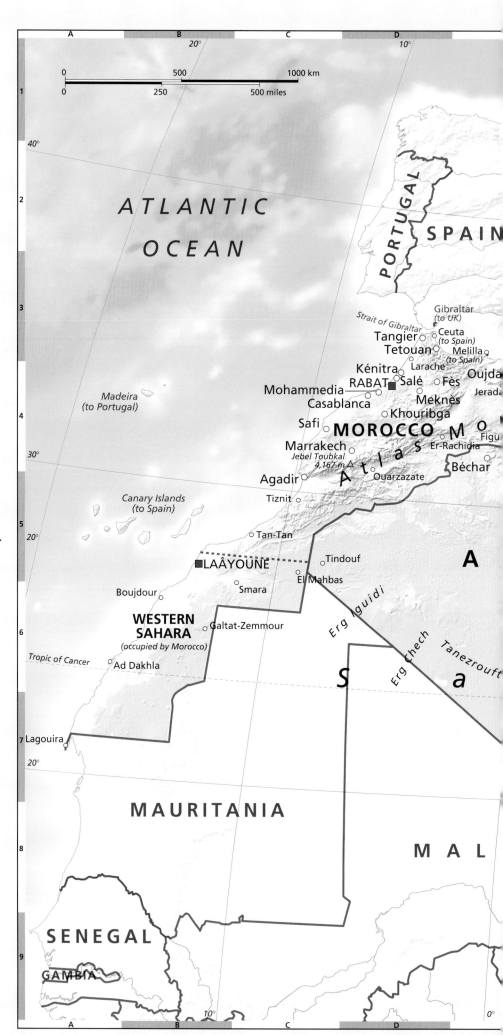

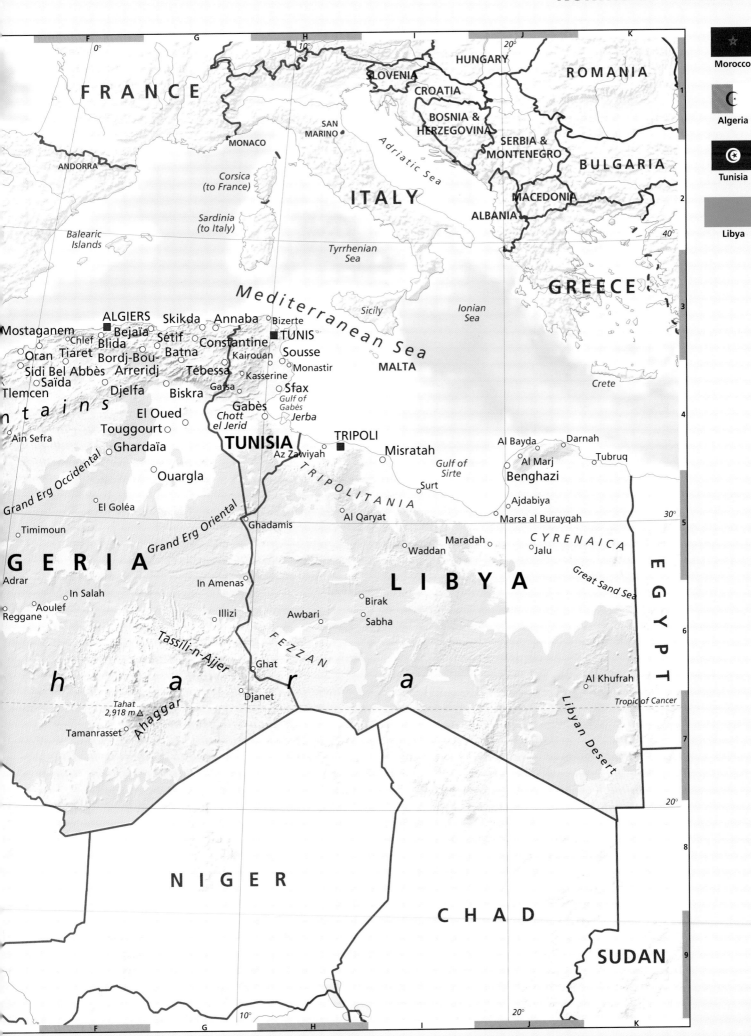

Morocco

Algeria

Tunisia

Libya

FRANCE

HUNGARY

ROMANIA

SLOVENIA

CROATIA

BOSNIA & HERZEGOVINA

SERBIA & MONTENEGRO

BULGARIA

MACEDONIA

ALBANIA

ANDORRA

MONACO

SAN MARINO

ITALY

GREECE

Corsica (to France)

Adriatic Sea

Balearic Islands

Sardinia (to Italy)

Tyrrhenian Sea

Ionian Sea

Sicily

Crete

MALTA

Mediterranean Sea

Mostaganem
ALGIERS
Skikda
Annaba
Bizerte
TUNIS
Chlef
Bejaïa
Sétif
Constantine
Blida
Oran
Tiaret
Bordj-Bou-
Batna
Kairouan
Sousse
Sidi Bel Abbès
Arreridj
Tébessa
Kasserine
Monastir
Saïda
Gafsa
Sfax
Tlemcen
Djelfa
Biskra
Gabès
Gulf of Gabès
Jerba
Ain Sefra
El Oued
Chott el Jerid
TUNISIA
TRIPOLI
Misratah
Al Bayda
Darnah
Touggourt
Az Zawiyah
Al Marj
Tubruq
Ghardaïa
Benghazi
Ouargla
Surt
Gulf of Sirte
Ajdabiya
El Goléa
Marsa al Burayqah

Grand Erg Occidental

Grand Erg Oriental

Timimoun
Ghadamis
CYRENAICA
GERIA
Waddan
Maradah
Jalu
Adrar
In Amenas
LIBYA
EGYPT
In Salah
Illizi
Birak
Great Sand Sea
Aoulef
Awbari
Sabha
Reggane
FEZZAN
Tassili-n-Ajjer
Ghat
Al Khufrah
h
a
r
a
Djanet
Libyan Desert
Tahat 2,918 m △
Ahaggar
Tropic of Cancer
Tamanrasset

TRIPOLITANIA

Al Qaryat

NIGER

CHAD

SUDAN

NORTHEAST AFRICA

The land in the northeastern part of Africa is mainly arid. To the north, Egypt and northern Sudan are desert areas. Only the Nile valley provides a narrow strip of fertile soil, where people can live and farm. Smaller deserts lie in Somalia, Ethiopia and Djibouti. There are some forests on Ethiopia's highlands, but much of the rest of this region is covered by dry scrubland and the occasional tree.

People settled in northeast Africa over 6,000 years ago, and by about 3000 BCE, one of the greatest early civilizations was established in

Egypt. For much of its history, this region was an important international centre of trade, with great cities and monuments. In 1867, the Suez Canal was opened to provide a shipping link between the Red and Mediterranean Seas.

Today, there are few big cities in northeast Africa, and most people live in the countryside and work the land. Farmers have to grow what crops they can in this hot, dry environment, where rainfall is rare and many rivers dry up for much of the year. Cotton and sugar cane are grown along the Nile river, dates grow well in

oases in the desert, and coffee is Ethiopia's main crop. Sheep, goats and cattle are raised on the grasslands, while the region's factories process food. There is also a local textile industry.

In the past few decades, life has been very hard for the people of this region. Rapid population growth has forced farmers to clear land to grow food and to cut down trees for fuel. The removal of trees and plants has allowed the wind to erode the soil, turning large areas into desert. A series of famines and wars have brought death and suffering to millions of people in this area.

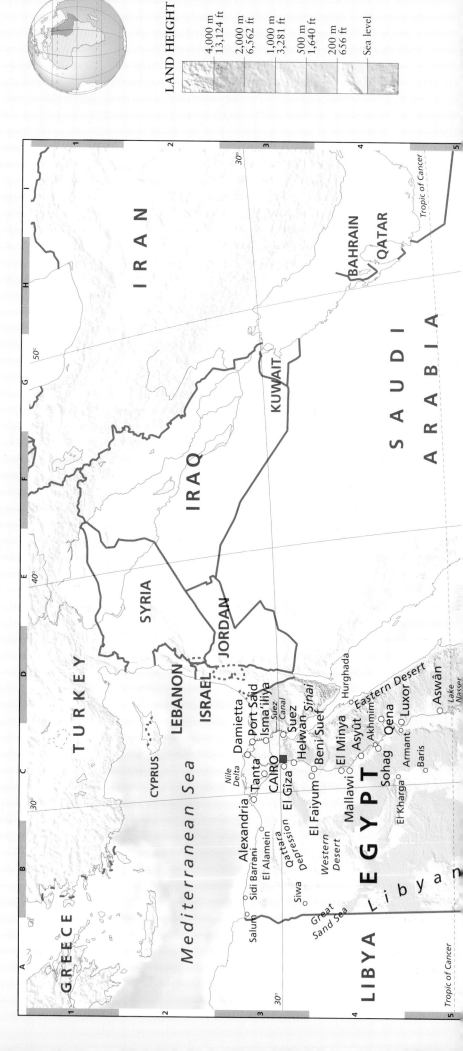

LAND HEIGHT	
4,000 m	13,124 ft
2,000 m	6,562 ft
1,000 m	3,281 ft
500 m	1,640 ft
200 m	656 ft
Sea level	

Egypt   Sudan   Eritrea   Ethiopia   Djibouti   Somalia

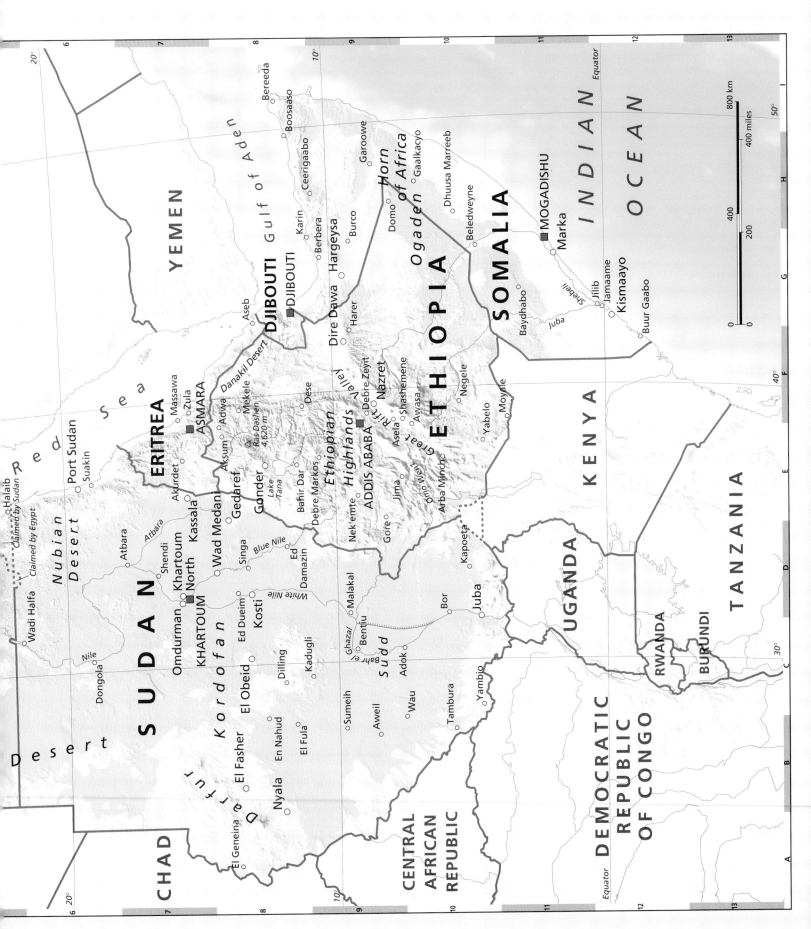

CHAD

SUDAN

Desert

Nubian Desert

Red Sea

Halaib
Claimed by Sudan
Claimed by Egypt

Wadi Halfa

Nile

Dongola

Atbara

Atbara

Shendi

Omdurman
Khartoum North
KHARTOUM

Port Sudan

Suakin

Akurdet

Kassala

ERITREA

Massawa
Zula
ASMARA

YEMEN

Gulf of Aden

Aseb

DJIBOUTI
DJIBOUTI

Karin

Berbera

Burco

Hargeysa

Dire Dawa

Harer

Danakil Desert

Mekele
Ras Dashen
4,620 m

Adwa
Aksum

Gedaref

Wad Medani

Gonder
Lake
Tana

Bahir Dar

Debre Markos

Dese

Ethiopian Highlands

Great Rift Valley

Debre Zeyit
ADDIS ABABA

Nazret

Asela

Shashemene

Awasa

Domo

Ogaden

ETHIOPIA

Horn of Africa

Bereeda

Boosaaso

Ceerigaabo

Garowe

Gaalkacyo

Dhuusa Marreeb

Beledweyne

SOMALIA

MOGADISHU
Marka

Baydhabo

Jilib

INDIAN

OCEAN

Equator

800 km

400 miles

400

200

Kismaayo
Jamaame

Buur Gaabo

Shebeli

Juba

Kordofan

Darfur

El Fasher

Nyala

El Geneina

En Nahud

El Fula

Dilling

Kadugli

El Obeid

Ed Dueim

Kosti

Singa
Blue Nile
Ed Damazin

White Nile

Malakal

Ghazal

Bentiu

Sudd

Bahr el

Adok

Bor

Juba

Kapoeta

Yambio

Tambura

Wau

Aweil

Sumeih

Sobat

Omo Wenz

Jima

Gore

Nek'emte

Yabelo

Negele

Moyale

Arba Minch

KENYA

UGANDA

CENTRAL AFRICAN REPUBLIC

DEMOCRATIC REPUBLIC OF CONGO

RWANDA

BURUNDI

TANZANIA

Equator

WEST AFRICA

In the northern part of this region, the edge of the Sahara meets a wide band of semi-desert scrubland called the Sahel, which stretches from Mauritania to Niger. South of the Sahel is a strip of grassland and further south, along the coast, is a region of land where higher rainfall feeds areas of tropical rainforest. Many rivers cross the southern half of this area. The longest of these is the Niger, which forms a vast, swampy delta at the coast.

Cash crops such as cotton, cocoa and peanuts are grown throughout the southern part of this region. Further north, farmers raise sheep and goats, and grow food crops such as yams and cassava. The biggest industries are connected with food – the processing of nuts to extract oil, for example. Many people in Nigeria also work in the chemical industry, or on wells that tap the region's rich supplies of gas and oil.

West Africa is an area with large deposits of minerals, ranging from iron ore to diamonds. In the past, it has been home to successful civilizations, such as the empires of Mali and Asante, which benefited from these resources. In spite of new wealth from oil and tourism, most west Africans remain poor. Their lives are made difficult by frequent droughts and the growth of the desert in the north of the region.

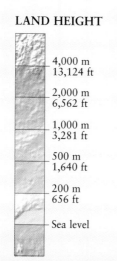

LAND HEIGHT

4,000 m
13,124 ft

2,000 m
6,562 ft

1,000 m
3,281 ft

500 m
1,640 ft

200 m
656 ft

Sea level

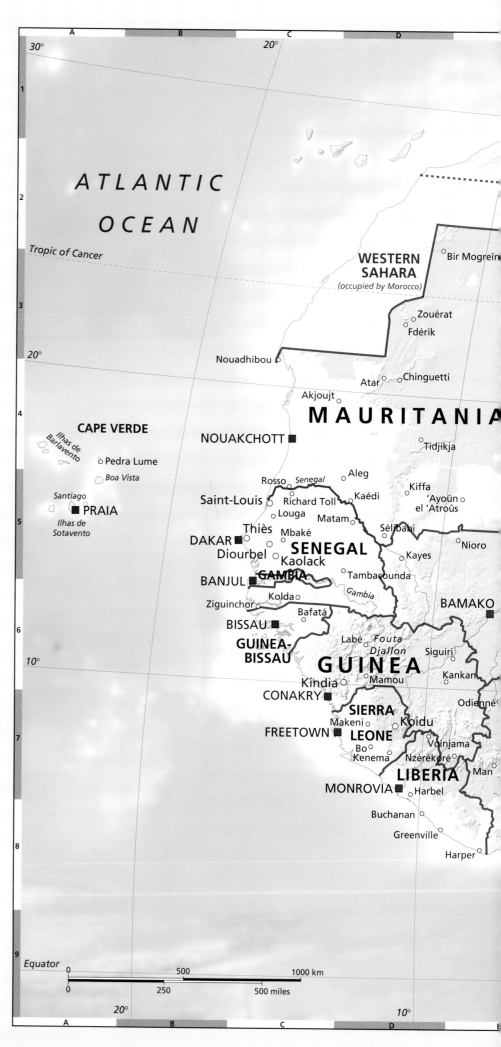

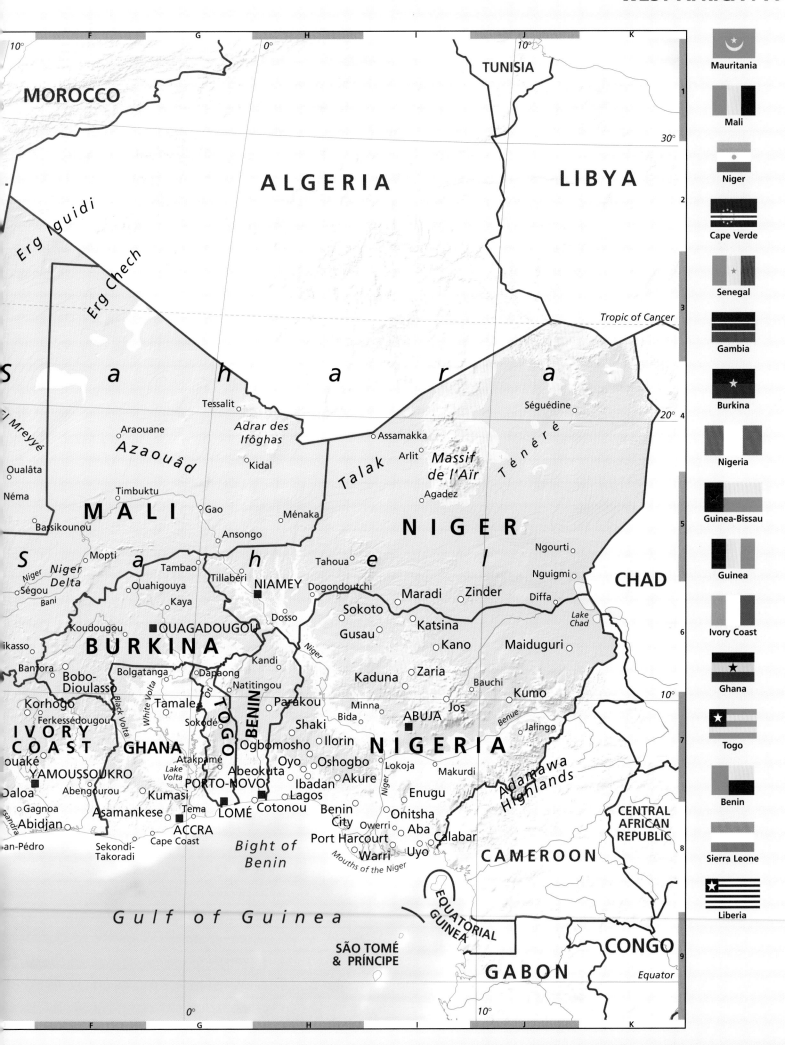

MOROCCO

MAURITANIA *(flag)* Mauritania

Mali *(flag)* Mali

TUNISIA

ALGERIA

LIBYA

Niger *(flag)* Niger

Cape Verde *(flag)* Cape Verde

Senegal *(flag)* Senegal

Gambia *(flag)* Gambia

Burkina *(flag)* Burkina

Nigeria *(flag)* Nigeria

Guinea-Bissau *(flag)* Guinea-Bissau

Guinea *(flag)* Guinea

Ivory Coast *(flag)* Ivory Coast

Ghana *(flag)* Ghana

Togo *(flag)* Togo

Benin *(flag)* Benin

Sierra Leone *(flag)* Sierra Leone

Liberia *(flag)* Liberia

Erg Iguidi
Erg Chech
El Mreyyé
S a h a r a
Tessalit
Araouane
Adrar des Ifôghas
Séguédine
Assamakka
Azaouâd
Oualâta
Néma
Kidal
Arlit
Massif de l'Aïr
Ténéré
Talak
Timbuktu
Agadez
Bassikounou
M A L I
Gao
Ménaka
N I G E R
S a h e l
Niger
Niger Delta
Mopti
Ségou
Bani
Tambao
Ansongo
Tahoua
Ngourti
Nguigmi
CHAD
Dogondoutchi
Maradi
Zinder
Diffa
Lake Chad
Tillabéri
NIAMEY
Dosso
Sokoto
Katsina
Kano
Maiduguri
Koudougou
OUAGADOUGOU
Kaya
Gusau
ikasso
B U R K I N A
Kandi
Kaduna
Zaria
Bauchi
Kumo
Banfora
Bobo-Dioulasso
Bolgatanga
Dapaong
Natitingou
Parakou
Minna
Jos
Korhogo
Tamale
Sokodé
Ilorin
Bida
ABUJA
Jalingo
Ferkessédougou
I V O R Y
C O A S T
GHANA
TOGO
BENIN
Shaki
N I G E R I A
Ogbomosho
ouaké
YAMOUSSOUKRO
Atakpamé
Lake Volta
Oyo
Oshogbo
Akure
Lokoja
Makurdi
Adamawa Highlands
Daloa
Abengourou
Kumasi
Abeokuta
PORTO-NOVO
Ibadan
Lagos
Enugu
CENTRAL AFRICAN REPUBLIC
Gagnoa
Asamankese
Tema
LOMÉ
Cotonou
Benin City
Onitsha
Aba
Calabar
Abidjan
ACCRA
Port Harcourt
Owerri
Uyo
an-Pédro
Sekondi-Takoradi
Cape Coast
Bight of Benin
Warri
CAMEROON
Mouths of the Niger
Gulf of Guinea
EQUATORIAL GUINEA
CONGO
SÃO TOMÉ & PRÍNCIPE
GABON
White Volta
Black Volta
Oti
Kaya

10°
0°
30°
20°
Tropic of Cancer
10°
10°
Equator

CENTRAL AND EAST AFRICA

This region extends from Africa's Atlantic coast to the Indian Ocean. In the west is the Congo, the continent's second-longest river. Its basin is covered by the Earth's largest tropical rainforest. So far, this area has survived well, but some parts of it are being cut away. In the east is the Great Rift Valley, which runs from the north to the south, and cuts through the uplands and grasslands of Uganda and Tanzania. The Nile river rises in the uplands, and flows north on its way to the Mediterranean Sea.

To the west, among the dense forests of the Democratic Republic of Congo, rubber and oil palm trees are grown in large plantations. The Congo river and its many tributaries provide a source of fish for the local people. Elsewhere, cattle and goats are herded. In the east, farmers grow crops for export, such as vegetables and coffee.

The Democratic Republic of Congo mines its rich supplies of copper, diamonds, silver and cobalt. Other countries, such as Kenya, have developed manufacturing industries. Tourism is growing steadily in Kenya and Tanzania, where each year, thousands of overseas visitors come to visit the countries' amazing wildlife. Although the tourist industry employs a great number of people here, most of the population still makes its living from the land.

LAND HEIGHT

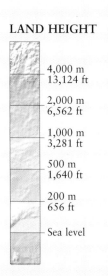

4,000 m	13,124 ft
2,000 m	6,562 ft
1,000 m	3,281 ft
500 m	1,640 ft
200 m	656 ft
Sea level	

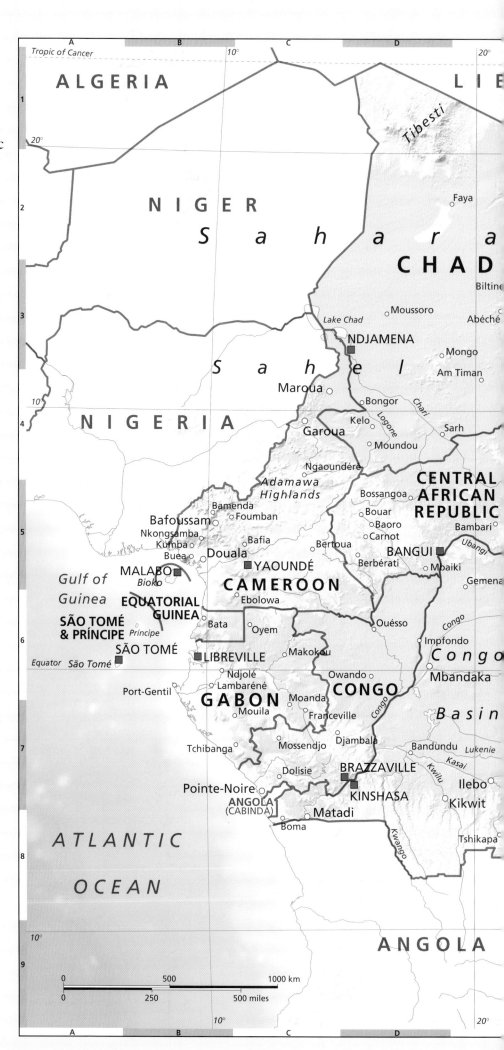

EGYPT

SAUDI
ARABIA

A

SUDAN

ERITREA

YEMEN

DJIBOUTI

ETHIOPIA

SOMALIA

Birao

*Massif
es Bongo*

Bria

Bangassou

Obo

Bondo   *Uele*

Bumba   Buta   Isiro   Mungbere   Watsa   *Nile*   Gulu   Lodwar   *Lake
Turkana*   Moyale

Yangambi   Kisangani   *Aruwimi*   Lira   Marsabit

EMOCRATIC   Ikoli   *Lake Albert*   UGANDA   Moroto

REPUBLIC   *Tshuapa*   Masindi   Mbale   KENYA

OF CONGO   KAMPALA   Tororo   Eldoret   Meru

Entebbe   Jinja   Kakamega   △ Kirinyaga 5,199 m

Kindu   *Lake Edward*   Mbarara   Kisumu   Nakuru   Nyeri   Garissa

Goma   Kabale   *Lake
Victoria*   Thika

Lomani   Bukavu   *Lake Kivu*   KIGALI   NAIROBI

Lualaba   RWANDA   Mwanza   Machakos   △ Kilimanjaro
5,895 m

Kananga   Kabinda   BUJUMBURA   *Serengeti
Plain*   Arusha   Moshi   Malindi

Mbuji-Mayi   Kasongo   BURUNDI   Shinyanga   *Masai
Steppe*   Mombasa

Mwene-Ditu   Kongolo   Kigoma   Singida   Tanga   *Pemba*

Kamina   Kalémié   Tabora   Zanzibar   *Zanzibar*   INDIAN

Kabalo   *Lake
Tanganyika*   DODOMA   Morogoro   OCEAN

Dilolo   Kolwezi   *Lake
Mweru*   Mpanda   TANZANIA   Dar es Salaam

Likasi   Sumbawanga   Iringa   *Rufiji*   *Mafia*

Kamina   Mbeya   *Aldabra Group
(to Seychelles)*

*Lake
Nyasa*   Makumbako   Mohoro

Lubumbashi   Masasi   Lindi

Songea   *Ruvuma*   Mtwara

ZAMBIA   MALAWI   MOZAMBIQUE   COMOROS

*Mayotte
(to France)*

Great Rift Valley

Equator

Chad

Cameroon

Central African
Republic

Democratic
Republic of Congo

Kenya

Uganda

Equatorial Guinea

Congo

São Tomé &
Príncipe

Gabon

Rwanda

Tanzania

Burundi

SOUTHERN AFRICA

This region has a huge variety of scenery, from the parched Namib and Kalahari deserts of the west to the eastern grasslands and the Drakensberg mountains in the southeast. Off the eastern coast of southern Africa is Madagascar, a large island that split from the mainland about 1,345 million years ago. Madagascar's wildlife, from lemurs to chameleons, includes many species of plants and animals that cannot be found anywhere else in the world.

Cattle are farmed on the grasslands, while much of the land in the south is used for growing fruit for the export market. With rich deposits of precious minerals and metals, such as diamonds and gold, South Africa is the wealthiest part of this region. The country also has many other industries, including food canning, steel production, manufacturing and textiles. These types of businesses are found in other countries in southern Africa, but on a smaller scale.

In many areas, trees have been cut down for fuel, and the soils have been blown away, leaving barren, infertile deserts. The region also has political problems. For much of the 20th century, the black South Africans were denied basic human rights by the South African government. This system, known as apartheid, was abolished in 1994, when black South Africans were allowed to vote for the first time, and the country became a truly democratic state.

LAND HEIGHT

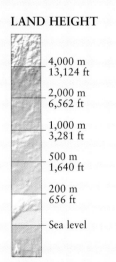

4,000 m	13,124 ft
2,000 m	6,562 ft
1,000 m	3,281 ft
500 m	1,640 ft
200 m	656 ft
Sea level	

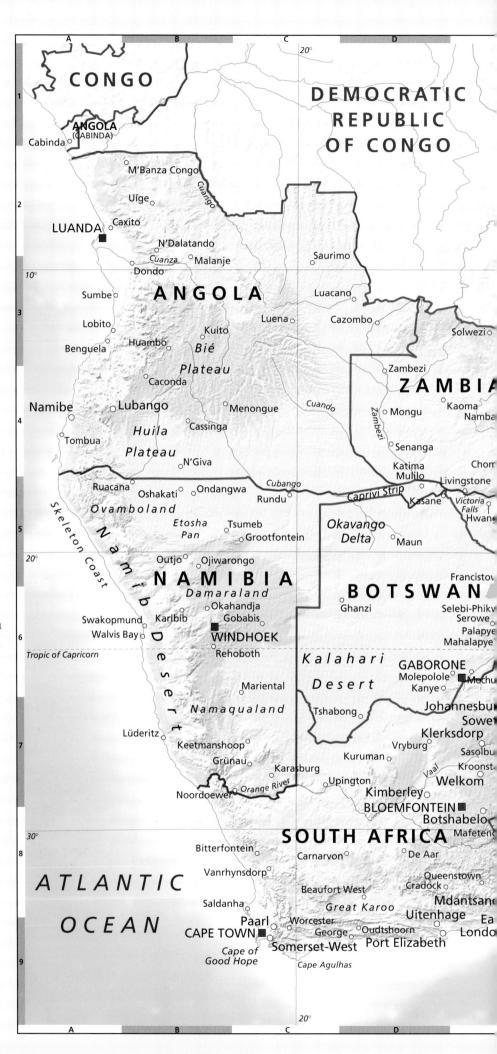

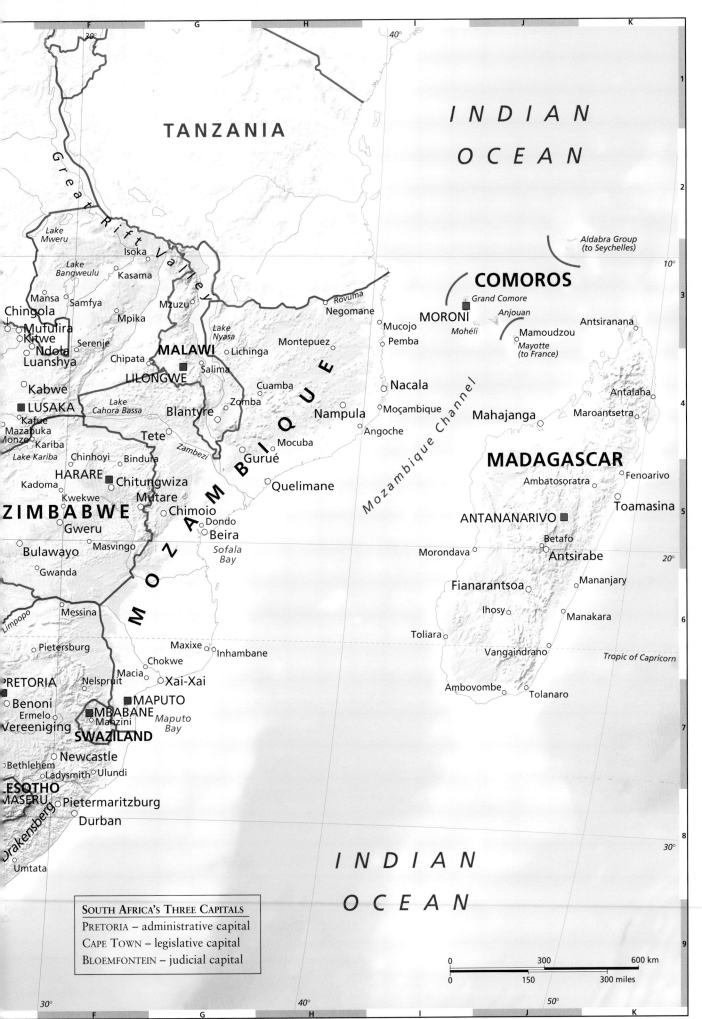

INDIAN
OCEAN

TANZANIA

Great Rift Valley

Lake Mweru
Isoka
Lake Bangweulu
Kasama
Mansa
Samfya
Mzuzu
Rovuma
Negomane
Mucojo
Pemba
COMOROS
Grand Comore
MORONI
Anjouan
Mohéli
Mamoudzou
Mayotte (to France)
Aldabra Group (to Seychelles)
Antsiranana
Chingola
Mufulira
Kitwe
Ndola
Luanshya
Serenje
Mpika
Chipata
MALAWI
Lichinga
Montepuez
Cuamba
Kabwe
LILONGWE
Lake Nyasa
LUSAKA
Kafue
Lake Cahora Bassa
Blantyre
Zomba
Nampula
Moçambique
Nacala
Angoche
Mahajanga
Antalaha
Maroantsetra
Mazabuka
Monze
Kariba
Tete
Lake Karie
Chinhoyi
Bindura
Zambezi
Gurué
Mocuba
MADAGASCAR
Fenoarivo
HARARE
Chitungwiza
Quelimane
Ambatosoratra
Toamasina
Kadoma
Kwekwe
Mutare
Chimoio
Dondo
Beira
ANTANANARIVO
Betafo
ZIMBABWE
Gweru
Sofala Bay
Antsirabe
Bulawayo
Masvingo
Morondava
Gwanda
Fianarantsoa
Mananjary
Messina
Ihosy
Manakara
Limpopo
Pietersburg
Maxixe
Inhambane
Toliara
Vangaindrano
Chokwe
Macia
Xai-Xai
PRETORIA
Nelspruit
Benoni
MAPUTO
Ambovombe
Tolanaro
Ermelo
MBABANE
Maputo Bay
Vereeniging
Manzini
SWAZILAND
Newcastle
Bethlehem
Ladysmith
Ulundi
LESOTHO
MASERU
Pietermaritzburg
Durban
Drakensberg
Umtata

Mozambique Channel

MOZAMBIQUE

INDIAN
OCEAN

SOUTH AFRICA'S THREE CAPITALS
PRETORIA – administrative capital
CAPE TOWN – legislative capital
BLOEMFONTEIN – judicial capital

0   300   600 km
0   150   300 miles

Angola

Zambia

Malawi

Mozambique

Comoros

Madagascar

Zimbabwe

Namibia

Botswana

South Africa

Swaziland

Lesotho

THE INDIAN OCEAN

From the coast of Africa in the west to Australia and the islands of southeast Asia in the east, the Indian Ocean measures almost 10,000 km across at its widest point. Under the water are three ridges that form an upside-down 'Y' shape. The ridges mark where three continental plates meet. Here, volcanic activity is common.

The climate of the Indian Ocean varies according to latitude. The regions in the north, near India, have a warm climate. In the south, freezing temperatures have created pack ice and icebergs. Monsoon winds bring heavy rainfall to many coastal countries. They also have an effect on the ocean's currents, which reverse direction completely between March and August.

For thousands of years, the Indian Ocean has provided important trade routes between the eastern and western parts of the world. Among the first traders to sail its waters were the ancient Egyptians, who travelled along the east African coast more than 4,000 years ago. In the 15th century, European explorers made pioneering journeys across the Indian Ocean to Asia. They were soon followed by merchants who brought back silks, spices and tea from India and China. Today, huge tankers carry oil from the Persian Gulf to many of the ocean's international ports. A large number of these boats travel along the Red Sea and through the Suez Canal to reach Europe.

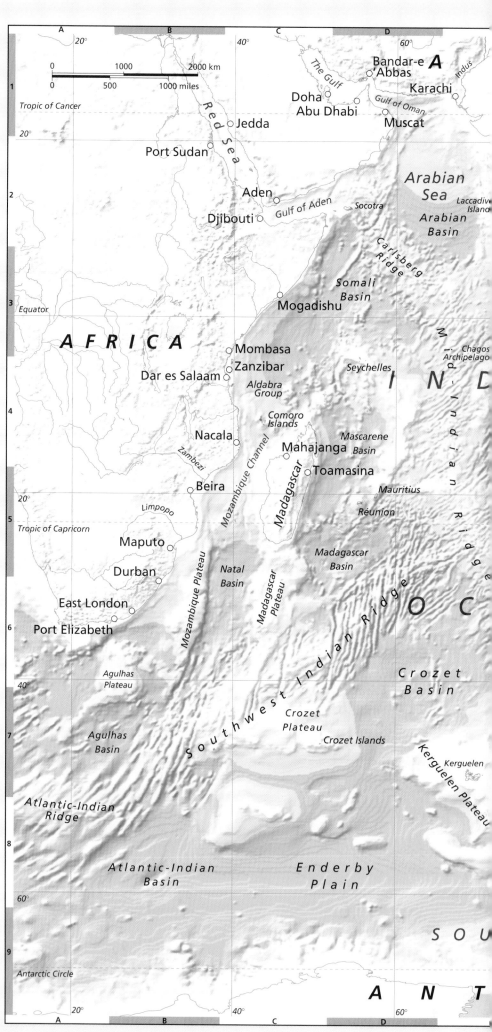

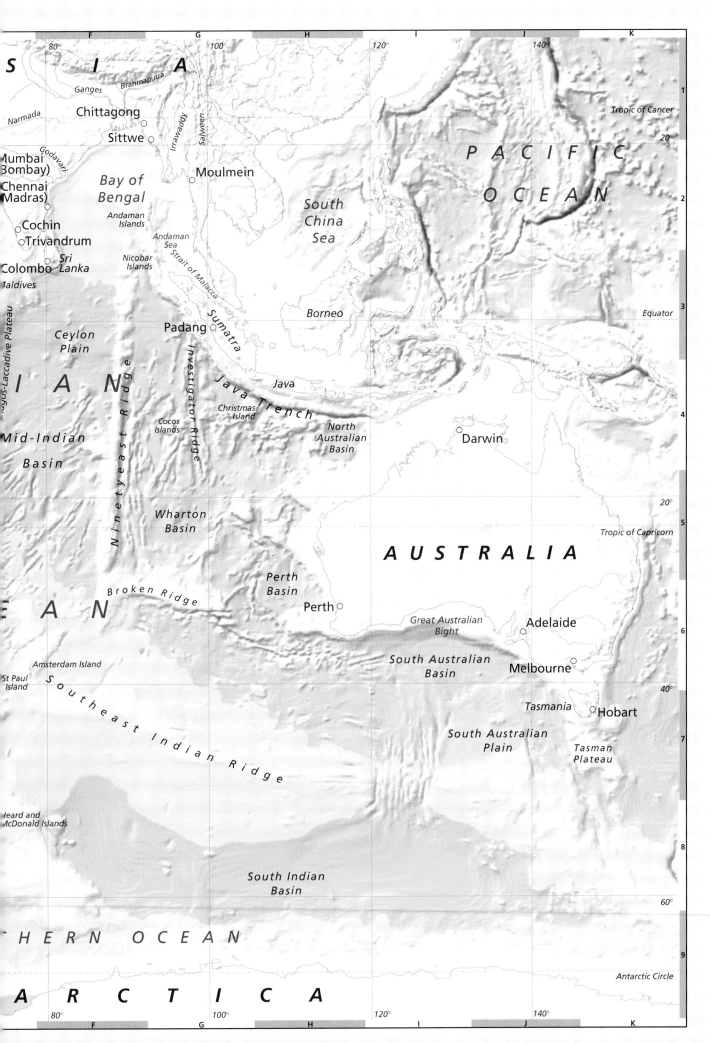

S I A

Narmada
Ganges
Brahmaputra
Chittagong
Sittwe
Irrawaddy
Salween
Moulmein

Mumbai
(Bombay)
Godavari
Chennai
(Madras)
Cochin
Trivandrum
Sri
Lanka
Colombo
Maldives

Bay of
Bengal
Andaman
Islands
Andaman
Sea
Nicobar
Islands
Strait of Malacca

P A C I F I C

O C E A N

Tropic of Cancer

*South
China
Sea*

Borneo

Chagos-Laccadive Plateau
Ceylon
Plain
Padang
Sumatra

I A N
Ninetyeast Ridge
Investigator Ridge
Java Trench
Java

Mid-Indian
Basin
Cocos
Islands
Christmas
Island
North
Australian
Basin

Equator

Darwin

Wharton
Basin

20°

E A N
Broken Ridge

Perth
Basin
Perth

Tropic of Capricorn

A U S T R A L I A

Great Australian
Bight
Adelaide

Amsterdam Island
St Paul
Island
Southeast Indian Ridge

South Australian
Basin
Melbourne

40°

Tasmania
Hobart

South Australian
Plain
Tasman
Plateau

Heard and
McDonald Islands

South Indian
Basin

60°

T H E R N   O C E A N

9

Antarctic Circle

A R C T I C A

80°
100°
120°
140°

ASIA

Stretching from the Black Sea in the west to Japan in the east, Asia is the world's largest continent. There are many types of landscapes, from the snowy Mount Everest, the world's highest mountain, to the Arabian Desert. Uplands stretch across much of the middle of Asia and there are great rivers, such as China's Yangtze and India's Ganges. The Earth's lowest place, the Dead Sea, is located on the border of Israel and Jordan.

Asia has a variety of peoples with many different beliefs, languages and lifestyles. The huge communist state of China is the most populous country in the world. India, with over 1 billion people, is the world's largest democratic nation. The break-up of the Soviet Union, which stretched from the eastern edge of the Russian Federation to Iran, created four countries in central Asia – Kazakhstan, Kyrgyzstan, Tajikistan and Turkmenistan. These, and the older states to the west, are mainly Muslim nations.

Few people live in the cold and windswept areas of central and northern Asia. Those who inhabit these regions are often poor, and live without many of the luxuries of modern life. Further south are some of the world's major cities, such as Mumbai, Beijing and Tokyo. The cities and countries of western Asia have grown rich from oil, while those of the Pacific coast have modern industries that have brought a high standard of living to many people.

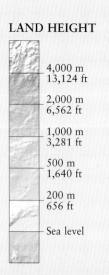

LAND HEIGHT

4,000 m
13,124 ft

2,000 m
6,562 ft

1,000 m
3,281 ft

500 m
1,640 ft

200 m
656 ft

Sea level

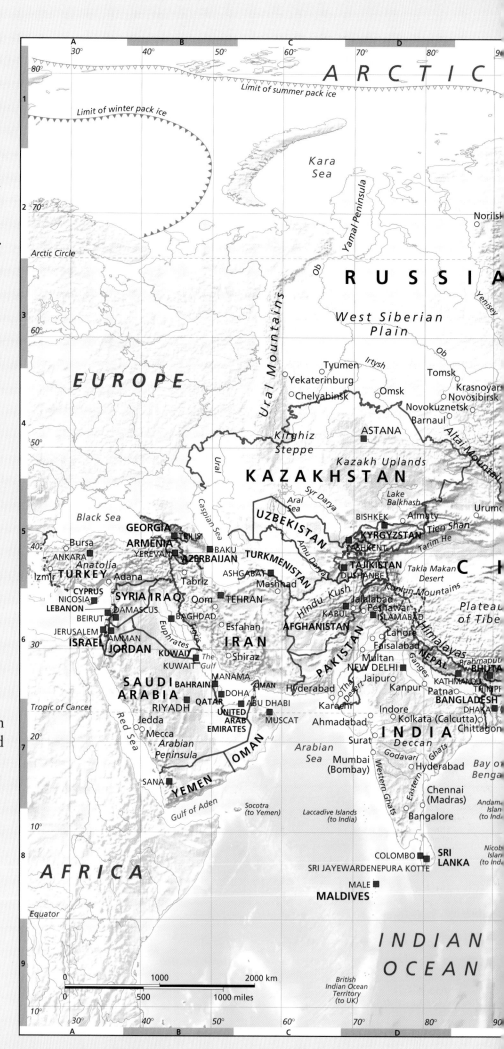

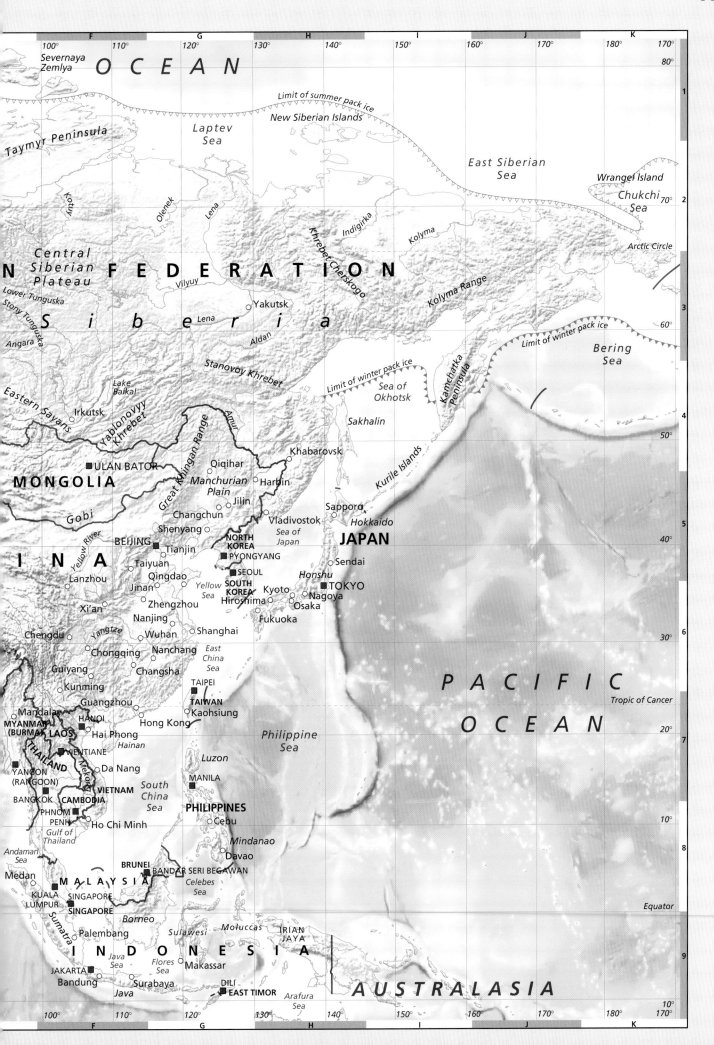

OCEAN

Severnaya
Zemlya

100°   110°   120°   130°   140°   150°   160°   170°   180°   170°   80°

Taymyr Peninsula

Laptev
Sea

Limit of summer pack ice

New Siberian Islands

East Siberian
Sea

Wrangel Island

Chukchi
Sea

70°

Arctic Circle

Central
Siberian
Plateau

N FEDERATION

Kotuy

Olenek

Lena

Vilyuy

Lower Tunguska

Stony Tunguska

Angara

Khrebet Cherskogo

Indigirka

Kolyma

Kolyma Range

Siberia

Yakutsk

Lena

Aldan

60°

Limit of winter pack ice

Bering
Sea

Stanovoy Khrebet

Limit of winter pack ice

Sea of
Okhotsk

Kamchatka Peninsula

Eastern Sayans

Lake
Baikal

Irkutsk

Yablonovyy
Khrebet

Sakhalin

50°

Great Khingan Range

Amur

Khabarovsk

Kurile Islands

ULAN BATOR

Qiqihar

Manchurian
Plain

Harbin

MONGOLIA

Changchun

Jilin

Vladivostok

Sapporo

Hokkaido

Gobi

Shenyang

Sea of
Japan

JAPAN

40°

INA

Yellow River

BEIJING

Tianjin

NORTH
KOREA

PYONGYANG

Sendai

Taiyuan

SEOUL

Honshu

Lanzhou

Qingdao

SOUTH
KOREA

Kyoto

TOKYO

Jinan

Yellow
Sea

Hiroshima

Nagoya

Xi'an

Zhengzhou

Osaka

Nanjing

Fukuoka

Chengdu

Yangtze

Wuhan

Shanghai

30°

Chongqing

Nanchang

East
China
Sea

Guiyang

Changsha

Kunming

TAIPEI

Guangzhou

TAIWAN

PACIFIC

Mandalay

HANOI

Kaohsiung

Tropic of Cancer

MYANMAR
(BURMA)

LAOS

Hai Phong

Hong Kong

OCEAN

20°

THAILAND

VIENTIANE

Hainan

Philippine
Sea

Da Nang

YANGON
(RANGOON)

Mekong

VIETNAM

Luzon

BANGKOK

CAMBODIA

South
China
Sea

MANILA

PHNOM
PENH

Ho Chi Minh

PHILIPPINES

10°

Gulf of
Thailand

Cebu

Andaman
Sea

Mindanao

Davao

Medan

BRUNEI

BANDAR SERI BEGAWAN

MALAYSIA

Celebes
Sea

KUALA
LUMPUR

SINGAPORE

SINGAPORE

Borneo

Equator

Sumatra

Palembang

Sulawesi

Moluccas

IRIAN
JAYA

INDONESIA

Java
Sea

Flores
Sea

Makassar

JAKARTA

Bandung

Surabaya

Java

DILI

EAST TIMOR

Arafura
Sea

AUSTRALASIA

100°   110°   120°   130°   140°   150°   160°   170°   180°   170°   10°

THE RUSSIAN FEDERATION

The western part of the Russian Federation falls in Europe, while the area east of the Ural Mountains is in Asia. Just east of the mountains is a flat region of marshes and streams, called the West Siberian Plain. The plain gradually rises to the Central Siberian Plateau, and then again to highlands in the south and east. Great coniferous forests cover most of this land. Much of European Russia lies on the North European Plain. This region is covered in large forests of birch and pine trees, and is watered by several great rivers, including the Volga. In the far north is frozen tundra.

In the east, a cold climate and harsh living conditions keep the population low. Many of those who do live here herd reindeer or work in forestry. The majority of people live in the west, where farmers grow root crops and wheat. This part of the country is highly industrialized, producing goods such as chemicals, cars and textiles. The region is also one of Europe's main sources of oil.

The Russian Federation was created when the communist Soviet Union broke up in 1991. The communists controlled farming, and they developed heavy industries, many of which caused pollution. Today, the country is modernizing its industries, and tackling the environmental problems caused during the Soviet period.

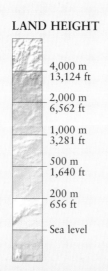

LAND HEIGHT

	4,000 m 13,124 ft
	2,000 m 6,562 ft
	1,000 m 3,281 ft
	500 m 1,640 ft
	200 m 656 ft
	Sea level

Russian Federation

ARCTIC OCEAN

UNITED STATES OF AMERICA
(ALASKA)

Bering Strait

Chukchi
Sea

Wrangel
Island

Bering
Sea

Arctic circle

Pevek

Anadyr

East Siberian
Sea

Franz Josef Land

Ostrov
Komsomolets

Ostrov
Oktyabrskoy
Revolyutsii

Cherskiy

Severnaya
Zemlya

Ostrov
Bolshevik

Laptev
Sea

New
Siberian
Islands

Indigirka

Kolyma

Kolyma Range

Palana

Gora
Pobeda
△3,003 m

Ust-Kamchatsk

Sopka Klyuchevskaya
4,750 m △

Taymyr
Peninsula

Tiksi

Khrebet Cherskogo

Olenek

Verkhoyanskiy Khrebet

Kamchatka
Peninsula

Gydanskiy
Poluostrov

Kotuy

Dudinka

Magadan

S i b e r i a

Lena

Petropavlovsk-
Kamchatskiy

Norilsk

Urengoy
Turukhansk

C e n t r a l

S i b e r i a n

P l a t e a u

Vilyuy

Yakutsk

Lower Tunguska

Yenisey

Tura

Aldan

Sea of
Okhotsk

Mirnyy

Olekminsk

Kurile Islands

Stony Tunguska

Bor

Aldan

Olekma

Nogliki

Ob

Angara

Ust-Ilimsk

Stanovoy Khrebet

Berkakit

Sakhalin

Tomsk

Kansk

Bratsk

Lena

Tynda

Komsomolsk-
na-Amure

Yuzhno-
Sakhalinsk

Kemerovo

Prokopyevsk

Krasnoyarsk

Eastern Sayans

Severobaykalsk

Vitim

Svobodnyy

Belogorsk

Sovetskaya
Gavan

Novokuznetsk

Biysk

Abakan

Angarsk

Lake Baikal

Chita

Karymskoye

Blagoveshchensk

Khabarovsk

Gorno-Altaysk

Kyzyl

Gora Munku-
Sardyk
3,492 m

Irkutsk

Ulan-Ude

Khilok

Aginskoye

Amur

Bikin

Yablonovyy Khrebet

Gora Belukha
4,506 m

Altai Mountains

MONGOLIA

Ussuriysk

Vladivostok

Nakhodka

Sea of
Japan

NORTH
KOREA

JAPAN

SOUTH
KOREA

C H I N A

0   500   1000 km

0   250   500 miles

WEST ASIA

In the north of west Asia lie the Taurus Mountains and the plateau of Anatolia. The eastern part of this region is also dominated by uplands, including the Elburz and Zagros Mountains. In the south is the huge Arabian Peninsula, which is separated from the rest of Asia by the valleys of the Tigris and Euphrates rivers. Mountains run along the peninsula's Red Sea coast, and much of the rest of this region is covered in dry, barren deserts.

West Asia has a long history. Some of the world's first great civilizations developed in Iraq about 5,000 years ago, and the Arabian Peninsula was the home of the prophet Muhammad, and the first Muslims. This region is still mainly Muslim, although it also contains the Jewish state of Israel.

Oil and natural gas are important sources of income for many of the countries in west Asia. Other industries produce a range of goods, from industrial machinery in Georgia to carpets in Iran. Cattle and sheep are raised in the north, while goats are herded on the southern tip of the Arabian Peninsula. Hazelnuts are the main crop along the Black Sea coast, root crops are produced in Anatolia, and olives, figs, grapes and peaches are cultivated on Turkey's southern coast. Wheat is harvested in the fertile valleys of the Euphrates and Tigris rivers. Cotton, dates and fruits for the export market are also grown here.

LAND HEIGHT

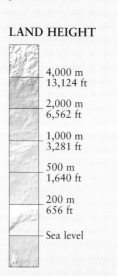

	4,000 m 13,124 ft
	2,000 m 6,562 ft
	1,000 m 3,281 ft
	500 m 1,640 ft
	200 m 656 ft
	Sea level

RUSSIAN FEDERATION
Caucasus
GEORGIA
Kutaisi
Batumi
Hopa
Trabzon
Gyumri
Vanadzor
ARMENIA
YEREVAN
rzurum
Bitlis
Van
Lake Van
Diyarbakir
Batman
Lake Urmia
Al Qamishli
Summel
Al Hasakah
Mosul
Al Jazirah
Dayr az Zawr
bu Kamal
Tikrit
Samarra'
Ba'qubah
Ar Ramadi
BAGHDAD
IRAQ
Karbala'
Al Hillah
An Najaf
Ar 'ar
Rafhah
Hafar al Batin
Nafud
Ha'il
Arabian
Buraydah
'Unayzah
Shaqra'
Peninsula
RIYADH
Al Kharj
Harad
Halaban
Zalim
Layla
SAUDI ARABIA
As Sulayyil
Ar Rub' al Khali (Empty Quarter)
Al Bahah
Tathlith
Abha
Najran
YEMEN
SANA
Jizan
Hodeida
Dhamar
Ibb
Ta'izz
Lawdar
Mocha
Zinjibar
Aden
DJIBOUTI
Gulf of Aden
Babel Mandeb
At Ta'if
Qunfidhah
Kazbek 5,047 m
TBILISI
Rustavi
Ganca
Sumqayit
BAKU
AZERBAIJAN
AZERBAIJAN
Naxçivan
Khvoy
Tabriz
Ardabil
Orumiyeh
Maragheh
Rasht
Caspian Sea
KAZAKHSTAN
UZBEKISTAN
TURKMENISTAN
Bojnurd
Gonbad-e Kavus
Neyshabur
Mashhad
Gorgan
Qolleh ye Damavand 5,881 m
Babol
Sari
Amol
Emamshahr
Sabzevar
Zanjan
Qazvin
Elburz Mountains
Karaj
TEHRAN
Semnan
Garmsar
As Sulaymaniyah
Sanandaj
Hamadan
Saveh
Qom
Bukan
Arbil
Kirkuk
Bakhtaran
Ilam
Arak
Kashan
Dasht-e Kavir
Tabas
Gonabad
AFGHANISTAN
Saray
Borujerd
Khorramabad
Najafabad
Esfahan
Iranian
IRAN
Birjand
Dezful
Al Kut
Al 'Amarah
Qomisheh
Yazd
Plateau
Dasht-e Lut
Zabol
Ahvaz
Al Qurnah
Khorramshahr
Abadan
Kazerun
Basra
Tigris
Euphrates
An
Nasiriyah
Shiraz
Zagros Mountains
Karun
Kerman
Zahedan
Bam
PAKISTAN
KUWAIT
KUWAIT
Al Ahmadi
Al Wari'ah
Bandar-e Bushehr
Sirjan
Iranshahr
Kangan
The Gulf
Ad Dahna
Ad Dammam
Al Majma'ah
Dhahran
Al Hufuf
Bandar-e Lengeh
Qeshm
Bandar-e 'Abbas
Al Khasab
Strait of Hormuz
Jask
Chabahar
BAHRAIN
MANAMA
DOHA
QATAR
ABU DHABI
UNITED ARAB EMIRATES
Ajman
Sharjah
Dubai
OMAN
Fujairah
'Ayn
Ar Rustaq
Suhar
Gulf of Oman
MUSCAT
'Ibri
Nizwa
Sur
OMAN
Masirah
Gulf of Masirah
Hayma'
Mughshin
Zufar
Arabian Sea
Raysut
Salalah
Al Mahrah
Nishtun
Shibam
Hawra
Sayhut
Hadramawt
Al Mukalla
Socotra (to Yemen)
'Abd Al Kuri
INDIAN OCEAN
Tropic of Cancer

RUSSIAN FEDERATION
khumi

Turkey

Georgia

Armenia

Azerbaijan

Iran

Syria

Iraq

Cyprus

Lebanon

Israel

Jordan

Saudi Arabia

Kuwait

Bahrain

Oman

Qatar

United Arab Emirates

Yemen

CENTRAL ASIA

A wall of mountains cuts through central Asia in a diagonal line from the Tien Shan in the northeast, through the Pamirs in the centre, to the Hindu Kush in the southwest. In the northwest are the sandy deserts of Uzbekistan and Turkmenistan. There are rolling grasslands in Kazakhstan, in the north. Central Asia receives very little rain and the region experiences extremes of temperature – winters are cold and summers are very hot.

With very few large cities, the peoples of central Asia live mainly in rural areas and make their

living from the land. Farming is difficult in the desert and mountain regions, so agriculture is concentrated around the river valleys in the east. Here, a variety of cereals and fruits, including peaches, melons and apricots, are grown. Cotton, which is central Asia's main export, is grown on land irrigated by the Amu Darya river. Herds of cattle, sheep and goats are raised in the south and east, and on the grasslands of Kazakhstan in the north.

Fossil fuels, including oil, gas and coal, are extracted and processed throughout the region.

There are a number of traditional industries, which make products such as carpets and leather goods. The main industrial area is located in the east, in the Fergana Valley, where old-fashioned factories cause air pollution.

Once the fourth largest lake in the world, the Aral Sea has shrunk by almost half its size since 1960. This is because the rivers feeding the lake have been diverted to irrigate fields of cotton. The dry climate, combined with poor vegetation cover, means that desertification is another environmental problem in central Asia.

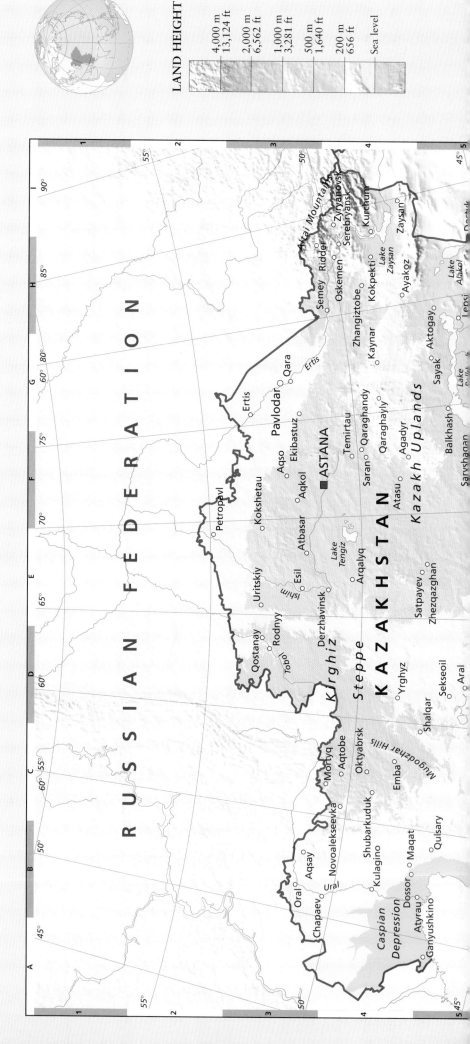

LAND HEIGHT

4,000 m 13,124 ft
2,000 m 6,562 ft
1,000 m 3,281 ft
500 m 1,640 ft
200 m 656 ft
Sea level

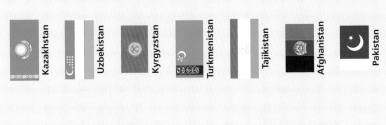

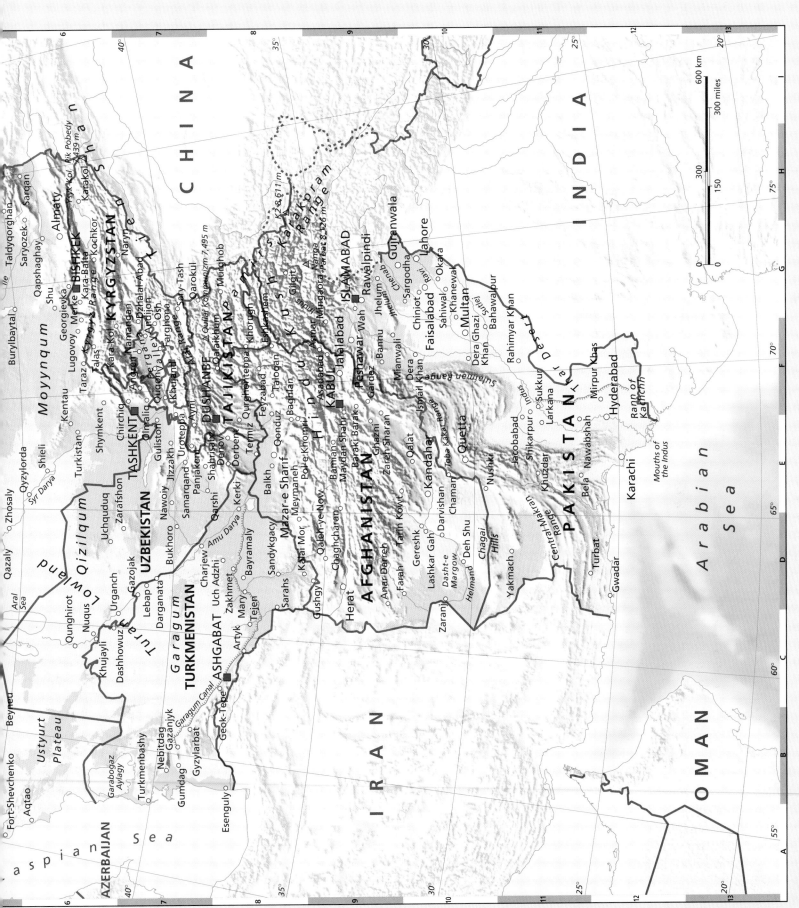

SOUTH ASIA

South Asia is separated from the rest of Asia by the Thar Desert in the northwest and a wall of mountains, including the towering Himalayas, in the north and east. The great floodplains of the Ganges, Brahmaputra and Indus rivers lie at the foothills of the mountains. Further south are rolling plateaux, which are fringed by a line of coastal hills, called the Eastern and Western Ghats. To the southeast are the mountainous islands of Sri Lanka.

More than half of south Asia's population makes its living from agriculture. Farmers grow rice in the wet areas of the east and west, while corn and millet are the main crops on the Deccan plateau. Elsewhere, groundnuts are grown for cooking oil, and tea for the export market is harvested on huge plantations. Livestock are raised throughout the region, and fishing is common along the entire coast.

Large-scale industries, from car manufacturing to chemicals, have expanded in the region's cities in recent years. Service industries are also growing steadily. In the countryside, a number of people work in traditional trades, providing goods to the local people. Products such as clothing, leather and jewellery are among south Asia's leading exports.

This part of Asia's huge population is growing rapidly. The majority of the people live in rural areas, but increasing numbers are moving to the cities in search of work. There is serious overcrowding in both rural and urban regions, and slums have developed in the larger cities. Deforestation is also a major problem, with trees being cut down in the southern and Himalayan regions for fuel.

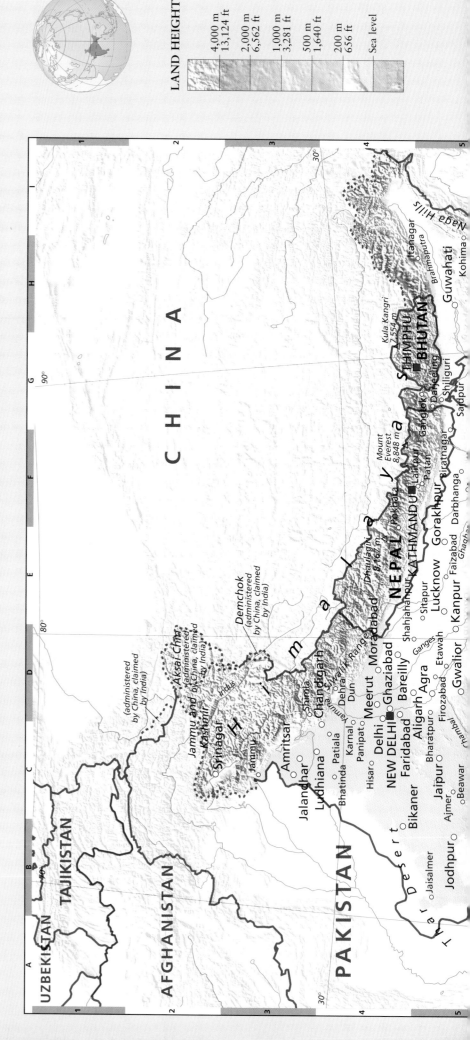

LAND HEIGHT	
4,000 m	13,124 ft
2,000 m	6,562 ft
1,000 m	3,281 ft
500 m	1,640 ft
200 m	656 ft
Sea level	

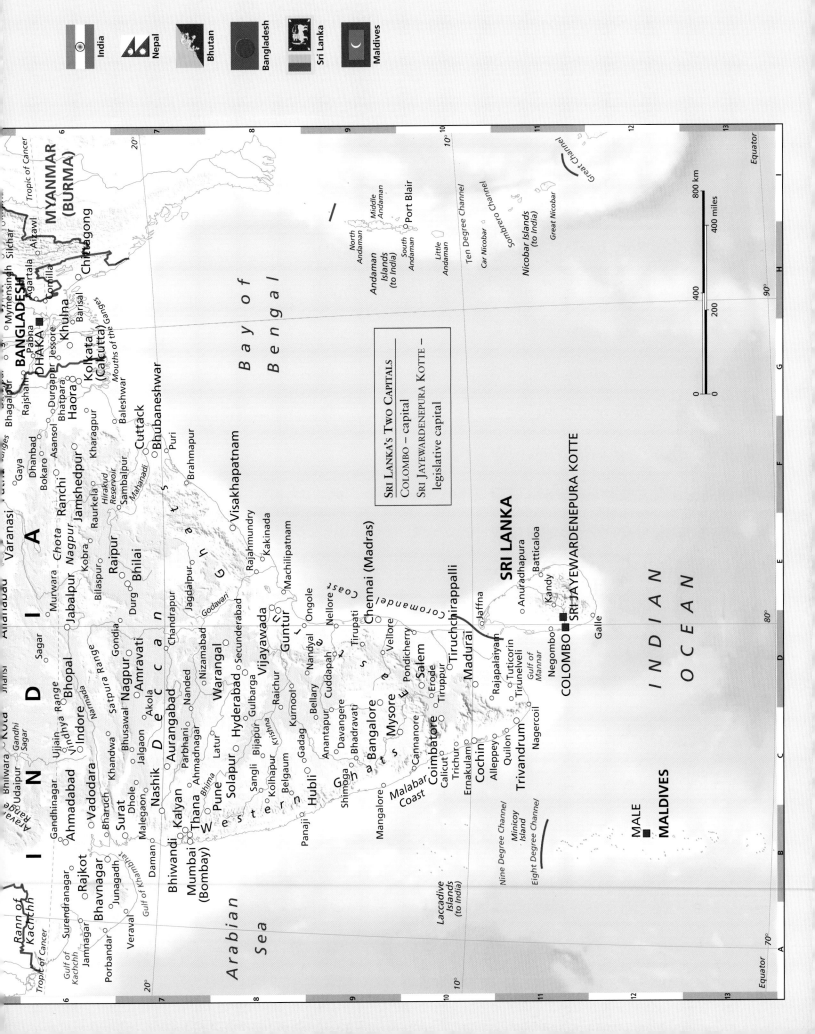

India

Nepal

Bhutan

Bangladesh

Sri Lanka

Maldives

SRI LANKA'S TWO CAPITALS
COLOMBO – capital
SRI JAYEWARDENEPURA KOTTE –
legislative capital

MYANMAR (BURMA)

Tropic of Cancer

Silchar
Aizawl
Agartala
Comilla
Mymensingh

BANGLADESH
DHAKA
Rajshahi
Pabna
Durgapur
Jessore
Khulna
Barisal
Chittagong

Kolkata (Calcutta)
Haora
Bhatpara
Kharagpur
Baleshwar
Mouths of the Ganges

Ganges

Bay of Bengal

Cuttack
Bhubaneshwar
Puri
Brahmapur

North Andaman
Middle Andaman
South Andaman
Port Blair
Little Andaman

Andaman Islands (to India)

Ten Degree Channel

Car Nicobar
Sombrero Channel
Nicobar Islands (to India)
Great Nicobar

Great Channel

10°

Equator

800 km

400 miles

400

200

0

0

90°

I

H

G

F

E

D

C

B

A

Allahabad
Varanasi
Gaya
Dhanbad
Bokaro
Ranchi
Murwara
Jabalpur
Chota Nagpur
Kobra
Bilaspur
Raurkela
Hirakud Reservoir
Sambalpur
Mahanadi

Gandhi Sagar
Ujjain
Bhopal
Indore
Narmada
Satpura Range
Khandwa
Khandwa
Bhusawal
Jalgaon
Akola
Amravati
Nagpur
Durg
Bhilai
Raipur
Jagdalpur
Chandrapur
Godavari

INDIA

Deccan

Visakhapatnam
Rajahmundry
Kakinada
Machilipatnam

Bhilwara
Udaipur
Gandhi Sagar
Aravale Range

Gandhinagar
Ahmadabad
Vadodara
Bharuch
Surat
Daman

Gulf of Khambhat

Rajkot
Bhavnagar
Junagadh
Porbandar
Veraval

Gulf of Kachchh

Surendranagar
Jamnagar

Rann of Kachchh
Tropic of Cancer

Arabian Sea

Bhiwandi
Kalyan
Thana
Mumbai (Bombay)
Pune
Solapur
Ahmadnagar
Aurangabad
Parbhani
Nanded
Latur
Bhima
Nashik
Malegaon
Dhole

Vindhya Range

Bijapur
Sangli
Kolhapur
Belgaum
Panaji

Krishna
Gulbarga
Raichur
Gadag
Hubli
Bellary
Anantapur

Bhadravati
Shimoga
Davangere

Mangalore
Cannanore

Malabar Coast

Calicut
Trichur
Ernakulam
Cochin
Alleppey
Quilon
Trivandrum
Nagercoil

Coimbatore
Tiruppur
Erode
Salem

Bangalore
Mysore

Gonda

Warangal
Nizamabad
Secunderabad
Hyderabad
Vijayawada
Guntur
Nandyal
Kurnool
Cuddapah
Tirupati
Nellore
Ongole

Godavari

Western Ghats

Eastern Ghats

Coromandel Coast

Chennai (Madras)
Vellore
Pondicherry
Tiruchchirappalli
Madurai
Tirunelveli
Tuticorin

Gulf of Mannar

Rajapalaiyam

Jaffna

SRI LANKA
Anuradhapura
Kandy
Batticaloa

SRI JAYEWARDENEPURA KOTTE
COLOMBO
Negombo
Galle

INDIAN OCEAN

Laccadive Islands (to India)

Nine Degree Channel
Minicoy Island
Eight Degree Channel

MALE
MALDIVES

80°

70°

10°

Equator

6

7

8

9

10

11

12

13

SOUTHEAST ASIA

Southeast Asia is made up of many thousands of tropical islands and a mainland area. The landscape of the mainland is dominated by a string of mountain ranges, which are covered in dense forests and crossed by wide river valleys. The many islands to the southeast of the mainland are also forested. Most of these islands were formed by volcanoes, many of which are still active. In the centre of the region is the island of Borneo. The third-largest island in the world, it is divided between the countries of Malaysia, Indonesia and Brunei.

Rice is the main food crop in this region, while bananas, pineapples and sugar cane are grown as cash crops. Large quantities of fish are caught in the surrounding waters. Over the last few decades, the types of industries in southeast Asia have changed dramatically. There are still a number of traditional companies, which process the area's raw materials, including timber and metals, but many parts of the region now have large high-tech industries.

The forests of southeast Asia are home to thousands of unique species of plants and animals. This wildlife is now under threat, however, because vast numbers of trees are being cut away for use in the region's timber industry. In Indonesia, trees are burned to clear land for crops. The smoke from the fires creates terrible smog.

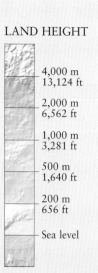

LAND HEIGHT

4,000 m	13,124 ft
2,000 m	6,562 ft
1,000 m	3,281 ft
500 m	1,640 ft
200 m	656 ft
Sea level	

Myanmar

Laos

Vietnam

Thailand

Philippines

Cambodia

Malaysia

Brunei

Singapore

Indonesia

East Timor

Tropic of Cancer

TAIWAN

Batan Islands

Luzon Strait

Babuyan Islands

Laoag ○ ○ Aparri

Luzon

San Fernando ○ ○ Ilagan

Dagupan ○ ○ Baguio

○ Cabanatuan

Angeles ○ ○ San Fernando

■ MANILA

Batangas ○ *Catanduanes*

○ Naga

○ Legaspi

Mindoro

Calbayog ○ *Samar*

Calamian Group ○ Roxas City *Masbate*

Panay Leyte ○ Tacloban

PHILIPPINES Iloilo ○ Cadiz ○ Ormoc

San Carlos ○ Bacolod City

Cebu ○ Cebu

○ Bohol

Negros

Puerto Princesa ○ Dumaguete ○ Surigao

○ Butuan

○ Cagayan de Oro

Iligan ○ *Mindanao*

Zamboanga ○ Mount Apo △ Davao

Basilan 2,954 m

Kudat ○ Jolo ○ General Santos

Kota Kinabalu Gunung Kinabalu

△ 4,094 m Sandakan

Ranau *Tawitawi*

Sulu Archipelago

SABAH

■ **BRUNEI**

Miri ○

ARAWAK

Rajang

Kapuas Mountains

Samarinda ○ *Mahakan*

KALIMANTAN

Balikpapan ○

Barito

anjarmasin ○

Martapura ○

Makassar ○

Selayar

Madura

Surabaya ○

Jember *Bali* *Lombok* *Sumbawa*

Malang

Denpasar ○ Mataram ○

PACIFIC

OCEAN

MICRONESIA

PALAU

Talaud Islands

Celebes Sea

Sangir Islands

Morotai

Halmahera

Manado ○

Ternate ○

Gorontalo ○ *Waigeo*

Manokwari ○

Gulf of Tomini *Molucca Sea* *Halmahera Sea* Sorong ○ Biak ○

Palu ○ Bacan *Jazirah Doberai*

Poso ○ *Peleng* Obi Yapen ○ Jayapura

Sulawesi *Moluccas* *Misool* **IRIAN JAYA**

Sula Islands *Ceram Sea* *Seram* Puncak Jaya △ *Pegunungan Maoke*

Malunda ○ Buru ○ Ambon 5,030 m

Parepare ○ Kendari ○

Muna *Kai Islands* Aru Islands

Buton

Flores Sea *Banda Sea*

Wetar *Tanimbar Islands* Yos Sudarso

Flores Alor

Lomblen ■ DILI

EAST TIMOR

Sumba *Timor*

Kupang ○ *Timor Sea*

Arafura Sea

AUSTRALIA

South China Sea

Spratly Islands

Palawan

Sulu Sea

Balabac Strait

IA

EGAWAN

rneo

Tarakan ○

Tanjungredeb ○

Makassar Strait

PAPUA NEW GUINEA

Equator

Mamberamo

ea

Madura

Lesser Sunda Islands

EAST ASIA

East Asia's landscape may be divided into four main areas. In the southwest is the Plateau of Tibet. Here, high mountain peaks surround small areas of pasture and arid deserts. There are dry highlands in the northwest, and in the north there are cold deserts. Great plains lie to the east. These plains were formed from soils that were carried to the region by China's rivers.

Although most of China's land is either too poor or too mountainous for cultivation, almost three-quarters of this country's enormous population of almost 1.3 billion people make their living from farming. The majority of the people live in the east, where the land is flatter and more fertile. Wheat, corn, soya beans and cotton are grown on the plains, and further south, rice is the main crop. Pigs are raised here in large numbers. In Mongolia, in the north, farmers mainly herd sheep.

China became a communist country in 1949, and since then, it has become a major industrial nation. The country's industries, including iron and steel production, chemicals, engineering and textiles, are concentrated in the cities on the east coast, such as Qingdao and Shanghai. Hong Kong and Beijing are also major financial centres. Taiwan exports electronic goods, shoes and textiles throughout the world, while Mongolia's economy is mainly based on agriculture.

LAND HEIGHT

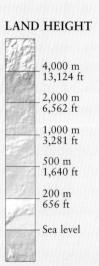

- 4,000 m / 13,124 ft
- 2,000 m / 6,562 ft
- 1,000 m / 3,281 ft
- 500 m / 1,640 ft
- 200 m / 656 ft
- Sea level

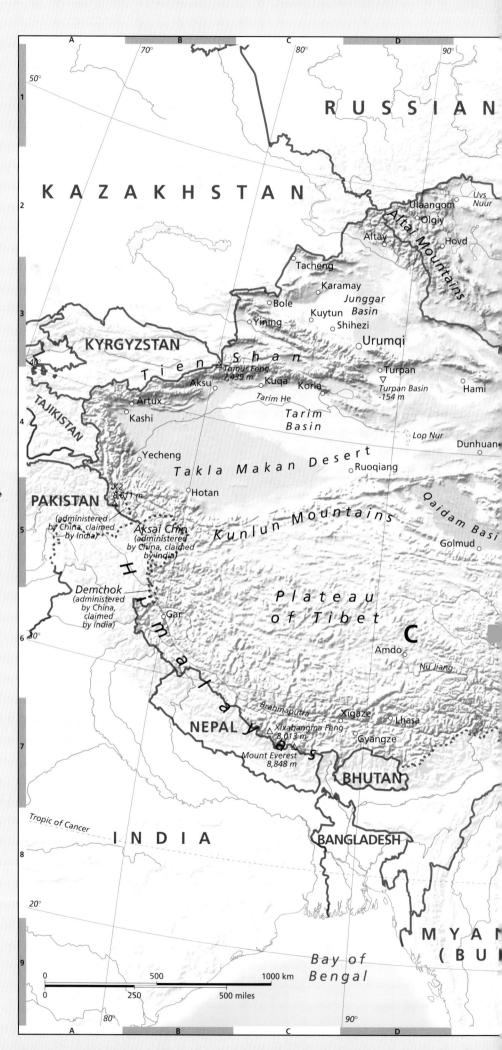

FEDERATION

Mongolia

China

Taiwan

100° F 110° G 120° H I 130° J K 50°

Amur (Heilong Jiang)

Argun (Ergun He)

Hovsgol Nuur

Moron

Halban

Suhbaatar

Manzhouli

Yakeshi

Hailar

Hulun Nur

Yichun

Hegang

Jiamusi

Shuangyashan

1

Uliastay

Tsetserleg

Bulgan

Erdenet

Darhan

Choybalsan

Nianzishan

Zalantun

Suihua

Qiqihar

Jixi

Lake Khanka

2

Altay

Bayanhongor

MONGOLIA

Lun

Dzuunmod

ULAN BATOR

Ondorhaan

Choyr

Baruun-Urt

Ulanhot

Daqing

Zhaodong

Harbin

Mudanjiang

Arvayheer

Mandalgovi

Saynshand

Xilinhot

Manchurian Plain

Baicheng

Changchun

Jilin

3

Dalandzadgad

Erenhot

Tongliao

Siping

Liaoyuan

Baishan

Tonghua

40°

Gobi

Ejin Qi

Jining

Baotou

Hohhot

Zhangjiakou

Liao He

Chifeng

Shenyang

Tieling

Fuxin

Fushun

Benxi

Ansham

NORTH KOREA

Yalu

Sea of Japan

Linhe

Datong

Dongsheng

BEIJING

Baoding

Beipiao

Jinzhou

Haicheng

Dandong

Luan He

Chengde

Qinhuangdao

Korea Bay

Dalian

Tangshan

Tianjin

Bo Hai

SOUTH KOREA

4

Yumen

Jiuquan

Shandan

Jinchang

Wuhai

Yinchuan

Ordos Desert

Yellow River

Yangquan

Taiyuan

Cangzhou

Dezhou

Yantai

Binzhou

Dongying

Zibo

Qingdao

Yellow Sea

Korea Strait

JAPAN

5

Qilian Shan

Tianjun

Wuwei

Qinghai Hu

Xining

Lanzhou

Yanan

Linfen

Changzhi

Handan

Anyang

Fen He

Yellow River

Jinan

Jining

Lianyungang

Shijiazhuang

Xingtai

Tongchuan

Xianyang

Sanmenxia

Zhengzhou

Kaifeng

Xinxiang

Xuzhou

Zaozhuang

Yancheng

6

Tianshui

Baoji

Xi'an

Wei He

Weinan

Pingdingshan

Luoyang

Suzhou

Bengbu

Huainan

Nanjing

Changzhou

Shanghai

30°

Hanzhong

Nanyang

Laohekou

Xinyang

Huai He

Hefei

Wuhu

Wuxi

Suzhou

Jiaxing

Ningbo

Guangyuan

Dachuan

Xiangfan

Suizhou

Anqing

Yangtze

Hangzhou

Shaoxing

Mianyang

Deyang

Nanchong

Wanxian

Yichang

Shashi

Wuhan

Huangshi

Jinhua

East China Sea

Chengdu

Sichuan Basin

Fuling

Changde

Jiujiang

Jingdezhen

Quzhou

Jiaojiang

Wenzhou

Leshan

Neijiang

Chongqing

Yiyang

Yueyang

Nanchang

Shangrao

7

Zigong

Yibin

Luzhou

Jishou

Huaihua

Xiangtan

Zhuzhou

Changsha

Pingxiang

Linchuan

Nanping

Fuzhou

Xichang

Zunyi

Shaoyang

Hengyang

Gan Jiang

Putian

Quanzhou

TAIPEI

Taichung

Tropic of Cancer

Zhaotong

Panzhihua

Dongchuan

Guiyang

Kaili

Zi Shui

Chenzhou

Ganzhou

Xiamen

Chiai

TAIWAN

Tainan

Taiwan Strait

Dali

Chuxiong

Anshun

Qujing

Duyun

Guilin

Xian Jiang

Shaoguan

Meizhou

Chaozhou

Kaohsiung

8

Kunming

Liuzhou

Wuzhou

Xi Jiang

Guangzhou

Shantou

20°

Kaiyuan

Bose

Foshan

Jiangmen

Shenzhen

Gejiu

Nanning

Yulin

Macao

Hong Kong

Hekou

Qinzhou

Maoming

Jinghong

VIETNAM

Beihai

Zhanjiang

Xuwen

Luzon Strait

PHILIPPINES

Gulf of Tongking

Haikou

South China Sea

PACIFIC OCEAN

9

THAILAND

Hainan

Sanya

100° G 110° H I 120° K

JAPAN AND THE KOREAS

South and North Korea lie on a peninsula that juts out from the northeast coast of China. To the east is Japan, a long chain of more than 4,000 islands in the Pacific Ocean. Mountains and hills dominate the landscape of these three countries, so most of this region's cities and towns are located on lower-lying land near the coasts.

Rice is grown throughout this region, and large quantities of fish are caught off the coasts. North Korea's communist government controls its industries and farms, and this country does very little trade with other nations. South Korea and Japan, however, export goods all over the globe. These two countries have few natural resources, so they have specialized in the production of high-value goods. South Korea makes cars, ships and textiles, while Japan is a world leader in the production of high-tech goods, such as cameras, computers and electronics, as well as cars.

Japan's environment suffers from acid rain caused by pollution from the factories of North Korea and the Russian Federation. Nuclear waste is dumped in the Sea of Japan. This country is also located in a major earthquake zone. Although buildings are constructed to withstand tremors, major quakes, such as the one that destroyed Kobe in 1995, are still a big threat in Japan.

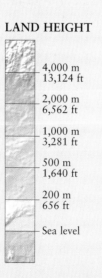

LAND HEIGHT

4,000 m
13,124 ft

2,000 m
6,562 ft

1,000 m
3,281 ft

500 m
1,640 ft

200 m
656 ft

Sea level

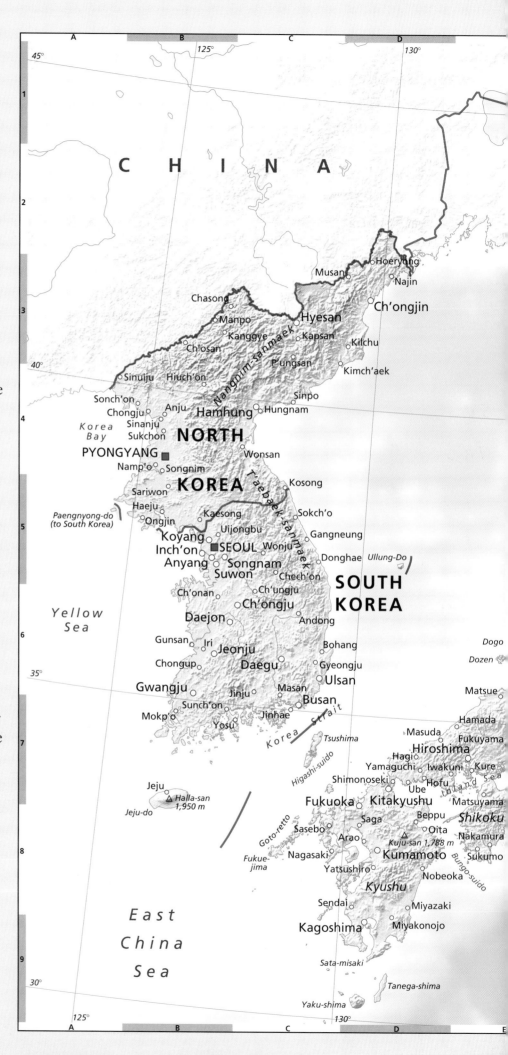

CHINA

Hoeryong
Musan
Najin
Chasong
Ch'ongjin
Manpo
Hyesan
Kanggye
Kapsan
Ch'osan
Kilchu
P'ungsan
Sinuiju
Hiuch'on
Kimch'aek
Sonch'on
Sinpo
Chongju
Anju
Hamhung
Sinanju
Hungnam
Korea
Bay
Sukchon
NORTH
PYONGYANG
Wonsan
Namp'o
Songnim
KOREA
Kosong
Sariwon
Haeju
Taebaek-sannaek
Ongjin
Kaesong
Sokch'o
Paengnyong-do
(to South Korea)
Uijongbu
Gangneung
Koyang
Inch'on
SEOUL
Wonju
Ullung-Do
Anyang
Songnam
Donghae
Suwon
Chech'on
SOUTH
Ch'onan
Ch'ungju
KOREA
Yellow
Ch'ongju
Andong
Sea
Daejon
Gunsan
Iri
Bohang
Jeonju
Chongup
Daegu
Gyeongju
Gwangju
Jinju
Masan
Ulsan
Mokp'o
Sunch'on
Jinhae
Busan
Yosu
Korea Strait
Dogo
Dozen
Matsue
Tsushima
Masuda
Hamada
Higashi-suido
Hagi
Fukuyama
Hiroshima
Jeju
Yamaguchi
Iwakuni
Kure
Shimonoseki
Hofu
Ube
Inland Sea
Halla-san
1,950 m
Fukuoka
Kitakyushu
Matsuyama
Jeju-do
Goto-retto
Saga
Beppu
Shikoku
Sasebo
Oita
Nakamura
Arao
Kuju-san 1,788 m
Sukumo
Fukue-jima
Nagasaki
Kumamoto
Bungo-suido
Yatsushiro
Nobeoka
Kyushu
Sendai
Miyazaki
Kagoshima
Miyakonojo
East
China
Sea
Sata-misaki
Tanega-shima
Yaku-shima

Nangnim-sannaek

Japan

North Korea

South Korea

RUSSIAN FEDERATION

Sea of Okhotsk

La Perouse Strait
Soya-misaki
Rebun-to
Rishiri-to
Wakkanai

Kurile Islands (administered by Russian federation)

45°

Nayoro
Shiretoko-misaki
Monbetsu
Abashiri
Rumoi
Kitami
Asahikawa
Shibetsu
Takikawa
△ Asahi-dake
2,290 m
Kussharo-ko
Nemuro
Otaru
Ebetsu
Hokkaido
Iwanai
Sapporo
Chitose
Kushiro
Obihiro
Tomakomai
Uchiura-wan
Muroran
Erimo-misaki

Okushiri-to
Hakodate
Tsugaru-kaikyo

Shimokita-hanto
Mutsu-wan
Aomori
Hirosaki
Hachinohe
Noshiro

40°

Oga
Morioka
Akita
Miyako
Yokote
Kesennuma
Sakata
Furukawa
Ishinomaki
Sado-shima
Yamagata
Ryotsu
Sendai
Niigata
Sendai-wan
Fukushima
Nagaoka
Honshu
Koriyama
Noto-hanto
Joetsu
Iwaki
JAPAN
Toyama-wan
Nikko
Kuroiso
Takaoka
Toyama
Utsunomiya
Hitachi
Kanazawa
Nagano
Matto
Maebashi
Mito
Komatsu
Matsumoto
Takasaki
Oyama
Tsuchiura
Fukui
Takayama
Chino
Urawa
Wakasa-wan
Tsuruga
Kofu
TOKYO
Funabashi
Choshi
ki-shoto
Ogaki
Gifu
Fujinomiya
Kawasaki
Chiba
Tottori
Maizuru
Otsu
Yokkaichi
△ Mount
Fuji
Ichihara
onago
Biwa-ko
Nagoya
Fuji
3,776 m
Yokohama
Okayama
Himeji
Okazaki
Toyota
Shizuoka
Kobe
Nara
Tsu
Toyohashi
Yaizu
Nojima-zaki
Kurashiki
Sakai
Osaka
Ise
Fujieda
Hamamatsu
Takamatsu
Wakayama
Ise-wan
ijhima
Tokushima
Sagami-nada
Tanabe
Ki-suido
Izu-shoto
Kochi
osa-
Muroto-zaki
Shiono-misaki
van

Sea of Japan

PACIFIC OCEAN

35°

0   200   400 km
0   100   200 miles

PACIFIC OCEAN

0   200   400 km
0   100   200 miles

East China Sea
Amami-o-shima
Naze
Tokuno-shima
Ryukyu Islands
Okinawa
Kume-jima
Okinawa
Naha
Iriomote-jima
Ishigaki-jima
Miyako-jima
Philippine Sea

30°

135°   140°   145°

AUSTRALASIA AND OCEANIA

Australasia and Oceania is made up of 14 countries. They include the vast landmass of Australia, the islands of New Zealand and Papua New Guinea, and the many thousands of coral atolls and islands that extend into the Pacific Ocean.

Before European explorers started to visit this part of the globe during the 16th century, the region was occupied by native peoples who lived by traditional means, such as hunting and gathering. Eventually, the Europeans began to settle and take over these lands. Some of the islands became overseas territories of the United Kingdom, France and the USA. In the past 20 years, a number of these dependencies, such as Palau, have become independent nations.

Natural resources are of major economic importance throughout Australasia and Oceania. Australia exports raw materials, such as coal, iron ore and bauxite. Sheep are raised for their wool and meat in New Zealand and Australia, and fishing is important throughout the Pacific islands. Manufacturing companies are found only in the large coastal cities of Australia and New Zealand. Until recently, both of these countries relied on Europe for trade. However, they have now begun to form trade links with the neighbouring countries of east and southeast Asia.

LAND HEIGHT

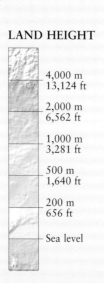

4,000 m	13,124 ft
2,000 m	6,562 ft
1,000 m	3,281 ft
500 m	1,640 ft
200 m	656 ft
Sea level	

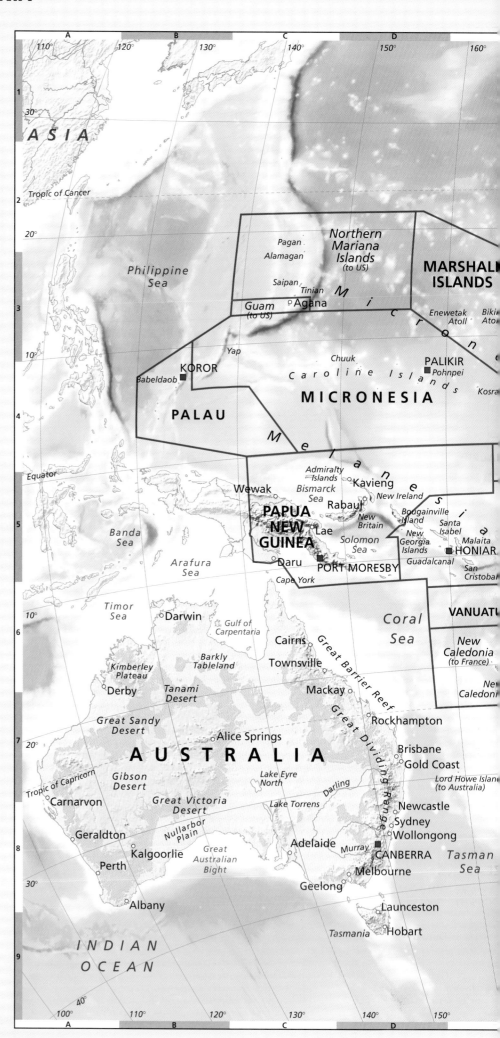

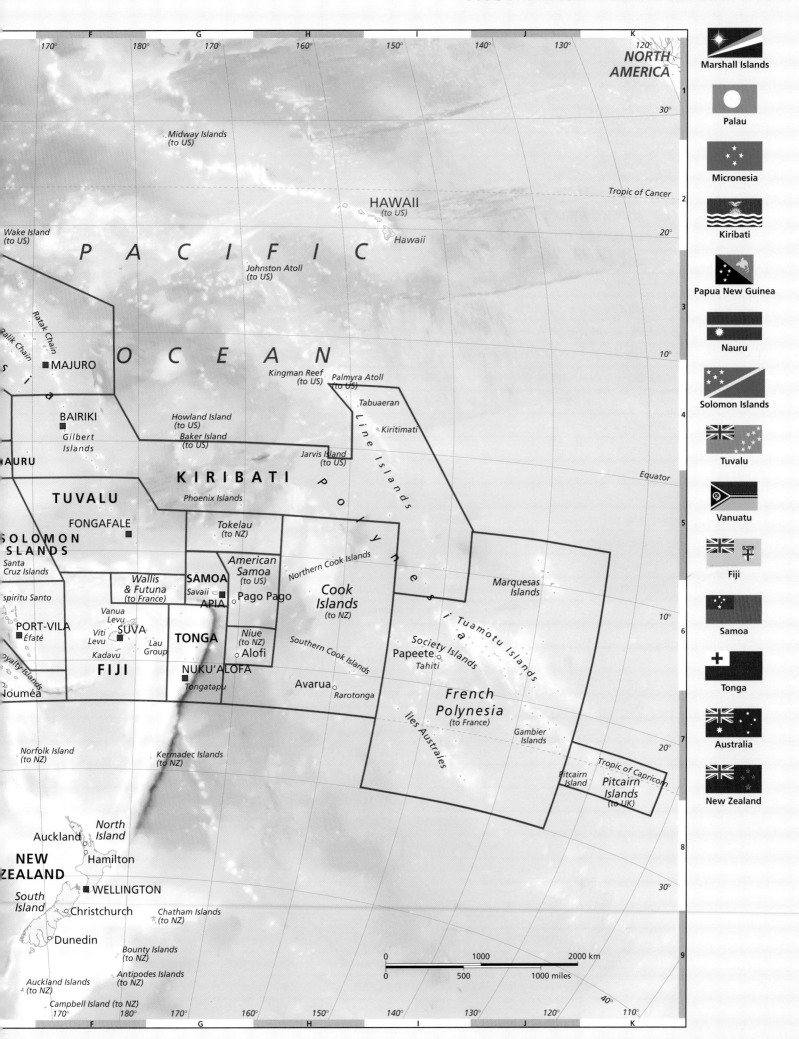

NORTH
AMERICA

Midway Islands
(to US)

Tropic of Cancer

HAWAII
(to US)

Hawaii

Wake Island
(to US)

PACIFIC

Johnston Atoll
(to US)

OCEAN

Ratak Chain
Ralik Chain

MAJURO

Kingman Reef
(to US)

Palmyra Atoll
(to US)

Tabuaeran

Line Islands

Kiritimati

BAIRIKI

NAURU

Howland Island
(to US)

Baker Island
(to US)

Gilbert
Islands

Jarvis Island
(to US)

Equator

KIRIBATI

TUVALU

Phoenix Islands

P   o   l   y   n   e   s   i   a

FONGAFALE

SOLOMON
ISLANDS

Tokelau
(to NZ)

American
Samoa
(to US)

Northern Cook Islands

Marquesas
Islands

Santa
Cruz Islands

Espiritu Santo

Wallis
& Futuna
(to France)

SAMOA

Savaii

APIA

Pago Pago

Cook
Islands
(to NZ)

Tuamotu Islands

PORT-VILA
Éfaté

Vanua
Levu

Viti
Levu

SUVA

Lau
Group

TONGA

Niue
(to NZ)

Alofi

Southern Cook Islands

Society Islands

Papeete

Tahiti

Loyalty Islands

Nouméa

Kadavu

FIJI

NUKU'ALOFA

Tongatapu

Avarua

Rarotonga

French
Polynesia
(to France)

Îles Australes

Gambier
Islands

Pitcairn
Island

Tropic of Capricorn

Pitcairn
Islands
(to UK)

Norfolk Island
(to NZ)

Kermadec Islands
(to NZ)

North
Island

Auckland

Hamilton

NEW
ZEALAND

South
Island

WELLINGTON

Christchurch

Chatham Islands
(to NZ)

Dunedin

Bounty Islands
(to NZ)

Antipodes Islands
(to NZ)

Auckland Islands
(to NZ)

Campbell Island (to NZ)

0   1000   2000 km

0   500   1000 miles

Marshall Islands

Palau

Micronesia

Kiribati

Papua New Guinea

Nauru

Solomon Islands

Tuvalu

Vanuatu

Fiji

Samoa

Tonga

Australia

New Zealand

AUSTRALIA

One of the world's largest countries, Australia is located in the southern Pacific Ocean. Despite its huge size, this nation has a relatively small population of almost 19.5 million people, because much of the land is dry. In the west are semi-arid plains of scrub and grassland, while in the east the land rises to the peaks of the Great Dividing Range. In the north, there are tropical rainforests and mangrove swamps.

Sugar cane is harvested near the east coast. In the south and west, grapes for Australia's successful wine industry are produced, along with wheat. Large numbers of sheep and cattle are raised in the southwest and on the Great Artesian Basin in the east. These provide meat and wool for export.

The first inhabitants of Australia were the Aboriginal peoples. Today, they are a tiny minority, and the majority of Australians are of European origin. Most people work and live in cities in the south and east, and around Perth in the west. In these urban areas are engineering and manufacturing businesses, and thriving service industries.

Australia has one of the world's biggest mining industries, which exploits the rich resources of gold, copper, coal and iron ore. Tourism is another important source of income, especially along the northeast coast, where people come to visit the sunny beaches and the Great Barrier Reef.

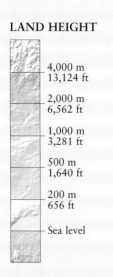

LAND HEIGHT

4,000 m
13,124 ft

2,000 m
6,562 ft

1,000 m
3,281 ft

500 m
1,640 ft

200 m
656 ft

Sea level

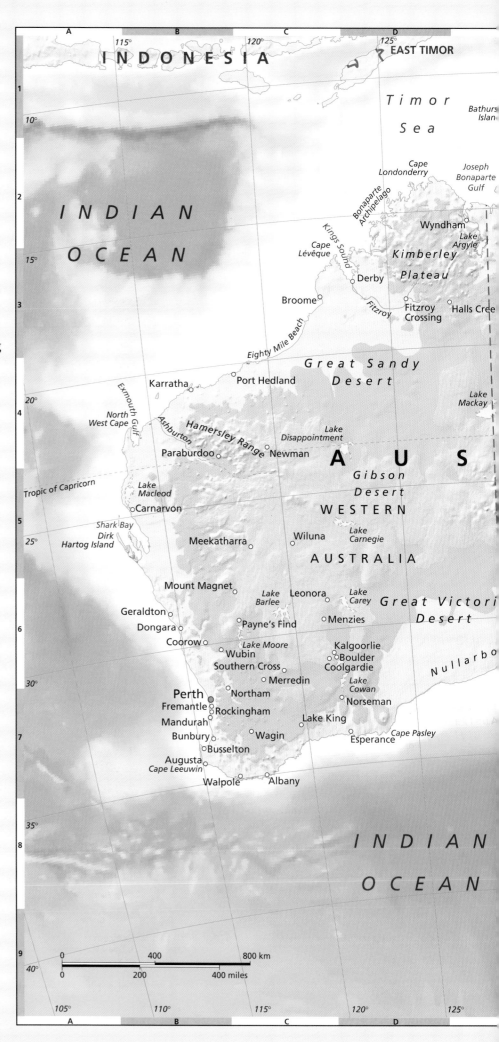

Australia

PAPUA NEW GUINEA

Torres Strait

Arafura Sea

Melville
Island

*Van
Diemen
Gulf*

Darwin

*Wessel
Islands*

Prince of
Wales Island

Cape York

Cape
Arnhem

*Arnhem
Land*

*Cape
York
Peninsula*

*Princess
Charlotte
Bay*

*Gulf of
Carpentaria*

*Groote
Eylandt*

Katherine

Mataranka

Victoria

Victoria River Roadhouse

Daly Waters

*Sir Edward
Pellew Group*

*Wellesley
Islands*

Cooktown

Cairns

*Coral
Sea*

Barkly Tableland

*Lake
Woods*

Normanton

Croydon

Georgetown

Great Barrier Reef

*Tanami
Desert*

Tennant Creek

Camooweal

Forsayth

NORTHERN

Cloncurry

Richmond

Charters Towers

Townsville

TERRITORY

Mount Isa

Duchess

Hughenden

Torrens Creek

Proserpine

Georgina

Boulia

Winton

Great Dividing Range

Mackay

*Cape
Townshend*

Macdonnell Ranges

Alice Springs

QUEENSLAND

Clermont

*Lake
Amadeus*

Longreach

Jericho

Emerald

Rockhampton

Diamantina

Great Artesian

Blackall

Gladstone

△ Uluru
(Ayers Rock)
867 m

*Simpson
Desert*

Thomson

Birdsville

Basin

*Buckland
Tableland*

Theodore

Bundaberg

Tropic of Capricorn

Charleville

Mitchell

Injune

Maryborough

Fraser Island

Hervey Bay

T R A L I A

Oodnadatta

*Lake
Eyre North*

*Sturt
Desert*

Cooper Creek

Quilpie

Durham
Downs

Roma

Miles

Gympie

Maroochydore-Mooloolaba

Caloundra

SOUTH AUSTRALIA

Coober Pedy

*Lake
Eyre South*

*Lake
Blanche*

Marree

Cunnamulla

Warrego

Saint George

Toowoomba

Ipswich

Brisbane

Dirranbandi

Warwick

Gold Coast

Talwood

Goondiwindi

Ballina

Tarcoola

Lake Torrens

*Lake
Frome*

Bourke

Moree

Lismore

Grafton

lain

Flinders Ranges

Darling

Walgett

Coffs Harbour

Lake Everard

Penong

*Lake
Gairdner*

Broken Hill

Wilcannia

Coonamble

Armidale

Ceduna

Whyalla

Port Augusta

**NEW SOUTH
WALES**

Tamworth

Port Macquarie

Streaky Bay

Kyancutta

Port Pirie

Ivanhoe

Dubbo

Forster-Tuncurry

*Great
Australian
Bight*

Elliston

Lachlan

Orange

Newcastle

Port Lincoln

Gawler

Waikerie

Mildura

Hay

Bathurst

Gosford

Spencer Gulf

Adelaide

Balranald

Wagga
Wagga

Sydney

York Peninsula

Murray Bridge

Murray

Albury

Goulburn

Wollongong

Gulf St Vincent

Keith

CANBERRA

AUSTRALIAN CAPITAL TERRITORY

Kangaroo Island

VICTORIA

Wodonga

Cooma

Naracoorte

Horsham

Bendigo

Great

Mount Kosciuszko
2,230 m

Ballarat

Mount Gambier

Hamilton

Melbourne

Sale

Cape Howe

Portland

Geelong

Cape Otway

Bass Strait

South East Point

*Tasman
Sea*

King Island

Flinders Island

Stanley

Burnie

*Furneaux
Group*

Devonport

Launceston

△ Mount Ossa 1,617 m

TASMANIA

Hobart

NEW ZEALAND

New Zealand lies in the southern Pacific Ocean, 1,600 km southeast of Australia. This country consists of two large islands – North Island and South Island – and many smaller ones. In the far north of North Island are coastal inlets, which are fringed by mangrove swamps. Further south are geysers, boiling mud pools and fertile plains that rise to volcanic peaks, such as Mount Egmont and Mount Ruapehu. There are also volcanoes in South Island, where the landscape is dominated by the Southern Alps. This towering mountain range stretches more than 480 km along the western side of the island. Many rivers flow down from these uplands to the east coast.

The first inhabitants of New Zealand were the Maori, a Polynesian people. In the 19th century, Europeans began to settle here, and they now make up more than 90 per cent of the whole population. The people are mainly concentrated in the country's coastal towns and cities, especially in Auckland, on North Island.

New Zealand has rich and fertile land that provides good pasture for millions of sheep and cattle. Fruits, such as apples, peaches, oranges and kiwi fruit, are grown and exported to many countries throughout the world.

New Zealand has a strong timber industry, and in the cities, high-tech businesses that produce electronic goods and computers are expanding. Agricultural products, however, such as lamb, wool and milk, remain the country's major exports. Tourism is also an important source of income. New Zealand's environment is generally unpolluted due to its low population and lack of heavy industries.

LAND HEIGHT

4,000 m / 13,124 ft
2,000 m / 6,562 ft
1,000 m / 3,281 ft
500 m / 1,640 ft
200 m / 656 ft
Sea level

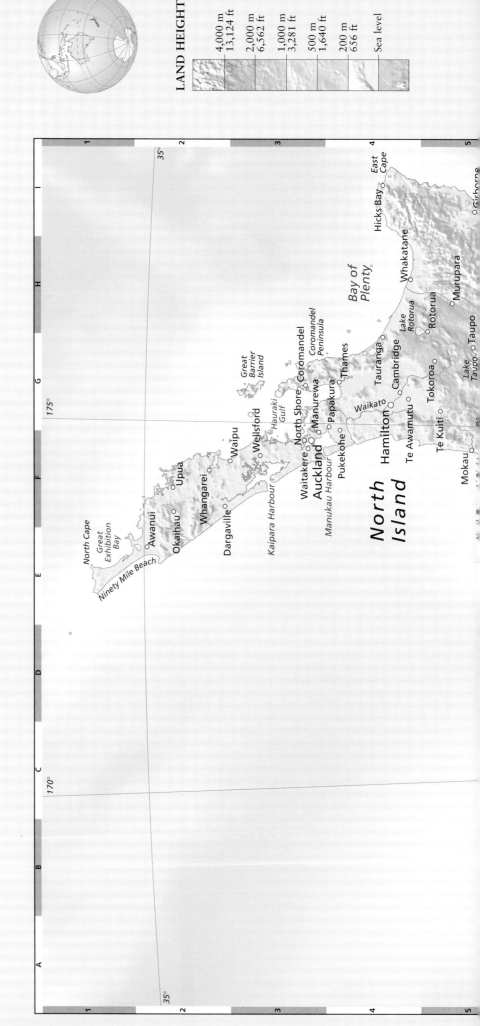

New Zealand

NEW ZEALAND

Tasman Sea

South Island

Southern Alps

Fiordland

Stewart Island

PACIFIC OCEAN

Cook Strait

Tasman Bay

Golden Bay

Canterbury Plains

Pegasus Bay

Banks Peninsula

Otago Peninsula

Foveaux Strait

Canterbury Bight

South Taranaki Bight

Karamea Bight

Hawke Bay

Mahia Peninsula

WELLINGTON
Christchurch
Dunedin

New Plymouth
Mount Egmont (Taranaki) △ 2,518 m
Cape Egmont
Opunake
Hawera
Stratford
△ Mount Ngauruhoe 2,291 m
△ Mount Ruapehu 2,797 m
Waiouru
Wanganui
Waimangaroa
Mangaweka
Feilding
Palmerston North
Napier
Hastings
Waipukurau
Herbertville
Wairoa
Masterton
Levin
Porirua
Lower-Hutt
Cape Palliser
Cloudy Bay
Clarence
Kaikoura
Parnassus
Picton
Blenheim
D'Urville Island
Cape Farewell
Collingwood
Motueka
Nelson
Owen River
Reefton
Westport
Cape Foulwind
Greymouth
Hokitika
Rotherham
Waipara
Rangiora
Sheffield
Dunsandel
Ashburton
Lake Ellesmere
Lake Tekapo
Fox Glacier
△ Mount Cook 3,754 m
△ Mount Aspiring 3,030 m
Haast
Cascade Point
Lake Wanaka
Lake Hawea
Omarama
Wanaka
Cromwell
Alexandra
Roxburgh
Beaumont
Clutha
Balclutha
Milton
Timaru
Kurow
Oamaru
Palmerston
Mataura
Lake Wakatipu
Queenstown
Kingston
Mossburn
Lumsden
Gore
Ohai
Waiau
Lake Te Anau
Te Anau
Tuatapere
Invercargill
Halfmoon Bay
West Cape
South West Cape
Resolution Island
Milford Sound

200 km
100 miles
100
50

THE PACIFIC OCEAN

Stretching over about one-third of the Earth's surface, the Pacific is the planet's largest ocean. It extends east from Japan to the Americas, and south from the Arctic Ocean to Antarctica. The ocean's floor is generally deeper in the west than in the east, and at its deepest point, the Mariana Trench, the Pacific plunges to –11,034 m.

The many thousands of islands scattered across the Pacific Ocean were created by volcanic eruptions. Some of these islands became fringed with coral, and the islands eventually dropped back into the sea, leaving circles of coral, or atolls. A string of active volcanoes, known as the 'Ring of Fire', surrounds the ocean. The Pacific region is plagued by tropical storms, called typhoons. The area is also prone to tidal waves, which are caused by volcanic eruptions or underwater earthquakes.

The peoples of the Pacific mainly grow food for their own consumption, although a few islands grow crops, such as coconuts and oil palms, for export. Many of the small islands rely heavily on fishing for much-needed foreign income. These fish industries tend to be small and are forced to compete with the large fishing fleets of Japan and the Russian Federation. With palm-fringed beaches, spectacular coral reefs and a warm, sunny climate, the islands of the Pacific Ocean have become popular tourist destinations.

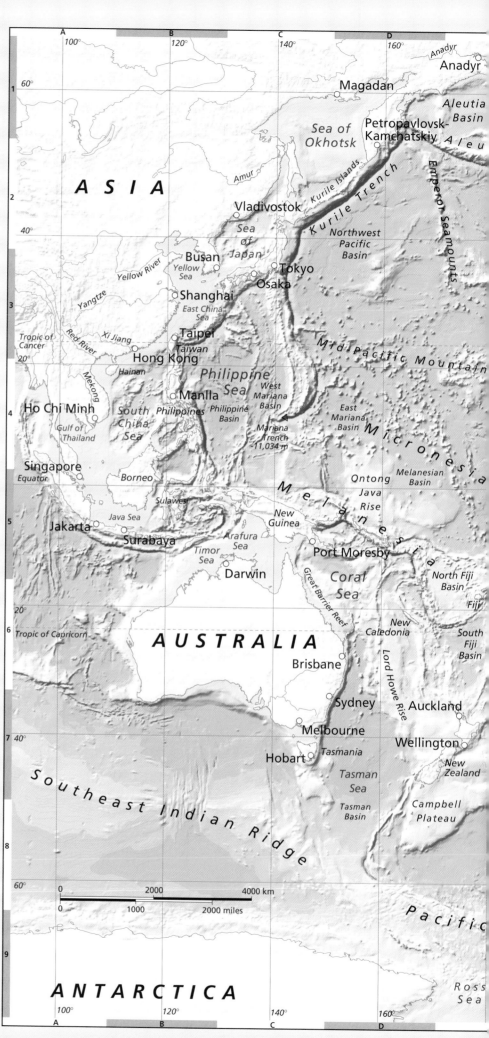

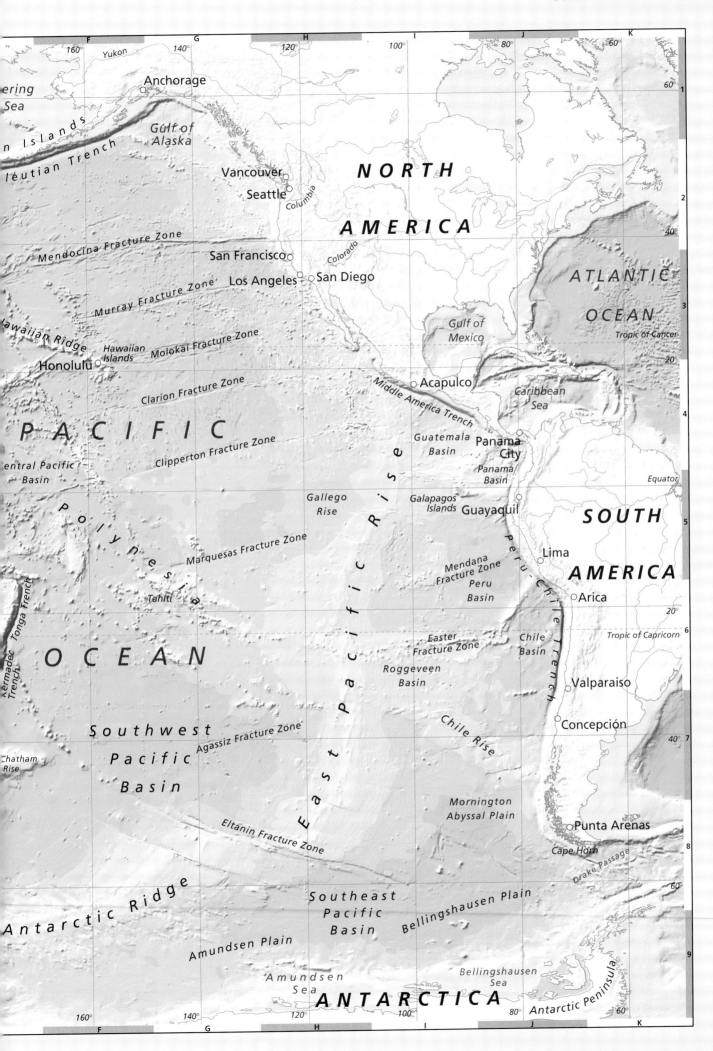

NORTH AMERICA

ATLANTIC OCEAN

SOUTH AMERICA

ANTARCTICA

PACIFIC OCEAN

Bering Sea

Aleutian Islands

Aleutian Trench

Yukon

Anchorage

Gulf of Alaska

Vancouver

Seattle

Columbia

Mendocina Fracture Zone

San Francisco

Colorado

Los Angeles

San Diego

Murray Fracture Zone

Hawaiian Ridge

Hawaiian Islands

Molokai Fracture Zone

Honolulu

Clarion Fracture Zone

Central Pacific Basin

Clipperton Fracture Zone

Polynesia

Marquesas Fracture Zone

Tahiti

Tonga Trench

Kermadec Trench

Gallego Rise

Middle America Trench

Acapulco

Guatemala Basin

Panama City

Panama Basin

Galapagos Islands

Guayaquil

East Pacific Rise

Mendana Fracture Zone

Peru Basin

Lima

Peru-Chile Trench

Arica

Gulf of Mexico

Caribbean Sea

Tropic of Cancer

Equator

Easter Fracture Zone

Roggeveen Basin

Chile Basin

Chile Rise

Tropic of Capricorn

Valparaiso

Concepción

Southwest Pacific Basin

Agassiz Fracture Zone

Chatham Rise

Mornington Abyssal Plain

Eltanin Fracture Zone

Punta Arenas

Cape Horn

Drake Passage

Antarctic Ridge

Southeast Pacific Basin

Bellingshausen Plain

Amundsen Plain

Amundsen Sea

Bellingshausen Sea

Antarctic Peninsula

GLOSSARY

The following glossary explains certain geographical and technical terms used in this atlas.

Acid rain
Rain and snow that has absorbed gases released by power stations and vehicle exhausts. Acid rain can cause severe environmental damage.

Arctic Circle
An imaginary line (latitude) that runs east-west around the Earth. The Arctic Circle lies at a latitude of 66° 32'N.

Biodiversity
The quantity of different plant or animal species in a given area.

Cash crops
Crops grown for sale, often for the export market, rather than for consumption in the area in which they are grown.

Climate
The average weather conditions in a given region.

Deforestation
The cutting down of large areas of forest for timber, farmland or urban development. It can lead to soil erosion, flooding and landslides.

Delta
A low-lying, fan-shaped area at a river mouth. It is formed when the river drops layers of sediment as it slows down when entering the sea.

Desertification
The gradual spread of desert conditions in arid or semi-arid regions. Desertification may be caused by changes in the climate or by human activities, such as overgrazing and **deforestation**.

Equator
The imaginary line (latitude) which circles the middle of the Earth. Lying at 0°, it is equidistant from the North and South Poles.

European Union (EU)
A group of European countries that have joined together to promote trade, industry and agriculture. The EU was formed in 1965, and was formerly known as the European Economic Community (EEC), then the European Community (EC).

Flood plain
The broad, flat part of a river valley, bordering the river. Flood plains are formed by sediment deposited during flooding.

Heavy industry
A type of industry that uses vast amounts of energy and raw materials to make heavy goods such as machinery and ships.

High-tech industry
A type of industry that produces high-value, technologically advanced goods, such as computers and other electronic equipment.

Ice shelf
Floating ice attached to the edge of a coast. The edge facing the sea is usually a steep cliff up to 30 m high.

Irrigation
The artificial supply of water to land. It usually involves the construction of canals and the diversion of natural watercourses.

Manufacturing
A type of industry that makes vast quantities of finished goods, from clothes to cars, which are sold to large numbers of people.

Natural resources
Fuel and raw materials, such as oil, ores and timber, which occur naturally and are found in large quantities in a given area.

Peninsula
A thin strip of land that juts out into the sea, and is surrounded by water on three of its sides. Large examples include Florida and the Koreas.

Plain
A flat, level region of land. It is often relatively low-lying.

Service industry
A type of industry that does not produce goods, but provides services such as banking and tourism.

Shanty town
An area in or around a city where people live in makeshift shacks, usually without basic facilities such as running water.

Tropics
The area between the **Tropic of Cancer** and the **Tropic of Capricorn** where the **climate** is hot.

Tropic of Cancer
An imaginary circle around the Earth, north of the Equator. It lies at a latitude of 23° 28'N.

Tropic of Capricorn
An imaginary circle around the Earth, south of the Equator. It lies at a latitude of 23° 28'S.

United Nations (UN)
An association of countries that was established in 1945. It seeks to maintain international peace and security, and promote co-operation over economic, social, cultural and humanitarian problems.

INDEX

The following index lists all the placenames and features on the regional and continental maps in this atlas. The entry names are settlements unless otherwise indicated by the use of italicized definitions. Each name is located within a region, country, sea or ocean. Physical feature names that are made up of a proper name and a description, such as Mount Etna, are positioned alphabetically by the proper name. The description appears after the proper name. For example, Mount Etna appears as 'Etna, Mount' in the index.

The first number at the end of each entry is the page number of the map on which the feature or place may be found. The letter and figure after the page number give the grid square in which the name is located.

110 . APIA–BELIZE CITY

Apia *country capital* Samoa 101 G6
Apo, Mount *volcano* Philippines 95 H5
Appalachian Mountains *mountain range* E USA 23 F9, 31 H4, 32 E9
Appennino Lucano *mountain range* Italy 63 G8
Appleton Wisconsin, USA 32 C4
Apure *river* Venezuela 38 C2, 40 D2
Aqaba Jordan 88 D5
Aqkol Kazakhstan 90 F3
Aqsay Kazakhstan 90 B3
Aqso Kazakhstan 90 F3
Aqtao Kazakhstan 91 A6
Aqtobe Kazakhstan 90 C4
Aquitaine *cultural region* France 54 D7
Arabian Basin *undersea feature* N Indian Ocean 82 D2
Arabian Peninsula *peninsula* SW Asia 84 B7, 89 E5
Arabian Sea *sea* NW Indian Ocean 82 D2, 84 C7, 91 D13, 93 A8
Aracaju Brazil 41 J5
Arad Romania 69 F2
Arafura Sea *sea* W Pacific Ocean 85 H9, 95 I9, 100 B5, 103 F1
Aragón *cultural region* Spain 57 G3
Araguaia *river* Brazil 39 F6, 41 H5
Arak Iran 89 G3
Arakan Yoma *mountain range* Myanmar 94 A2
Aral Kazakhstan 90 D5
Aral Sea *inland sea* Kazakhstan/Uzbekistan 84 C5, 91 D5
Aranda de Duero Spain 57 E3
Aranjuez Spain 57 E5
Arao Japan 98 D8
Araouane Mali 77 F4
Arapiraca Brazil 41 J5
'Ar'ar Saudi Arabia 89 E4
Aravali Range *mountain range* India 93 B6
Arba Minch Ethiopia 75 E10
Arbil Iraq 89 F3
Arbon Switzerland 60 D4
Arcachon France 54 D6
Archangel Russian Federation 47 H2, 86 C3
Arctic Ocean *ocean* 20 B2
Ardabil Iran 89 G2
Ardennes *physical region* Belgium/France 53 E11
Arendal Norway 49 B10
Arequipa Peru 39 C6, 40 D6
Arezzo Italy 62 D5
Argenteuil France 55 F3
Argentina *country* S South America 39 C10, 43 D7
Argentine Basin *undersea feature* C Atlantic Ocean 45 D10
Argostoli Greece 69 E7
Argun *river* China/Russian Federation 97 I2
Argyle, Lake *salt lake* Western Australia, Australia 102 E2
Århus Denmark 49 B12
Arica Chile 42 C1
Arima Trinidad & Tobago 37 J8
Arizona *state* USA 27 G10
Arjeplog Sweden 48 E5
Arkansas *river* C USA 23 E9, 29 G8, 31 F4
Arkansas *state* USA 31 E4
Arkansas City Kansas, USA 29 H8
Arles France 55 H7
Arlington Texas, USA 30 E5
Arlington Virginia, USA 33 G7
Arlit Niger 77 I4
Arlon Belgium 53 G12
Armant Egypt 74 C4
Armenia *country* SW Asia 84 B5, 89 F2
Armenia Colombia 40 C2
Armidale New South Wales, Australia 103 J6
Arnhem Netherlands 53 G6
Arnhem, Cape *headland* Northern Territory, Australia 103 G1
Arnhem Land *physical region* Northern Territory, Australia 103 F2
Arno *river* Italy 62 D5
Arnsberg Germany 59 C6
Arnstadt Germany 59 F7
Arqalyq Kazakhstan 90 E4
Ar Ramadi Iraq 89 F3
Arran *island* Scotland, United Kingdom 51 D6
Ar Raqqah Syria 88 E3
Arras France 55 F1
Ar Rub' al Khali *desert* SW Asia 89 G7
Ar Rustaq Oman 89 I6
Arta Greece 69 E7
Artesia New Mexico, USA 30 B5
Artiagas Uruguay 42 G5
Artsyz Ukraine 65 D12
Artux China 96 B4
Artyk Turkmenistan 91 C8
Aruba *Dutch dependent territory* S West Indies 23 H12, 37 G8
Aru Islands *island* Indonesia 95 J8
Arusha Tanzania 71 H8, 79 I7
Aruwimi *river* Democratic Republic of Congo 79 F6
Arvayheer Mongolia 97 F3
Arvidsjaur Sweden 49 F5
Asadabad Afghanistan 91 F9
Asahi-dake *mountain* Japan 99 I2
Asahikawa Japan 99 I2
Asamankese Ghana 77 G8
Asansol India 93 F6
Ascension Island *island* C Atlantic Ocean 45 F8, 71 A9
Ascoli Piceno Italy 63 F6
Aseb Eritrea 75 G8
Asela Ethiopia 75 F9
Ashburton *river* Western Australia, Australia 102 B4
Ashburton New Zealand 105 D10
Asheville North Carolina, USA 31 I3
Ashgabat *country capital* Turkmenistan 84 C5, 91 C8
Ashland Oregon, USA 27 B5
Asia *continent* 84–99
Asir *mountain range* Saudi Arabia 89 E7
Askersund Sweden 49 D10
Asmar Afghanistan 91 F9
Asmara *country capital* Eritrea 70 H5, 75 E7
Aspen Colorado, USA 28 D7
Aspiring, Mount *mountain* New Zealand 105 B10
Assamakka Niger 77 I4
Assen Netherlands 52 H3
Assisi Italy 63 E6
As Sulaymaniyah Iraq 89 F3
As Sulayyil Saudi Arabia 89 F7
Astana *country capital* Kazakhstan 84 D4, 90 F4
Asti Italy 62 B4
Astoria Oregon, USA 26 B3
Astrakhan Russian Federation 47 J6, 86 B6
Asunción *country capital* Paraguay 39 E8, 42 G3
Aswân Egypt 70 G4, 74 D5
Asyût Egypt 70 G3, 74 C4
Atacama Desert *desert* Chile 39 C7, 42 C4
Atakpamé Togo 77 G7
Atar Mauritania 76 D4
Atasu Kazakhstan 90 F4
Atbara *river* NE Africa 70 G5, 75 D7
Atbara Sudan 75 D7
Atbasar Kazakhstan 90 E3
Ath Belgium 53 C10
Athabasca *river* Alberta, Canada 24 C6
Athabasca, Lake *lake* Alberta/Saskatchewan, Canada 23 E6, 24 D6
Athens *country capital* Greece 47 F8, 69 G7
Athens Georgia, USA 31 I4
Athlone Republic of Ireland 51 C9
Athus Belgium 53 G13
Atlanta Georgia, USA 23 F9, 31 I4
Atlantic City New Jersey, USA 33 H7
Atlantic-Indian Basin *undersea feature* Atlantic Ocean/Indian Ocean 45 G11, 82 B8
Atlantic-Indian Ridge *undersea feature* Atlantic Ocean/Indian Ocean 45 F12, 82 A8
Atlantic Ocean *ocean* 31 J5, 44–45, 50 A2
Atlas Mountains *mountain range* NW Africa 70 C2, 72 C5
At Ta'if Saudi Arabia 88 E7
Attersee Austria 61 H3
Atyrau Kazakhstan 90 B5
Auch France 54 E7
Auckland New Zealand 101 F8, 104 F3
Auckland Islands *island group* New Zealand 101 E9
Augsburg Germany 59 E11
Augusta Western Australia, Australia 102 B7
Augusta Georgia, USA 31 I4
Augusta *state capital* Maine, USA 33 J4
Augustow Poland 66 H3
Aurangabad India 93 C7
Aurora Colorado, USA 28 E7
Austin *state capital* Texas, USA 23 E10, 30 D6
Austin Minnesota, USA 29 I4
Australasia *continent* 100–105
Australes, Îles *island group* French Polynesia 101 I7
Australia *country* SW Pacific Ocean 100 B7, 102–103
Australian Capital Territory *state* Australia 103 I7
Austria *country* C Europe 46 E6, 61 H4
Austvågøy *island* Norway 48 D3
Auxerre France 55 G4
Avarua Cook Islands 101 H6
Aveiro Portugal 56 B4
Avellino Italy 63 F8
Averøya *island* Norway 48 B7
Avesta Sweden 49 E9
Avezzano Italy 63 E7
Aviemore Scotland, United Kingdom 50 E4
Avignon France 55 H7
Ávila Spain 56 D4
Avilés Spain 56 D1
Avola Italy 63 G12
Avon *river* England, United Kingdom 51 F11
Avranches France 54 D3
Awanui New Zealand 104 E2
Awasa Ethiopia 75 F10
Awbari Libya 73 H6
Aweil Sudan 75 B9
Axel Heiburg Island *island* Nunavut, Canada 25 F1
Axios *river* Greece/Macedonia 69 F5
Ayacucho Peru 40 C6
Ayakoz Kazakhstan 90 H4
Aydin Turkey 88 C2
Ayers Rock *see* Uluru
Ayní Tajikistan 91 E7
'Ayoûn El 'Atroûs Mauritania 76 E5
Ayr Scotland, United Kingdom 51 E7
Azahar, Costa del *coastal region* Spain 57 H5
Azaouâd *desert* Mali 77 G4
Azerbaijan *country* SE Asia 84 B5, 89 G2
Azores *island group* SW Europe 44 E5
Azov, Sea of *sea* NE Black Sea 47 H6, 65 H12
Azuaga Spain 56 D7
Azul Argentina 43 F7
Azur, Côte d' *coastal region* France 55 I8
Az Zarqa Jordan 88 D4
Az Zawiyah Libya 73 H4

B

Baarle-Hertog Belgium 53 E7
Babeldaob *island* Palau 100 B4
Bab el Mandeb *strait* Gulf of Aden/Red Sea 89 F9
Babol Iran 89 H3
Babruysk Belarus 65 E7
Babuyan Islands *island group* Philippines 95 G3
Bacan *island* Indonesia 95 H7
Bacau Romania 69 H2
Bacolod City Philippines 95 G5
Badajoz Spain 56 C6
Badalona Spain 57 I3
Bad Doberan Germany 58 F3
Baden Austria 61 J3
Baden Switzerland 60 C4
Baden-Baden Germany 59 C10
Bad Hersfeld Germany 59 D7
Bad Homburg vor der Höhe Germany 59 C8
Bad Ischl Austria 61 H4
Bad Kissingen Germany 59 E8
Badlands *physical region* North Dakota, USA 29 E3
Bad Mergentheim Germany 59 D9
Bad Waldsee Germany 59 D12
Bad Windsheim Germany 59 E9
Bafatá Guinea-Bissau 76 C6
Baffin Bay *bay* Canada/Greenland 20 A4, 22 G4, 25 G3, 44 C2
Baffin Island *island* Nunavut, Canada 22 G4, 25 F3
Bafia Cameroon 78 C5
Bafoussam Cameroon 78 B5
Bagé Brazil 41 G9
Baghdad *country capital* Iraq 84 B6, 89 F4
Bagheria Italy 63 E11
Baghlan Afghanistan 91 E8
Baguio Philippines 95 G3
Bahamas *country* N West Indies 23 G11, 36 D2
Bahawalpur Pakistan 91 F10
Bahir Dar Ethiopia 75 E8
Bahrain *country* SW Asia 84 B6, 89 H5
Baia Mare Romania 69 F1
Baicheng China 97 I3
Baikal, Lake *lake* Russian Federation 85 F4, 87 G6
Bairiki *country capital* Kiribati 101 F4
Baishan China 97 J3
Baja Hungary 67 E11
Baker Oregon, USA 26 D4
Baker Island *US dependent territory* C Pacific Ocean 101 G4
Bakersfield California, USA 27 C10
Bakhtaran Iran 89 G3
Baku *country capital* Azerbaijan 84 B5, 89 G2
Balabac Strait *strait* Malaysia/Philippines 95 F5
Balassagyarmat Hungary 67 F9
Balaton *lake* Hungary 67 D11
Balbina, Represa de *reservoir* Brazil 41 F3
Balclutha New Zealand 105 C12
Balearic Islands *island group* Spain 46 B8, 57 I5
Baleshwar India 93 G7
Bali *island* Indonesia 95 F9
Balikesir Turkey 88 C1
Balikpapan Indonesia 95 F7
Balingen Germany 59 C11
Balkan Mountains *mountain range* Bulgaria/Serbia & Montenegro 69 F4
Balkh Afghanistan 91 E8
Balkhash Kazakhstan 90 G5
Balkhash, Lake *lake* Kazakhstan 84 D5, 90 G5
Ballarat Victoria, Australia 103 H8
Ballina New South Wales, Australia 103 J6
Balranald New South Wales, Australia 103 H7
Balsas *river* Mexico 34 D6
Balti Moldova 65 D11
Baltic Sea *sea* NE Atlantic Ocean 47 E4, 58 H2, 64 A3, 66 D1
Baltimore Maryland, USA 23 G9, 33 G7
Balvi Latvia 64 D4
Bam Iran 89 I4
Bamako *country capital* Mali 71 B5, 76 E6
Bambari Central African Republic 78 E5
Bamberg Germany 59 E9
Bamenda Cameroon 78 B5
Bamian Afghanistan 91 E9
Banbury England, United Kingdom 51 G10
Bandaaceh Indonesia 94 A6
Bandar-e 'Abbas Iran 89 I5
Bandar-e Bushehr Iran 89 H5
Bandar-e Lengeh Iran 89 I5
Bandar Seri Begawan *country capital* Brunei 85 F8, 94 D6
Banda Sea *sea* Indonesia 95 H8
Bandundu Democratic Republic of Congo 78 D7
Bandung Indonesia 85 F9, 94 D9
Banff Alberta, Canada 24 C7
Banfora Burkina 77 F6
Bangalore India 84 D7, 93 D9
Bangassou Central African Republic 79 E5
Bangka *island* Indonesia 94 D7
Bangkok *country capital* Thailand 85 F7, 94 C4
Bangladesh *country* S Asia 84 E6, 93 G6
Bangor Maine, USA 33 J4
Bangor Northern Ireland, United Kingdom 51 D7
Bangor Wales, United Kingdom 51 E9
Bangui *country capital* Central African Republic 71 E7, 78 D5
Bangweulu, Lake Zambia 81 F3
Bani *river* Ivory Coast/Mali 77 F6
Banja Luka Bosnia & Herzegovina 68 D3
Banjarmasin Indonesia 95 F8
Banjul *country capital* Gambia 70 A5, 76 C5
Banks Island *island* Northwest Territories, Canada 22 E4, 24 B3
Banks Peninsula *peninsula* New Zealand 105 E10
Bannu Pakistan 91 F9
Banska Bystrica Slovakia 67 F9
Bantry Bay *bay* Republic of Ireland 51 A11
Baoding China 97 H4
Baoji China 97 G6
Baoro Central African Republic 78 D5
Baotou China 97 G4
Ba'qubah Iraq 89 F3
Baraki Barak Afghanistan 91 F9
Baranavichy Belarus 65 C7
Barbados *country* SE West Indies 23 I12, 37 K7
Barbuda *island* Antigua & Barbuda 37 J5
Barcelona Spain 46 C7, 57 I3
Barcelona Venezuela 40 E1
Bardejov Slovakia 67 G8
Bareilly India 92 D4
Barents Sea *sea* Arctic Ocean 20 D4, 44 I2
Bari Italy 46 E8, 63 H7
Barinas Venezuela 40 D2
Baris Egypt 74 C5
Barisal Bangladesh 93 G6
Barito *river* Indonesia 95 F8
Barkly Tableland *plateau* Northern Territory/Queensland, Australia 100 B6, 103 F2
Barlad Romania 69 H2
Barlavento, Ilhas de *island group* Cape Verde 76 A4
Bar-le-Duc France 55 H3
Barlee, Lake *seasonal lake* Western Australia, Australia 102 C6
Barletta Italy 63 H7
Barlinek Poland 66 C4
Barnaul Russian Federation 84 D4, 87 E6
Barnstaple England, United Kingdom 51 E11
Barquisimeto Venezuela 39 C2, 40 D1
Barra *island* Scotland, United Kingdom 50 C5
Barranquilla Colombia 38 B1, 40 C1
Barreiro Portugal 56 A6
Barrow *river* Republic of Ireland 51 C9
Barrow Alaska, USA 26 H1
Barry Wales, United Kingdom 51 F11
Bartoszyce Poland 66 G3
Baruun-Urt Mongolia 97 H3
Barysaw Belarus 65 D6
Basel Switzerland 60 B4
Basento *river* Italy 63 H8
Basilan *island* Philippines 95 G6
Basildon England, United Kingdom 51 H11
Basingstoke England, United Kingdom 51 G11
Basra Iraq 89 G4
Bassein Myanmar 94 A3
Basse Terre *island* Antigua & Barbuda 37 J6
Basse Terre Antigua & Barbuda 37 J6
Basseterre St Kitts & Nevis 37 J5
Bassikounou Mauritania 77 E5
Bass Strait *strait* Tasmania/Victoria, Australia 103 H8
Bassum Germany 58 D4
Bastia Corsica, France 55 K8
Bastogne Belgium 53 G11
Bata Equatorial Guinea 78 B6
Batangas Philippines 95 G4
Batan Islands *island group* Philippines 95 G2
Bath England, United Kingdom 51 F11
Bathurst New South Wales, Australia 103 I7
Bathurst Island *island* Northern Territory, Australia 103 E1
Batman Turkey 89 E2
Batna Algeria 73 G3
Baton Rouge *state capital* Louisiana, USA 23 E10, 31 F6
Battambang Cambodia 94 C4
Batticaloa Sri Lanka 93 E11
Battipaglia Italy 63 G8
Batumi Georgia 89 F1
Bauchi Nigeria 77 J6
Bavaria *cultural region* Germany 59 E11
Bavarian Alps *mountain range* Austria/Germany 60 B6, 61 F4
Bayamo Cuba 36 D4
Bayamón Puerto Rico 37 H5
Bayanhongor Mongolia 97 F3
Bay City Michigan, USA 32 D5
Baydhabo Sudan 75 G11
Bayonne France 54 D8
Bayramaly Turkmenistan 91 D8
Bayreuth Germany 59 F9
Baza Spain 57 F7
Beachy Head *headland* England, United Kingdom 51 H12
Bear *river* C USA 26 G5
Beaufort Sea *sea* Arctic Ocean 20 B2, 24 C2
Beaufort West South Africa 80 D8
Beaumont New Zealand 105 C12
Beaumont Texas, USA 31 F6
Beauvais France 55 F2
Beawar India 92 C5
Béchar Algeria 72 E4
Beckley West Virginia, USA 33 E8
Beckum Germany 59 C6
Bedford Indiana, USA 32 C7
Be'ér Sheva Israel 88 D4
Beihai China 97 H9
Beijing *country capital* China 85 G5, 97 I4
Beipiao China 97 I3
Beira Mozambique 71 G10, 81 G5
Beirut *country capital* Lebanon 84 A6, 88 D3
Beja Portugal 56 B7
Bejaïa Algeria 73 G3
Bekescsaba Hungary 67 G11
Bela Pakistan 91 E11
Belarus *country* E Europe 47 F5, 65 D7
Belchatow Poland 67 F6
Belcher Islands *island group* Québec, Canada 23 F6, 25 G6
Beledweyne Sudan 75 G10
Belém Brazil 38 G4, 41 H3
Belfast Northern Ireland, United Kingdom 46 B4, 51 D8
Belfort France 55 I4
Belgaum India 93 C8
Belgium *country* NW Europe 46 D5, 53 D9
Belgorod Russian Federation 86 A4
Belgrade *country capital* Serbia & Montenegro 47 F7, 69 E3
Belitung *island* Indonesia 94 D8
Belize *country* Central America 23 E12, 35 H6
Belize City Belize 35 H6

BELLARY–CAKOVEC . 111

Bellary India 93 C9
Belle Île *island* France 54 C4
Bellevue Washington, USA 26 C2
Bellingham Washington, USA 26 C1
Bellingshausen Plain *undersea feature* SE Pacific Ocean 107 I9
Bellingshausen Sea *sea* N Atlantic Ocean 21 A3
Bellinzona Switzerland 60 D6
Belluno Italy 62 E2
Belmopan *country capital* Belize 23 E12, 35 H6
Belogorsk Russian Federation 87 I6
Belo Horizonte Brazil 39 H7, 41 I7
Belukha, Gora *mountain* Russian Federation 87 E7
Bemidji Minnesota, USA 29 H2
Benavente Spain 56 D3
Bend Oregon, USA 26 C4
Bendigo Victoria, Australia 103 H8
Benesov Czech Republic 67 B7
Benevento Italy 63 F8
Bengal, Bay of *bay* N Indian Ocean 83 F2, 84 E7, 93 G8, 96 C9
Bengbu China 97 I6
Benghazi Libya 70 E2, 73 J4
Bengkulu Indonesia 94 C8
Benguela Angola 71 E9, 80 A3
Beni *river* Bolivia 39 C6, 40 D6
Benidorm Spain 57 H6
Benin *country* W Africa 71 C6, 77 G7
Benin, Bight of *bay* E Atlantic Ocean 76 H8
Benin City Nigeria 71 D6, 77 H8
Beni Suef Egypt 74 C4
Ben Macdhui *mountain* Scotland, United Kingdom 50 E5
Ben Nevis *mountain* Scotland, United Kingdom 50 E5
Benoni South Africa 81 E7
Bensheim Germany 59 C9
Bentiu Sudan 75 C9
Benue *river* Cameroon/Nigeria 71 D6, 77 J7
Benxi China 97 J4
Beppu Japan 98 D8
Berat Albania 68 E6
Berbera Somalia 75 G9
Berbérati Central African Republic 78 D5
Berchtesgaden *mountain* Germany 59 G12
Berdyansk Ukraine 65 H11
Berdychiv Ukraine 65 D9
Bereeda Somalia 75 I8
Berezina *river* Belarus 65 D6
Berezniki Russian Federation 86 C4
Bergamo Italy 62 C3
Bergen Norway 46 D3, 49 A8
Bergen op Zoom Netherlands 53 D7
Bergerac France 54 E6
Bergisch Gladbach Germany 59 B7
Bering Sea *sea* N Pacific Ocean 85 F3
Bering Strait *strait* Bering Sea/Chukchi Sea 22 C3, 26 G1
Berkakit Russian Federation 87 I5
Berkeley California, USA 27 B8
Berkner Island *island* Antarctica 21 B2
Berlin *country capital* Germany 46 E5, 58 H5
Berlin New Hampshire, USA 33 J4
Bermuda *island* NW Atlantic Ocean 45 C5
Bermuda *UK dependent territory* NW Atlantic Ocean 23 H10
Bern *country capital* Switzerland 46 D6, 60 B5
Bernese Alps *mountain range* Switzerland 60 B6
Bernina, Piz *mountain* Italy/Switzerland 60 D6
Beroun Czech Republic 67 B7
Bertoua Cameroon 78 C5
Berwick-upon-Tweed England, United Kingdom 51 F6
Besançon France 55 H4
Betafo Madagascar 81 J5
Betanzos Spain 56 B2
Bethlehem South Africa 81 E7
Béthune France 55 F1
Béticos, Sistemas *mountain range* Spain 56 D8
Beveren Belgium 53 D8
Beyneu Kazakhstan 91 B5
Béziers France 55 G8
Bhadravati India 93 C9
Bhagalpur India 93 F5
Bhamo Myanmar 94 B2
Bharatpur India 92 D5
Bharuch India 93 B6
Bhatinda India 92 C4
Bhatpara India 93 G6
Bhavnagar India 93 B6
Bhilai India 93 E7
Bhilwara India 93 C5
Bhima *river* India 93 C7
Bhiwandi India 93 B7
Bhopal India 93 D6
Bhubaneshwar India 93 F7
Bhusawal India 93 C7
Bhutan *country* S Asia 84 E6, 92 G4
Biak *island* Indonesia 95 J7
Biala Podlaska Poland 66 I5
Bialystok Poland 66 H4
Biarritz France 54 D8
Biberach Germany 59 D11
Bida Nigeria 77 H7
Biddeford Maine, USA 33 J5
Biel Switzerland 60 B4
Bielefeld Germany 59 C6
Biella Italy 62 B3
Bielsko-Biala Poland 67 F7
Bielsk Podlaski Poland 66 I4
Bien Hoa Vietnam 94 D5
Bié Plateau *plateau* Angola 71 E9, 80 B3
Bighorn *river* Montana/Wyoming, USA 28 D4
Bighorn Basin *physical region* Wyoming, USA 28 C4
Bighorn Mountains *mountain range* Wyoming, USA 28 D4
Big Spring Texas, USA 30 C5
Big Springs Nebraska, USA 29 F6
Bihac Bosnia & Herzegovina 68 C3
Bijapur India 93 C8
Bikaner India 92 B4
Bikin Russian Federation 87 J6
Bikini Atoll *island* Marshall Islands 100 E3
Bilaspur India 93 E6
Bila Tserkva Ukraine 65 E9
Bilbao Spain 46 B6, 57 F2
Bilhorod-Dnistrovskyy Ukraine 65 E11
Billings Montana, USA 28 D3
Billund Denmark 49 B12
Biloxi Mississippi, USA 31 G6
Biltine Chad 78 E3
Bindura Zimbabwe 81 F4
Binghamton New York, USA 33 H5
Binzhou China 97 I5
Bioko *island* Equatorial Guinea 78 B5
Birak Libya 73 H6
Birao Central African Republic 79 E4
Biratnagar Nepal 92 G5
Birch Mountains *mountain range* Alberta, Canada 24 C6
Birdsville Queensland, Australia 103 G5
Birjand Iran 89 I3
Birmingham England, United Kingdom 46 C5, 51 G4
Birmingham Alabama, USA 31 H4
Bir Mogreïn Mauritania 76 D2
Birzai Lithuania 64 C5
Bischofshofen Austria 61 H4
Bishkek *country capital* Kyrgyzstan 84 D5, 91 G6
Biskra Algeria 73 G4
Biskupiec Poland 66 G3
Bismarck *state capital* North Dakota, USA 29 F3
Bismarck Sea *sea* W Pacific Ocean 100 C5
Bissau *country capital* Guinea Bissau 71 A5, 76 C6
Bistrita Romania 69 G1
Bitlis Turkey 89 F2
Bitola Macedonia 69 F5
Bitonto Italy 63 H8
Bitterfontein South Africa 80 C8
Bitterroot Range *mountain range* Idaho/Montana, USA 26 E2, 28 A2
Biwa-ko *lake* Japan 99 F7
Biysk Russian Federation 87 E6
Bizerte Tunisia 73 H3
Bjørnøya *island* NW Europe 20 D4, 44 H2
Blackall Queensland, Australia 103 I5
Blackburn England, United Kingdom 51 F8
Black Forest *forest* Germany 59 C12
Blackpool England, United Kingdom 51 F8
Black River *river* China/Vietnam 94 C2
Black Sea *sea* Asia/Europe 47 H7, 65 F13, 69 J4, 84 A5
Black Sea Lowland *physical region* Ukraine 65 F11
Black Volta *river* W Africa 77 F7
Blackwater *river* Republic of Ireland 51 B10
Blagoevgrad Bulgaria 69 F5
Blagoveshchensk Russian Federation 87 I6
Blanca, Bahía *bay* Argentina 39 E10, 43 F8
Blanca, Costa *coastal region* Spain 57 H7
Blanche, Lake *seasonal lake* South Australia, Australia 103 G6
Blanc, Mont *mountain* France/Italy 46 C6, 55 I5, 62 A3
Blantyre Malawi 71 G10, 81 G4
Blenheim New Zealand 105 F8
Blida Algeria 73 F3
Bloemfontein *judicial capital* South Africa 71 F12, 80 E7
Blois France 55 F4
Blönduós Iceland 48 B2
Bloomington Illinois, USA 32 B6
Bloomington Indiana, USA 32 C7
Bloomington Minnesota, USA 29 I4
Bludenz Switzerland 60 D5
Bluefield West Virginia, USA 33 E8
Blue Mountains *mountain range* Oregon/Washington, USA 26 D3
Blue Nile *river* Ethiopia/Sudan 71 G5, 75 D8
Blue Ridge *mountain range* E USA 31 I3
Bo Sierra Leone 76 D7
Boa Vista Brazil 41 F3
Boa Vista *island* Cape Verde 76 A4
Bobo-Dioulasso Burkina 77 F6
Bocholt Germany 59 B6
Bochum Germany 59 B6
Boden Sweden 48 F5
Bodmin Moor *moorland* England, United Kingdom 51 E12
Bodø Norway 48 D4
Bodrum Turkey 88 B2
Bogen Norway 48 E3
Bogor Java, Indonesia 94 D8
Bogotá *country capital* Colombia 38 B3, 40 C2
Bogra Bangladesh 93 G5
Bo Hai *bay* China 97 I4
Bohang South Korea 98 C6
Bohemia *cultural region* Czech Republic 67 B7
Bohemian Forest *forest* C Europe 59 G10, 67 B8
Bohol *island* Philippines 95 H5
Boise *state capital* Idaho, USA 26 E4
Boise City Oklahoma, USA 30 C3
Bojnurd Iran 89 I2
Bokaro India 93 F6
Boknafjorden *fjord* Norway 49 A9
Bole China 96 C3
Boleslawiec Poland 67 C6
Bolgatanga Ghana 77 G6
Bolhrad Ukraine 65 D11
Bolivia *country* W South America 39 D6, 40 D6
Bollnäs Sweden 49 E8
Bologna Italy 46 D7, 62 D4
Bolovens Plateau *plateau* Laos 94 D4
Bolsena, Lake *lake* Italy 63 D6
Bolshevik, Ostrov *island* Russian Federation 87 G2
Bolzano Italy 62 D2
Boma Democratic Republic of Congo 78 C8
Bombay *see* Mumbai
Bonaire *island* Netherlands Antilles 37 H8
Bonaparte, Archipelago *island group* Western Australia, Australia 102 D2
Bondo Democratic Republic of Congo 79 F5
Bongo, Massif des *plateau* Central African Republic 79 E4
Bongor Chad 78 D4
Bonifacio Corsica, France 55 K9
Bonifacio, Strait of *strait* C Mediterranean Sea 55 K9, 63 B7
Bonn Germany 59 B7
Boosaaso Somalia 75 I8
Boothia, Gulf of *gulf* Nunavut, Canada 25 F3, 47 F3, 49 F7
Boothia Peninsula *peninsula* Nunavut, Canada 25 E3
Bor Russian Federation 87 F5
Bor Sudan 75 D10
Borås Sweden 49 C11
Bordeaux France 54 D6
Bordj-Bou-Arreridj Algeria 73 F3
Børgefjellet *mountain range* Norway 49 D5
Borger Texas, USA 30 C4
Borgholm Sweden 49 E11
Borlänge Sweden 49 D9
Borneo *island* Brunei/Indonesia/Malaysia 83 H3, 85 F9, 94 E7
Bornholm *island* Denmark 49 D12
Borujerd Iran 89 G3
Bose China 97 G8
Bosna *river* Bosnia & Herzegovina 68 D3
Bosnia & Herzegovina *country* SE Europe 47 E7, 68 D3
Bossangoa Central African Republic 78 D5
Boston Massachusetts, USA 23 H8, 33 J5
Botosani Romania 69 H1
Botshabelo South Africa 80 E7
Botswana *country* S Africa 71 F11, 80 D6
Bouaké Ivory Coast 77 F7
Bouar Central African Republic 78 D5
Bougainville Island *island* Papua New Guinea 100 D5
Boujdour Western Sahara 72 B6
Boulder Western Australia, Australia 102 C6
Boulder Colorado, USA 28 E6
Boulia Queensland, Australia 103 G4
Boulogne-sur-Mer France 55 F1
Bountiful Utah, USA 27 G6
Bounty Islands *island group* New Zealand 101 F9
Bourg-en-Bresse France 55 H5
Bourges France 55 F4
Bourke New South Wales, Australia 103 I6
Bournemouth England, United Kingdom 51 G12
Bouvet Island *island* SE Atlantic Ocean 45 G11
Bowling Green *state capital* Kentucky, USA 32 C8
Bozeman Montana, USA 28 C3
Brac *island* Croatia 68 C4
Bradenton Florida, USA 31 I7
Bradford England, United Kingdom 51 G8
Braga Portugal 56 B3
Bragança Portugal 56 C3
Brahmapur India 93 F7
Brahmaputra *river* S Asia 84 E6, 92 H5, 96 C7
Braila Romania 69 H3
Braine-l'Alleud Belgium 53 D9
Brainerd Minnesota, USA 29 I3
Branco *river* Brazil 38 D3, 41 F3
Brandenburg Germany 58 G5
Brandon Manitoba, Canada 24 E8
Braniewo Poland 66 F2
Brasília *country capital* Brazil 39 G6, 41 H6
Brasov Romania 69 G2
Bratislava *country capital* Slovakia 47 E6, 67 D9
Bratsk Russian Federation 87 G6
Braunschweig Germany 59 E5
Brava, Costa *coastal region* Spain 57 J3
Bravo del Norte, Río *river* Mexico/USA 34 C2 *see also* Grande, Rio
Brawley California, USA 27 E12
Brazil *country* South America 38 D5, 40 E4
Brazil Basin *undersea feature* W Atlantic Ocean 45 E 8
Brazilian Highlands *physical region* Brazil 39 G6, 41 H6
Brazos *river* Texas, USA 30 D4
Brazzaville *country capital* Congo 71 E8, 78 D7
Brcko Bosnia & Herzegovina 68 D3
Breclav Czech Republic 67 D9
Brecon Beacons *mountain range* Wales, United Kingdom 51 E10
Breda Netherlands 53 E7
Bregenz Switzerland 60 D4
Breidhafjördhur *bay* Iceland 48 A2
Bremen Germany 46 D5, 58 D4
Bremerhaven Germany 58 D3
Bremervörde Germany 58 D3
Brescia Italy 62 C3
Bressanone Italy 62 D2
Brest Belarus 65 D8
Brest France 54 B3
Bria Central African Republic 79 E5
Bridgeport Connecticut, USA 33 I6
Bridgetown *country capital* Barbados 37 K7
Brig Switzerland 60 C6
Brigham City Utah, USA 27 G6
Brighton England, United Kingdom 51 H12
Brilon Germany 59 C7
Brindisi Italy 63 I8
Brisbane *state capital* Queensland, Australia 100 D7, 103 J5
Bristol England, United Kingdom 51 F11
Bristol Bay *bay* Alaska, USA 22 B3, 26 G2
Bristol Channel *channel* England/Wales, United Kingdom 51 E11
British Colombia *province* Canada 24 B6
British Indian Ocean Territory *UK dependent territory* United Kingdom 84 D9
British Isles *island group* NW Europe 44 F3
British Virgin Islands *UK dependent territory* E West Indies 37 I5
Brittany *cultural region* France 54 C3
Brive-la-Gaillarde France 55 F6
Brno Czech Republic 67 D8
Broken Arrow Oklahoma, USA 30 E4
Broken Hill New South Wales, Australia 103 H6
Broken Ridge *undersea feature* C Indian Ocean 83 F6
Brooks Range *mountain range* Alaska, USA 26 H1
Broome Western Australia, Australia 102 C3
Browning Montana, USA 28 B2
Bruck an der Mur Austria 61 I4
Bruges Belgium 53 B8
Brunei *country* SE Asia 85 F8, 95 F6
Brunsbüttel Germany 58 D3
Brunswick Georgia, USA 31 J5
Brunswick Maine, USA 33 J4
Brussels *country capital* Belgium 46 D5, 53 D9
Bryansk Russian Federation 47 G5, 86 B4
Brzeg Poland 67 E6
Bucaramanga Colombia 38 B2, 40 C2
Buchanan Liberia 76 D8
Bucharest *country capital* Romania 47 G7, 69 H3
Buckland Tableland *plateau* Queensland, Australia 103 I5
Budapest *country capital* Hungary 47 G5, 67 F10
Búdhardalur Iceland 48 B2
Buea Cameroon 78 B5
Buenaventura Colombia 40 C2
Buenos Aires *country capital* Argentina 39 E10, 43 F6
Buffalo New York, USA 33 F5
Bug *river* N Europe 66 H5
Bujumbura *country capital* Burundi 71 G8, 79 G7
Bukan Iran 89 F3
Bukavu Democratic Republic of Congo 79 G7
Bukhoro Uzbekistan 91 D7
Bulawayo Zimbabwe 71 F11, 81 E5
Bulgan Mongolia 97 F2
Bulgaria *country* SE Europe 47 F7, 69 G5
Bumba Democratic Republic of Congo 79 E6
Bunbury Western Australia, Australia 102 B7
Bundaberg Queensland, Australia 103 J5
Bungo-suido *strait* Japan 98 E8
Buraydah Saudi Arabia 89 F5
Burco Somalia 75 G9
Burgas Bulgaria 47 G7, 69 H4
Burgos Spain 57 E3
Burgundy *cultural region* France 55 G4
Burkina *country* W Africa 71 C5, 77 G6
Burlington Colorado, USA 29 F7
Burlington Iowa, USA 29 J6
Burlington Vermont, USA 33 I4
Burma *see* Myanmar
Burnie Tasmania, Australia 103 H9
Burns Oregon, USA 26 D4
Bursa Turkey 84 A5, 88 C1
Buru *island* Indonesia 95 H8
Burundi *country* C Africa 71 G8, 79 G7
Burylbaytal Kazakhstan 91 G5
Busan South Korea 98 C7
Busselton Western Australia, Australia 102 B7
Buta Democratic Republic of Congo 79 F6
Buton *island* Indonesia 95 G8
Butte Montana, USA 28 B3
Butuan Philippines 95 H5
Buur Gaabo Somalia 75 F12
Buzau Romania 69 H3
Bydgoszcz Poland 66 E4
Bytom Poland 67 F7
Bytow Poland 66 E3

C

Caaguazú Paraguay 42 G3
Cabanatuan Philippines 95 G4
Cabinda *province* Angola 71 D8, 80 A1
Cacak Serbia & Montenegro 69 E4
Cáceres Spain 56 C5
Caconda Angola 80 B4
Cader Idris *mountain* Wales, United Kingdom 51 E10
Cadiz Philippines 95 G5
Cádiz Spain 56 C8
Cádiz, Gulf of *gulf* Portugal/Spain 56 B8
Caen France 54 E2
Caernarfon Wales, United Kingdom 51 E9
Cagayan de Oro Philippines 95 H5
Cagliari Italy 46 D8, 63 B9
Caguas US 37 H5
Cahora Bassa, Lake Mozambique 81 F4
Cahors France 55 F7
Cahul Moldova 65 D12
Cairns Queensland, Australia 100 C6, 103 I3
Cairo *country capital* Egypt 70 G3, 74 C3
Cajamarca Peru 40 C5
Cakovec Croatia 68 C2

112 . CALABAR–COLORADO

Calabar Nigeria 77 I8
Calabria *cultural region* Italy 63 H10
Calafat Romania 69 F4
Calais France 55 F1
Calama Chile 42 C2
Calamian Group *island group* Philippines 95 F4
Calarasi Romania 69 H3
Calatayud Spain 57 G4
Calbayog Philippines 95 H4
Calcutta *see* Kolkata
Caldas de Rainha Portugal 56 A5
Caldwell Idaho, USA 26 E4
Calgary Alberta, Canada 23 D6, 24 C7
Cali Colombia 38 B3, 40 C3
Calicut India 93 C10
California *state* USA 27 B9
California, Gulf of *gulf* Mexico 23 C10, 34 A2
Callao Peru 39 B6, 40 C5
Caloundra Queensland, Australia 103 J5
Caltanissetta Italy 63 F11
Camagüey Cuba 36 D4
Camargue *physical region* France 55 G7
Cambodia *country* SE Asia 85 F7, 94 C4
Cambrian, Mountains *mountain range* Wales, United Kingdom 51 E10
Cambridge New Zealand 104 G4
Cambridge England, United Kingdom 51 H10
Cameroon *country* W Africa 71 D7, 78 C5
Camooweal Queensland, Australia 103 G3
Campbell Island *island* New Zealand 101 F9
Campeche Mexico 35 G5
Campeche, Bay of *bay* S Gulf of Mexico 35 F5
Cam Pha Vietnam 94 D2
Campina Grande Brazil 41 F7
Campinas Brazil 39 G8, 41 H7
Campobasso Italy 63 G7
Campo Grande Brazil 39 F7, 41 G7
Campos Brazil 41 I7
Cam Ranh Vietnam 94 D4
Canada *country* N North America 23 D6, 24 C6
Canadian *river* SW USA 30 C3
Canadian Shield *physical region* C Canada 24 E6
Canary Islands *island group* NW Africa 45 F6, 70 A3, 72 B5
Canaveral, Cape *headland* Florida, USA 31 J6
Canberra *country capital* Australian Capital Territory, Australia 100 D8, 103 I7
Cancún Mexico 35 H5
Cangzhou China 97 I4
Canicatti Italy 63 F11
Cannanore India 93 C10
Cannes France 55 I7
Cantábrica, Cordillera *mountain range* Spain 56 C2
Canterbury England, United Kingdom 51 I11
Canterbury Bight *bay* New Zealand 105 D10
Canterbury Plains *physical region* New Zealand 105 D10
Can Tho Vietnam 94 D5
Cape Basin *undersea feature* SE Atlantic Ocean 45 G10
Cape Breton Island *island* Nova Scotia, Canada 23 I8, 25 J7
Cape Coast Ghana 77 G8
Cape Coral Florida, USA 31 J7
Cape Town *legislative capital* South Africa 71 E13, 80 C9
Cape Verde *country* W Africa 76 A4
Cape Verde Basin *undersea feature* E Atlantic Ocean 45 E6
Cape Verde Islands *island group* W Africa 45 E6
Cape York Peninsula *peninsula* Queensland, Australia 103 H1
Cap-Haïten Dominican Republic 37 F4
Capri *island* Italy 63 F8
Caprivi Strip *cultural region* Namibia 80 D5
Caquetá *river* Brazil/Colombia 38 C3, 40 C3 *see also* Japurá
Caracas *country capital* Venezuela 38 C1, 40 D1
Caransebes Romania 69 F3
Caratasca, Laguna de *lagoon* Honduras 35 I7
Carbonara, Capo *headland* Italy 63 B10
Carbondale Illinois, USA 32 B8
Carbonia Italy 63 B10
Carcassonne France 55 F8
Cardiff Wales, United Kingdom 46 C5, 51 F11
Cardigan Bay *bay* SE Irish Sea 51 E10
Carey, Lake *seasonal lake* Western Australia, Australia 102 D6
Caribbean Sea *sea* W Atlantic Ocean 35 J7, 36 C6, 45 C7
Caribou Mountains *mountain range* Alberta, Canada 24 C5
Carlisle England, United Kingdom 51 F7
Carlsberg Ridge *undersea feature* N Indian Ocean 82 D2
Carmarthen Wales, United Kingdom 51 E11
Carmen Mexico 35 G6
Carmona Spain 56 D7
Carnarvon Western Australia, Australia 100 A7, 102 B5
Carnarvon South Africa 80 D8
Carnegie, Lake *seasonal lake* Western Australia, Australia 102 D5
Carney Island *island* Antarctica 21 A4
Car Nicobar *island* Nicobar Islands, India 93 I10
Carnot Central African Republic 78 D5
Caroline Islands *island group* Micronesia 100 C4
Carpathian Mountains *mountain range* C Europe 47 F6, 65 B10, 67 G8, 69 G1
Carpentaria, Gulf of *gulf* Northern Territory, Australia 100 B6, 103 G2
Carpi Italy 62 D4
Carrara Italy 62 C4
Carson City *state capital* Nevada, USA 27 C7
Cartagena Colombia 38 B2, 40 C1
Cartagena Spain 57 G7
Caruarú Brazil 41 J5
Casablanca Morocco 70 B2, 72 D4
Casa Grande Arizona, USA 27 G12
Cascade Point *headland* New Zealand 105 B10
Cascade Range *mountain range* Oregon/Washington, USA 26 B5
Cascavel Brazil 41 G8
Cascina Italy 62 C5
Caserta Italy 63 F8
Casper Wyoming, USA 28 D5
Caspian Depression *physical region* Kazakhstan/Russian Federation 90 A4
Caspian Sea *inland sea* Asia/Europe 47 J6, 84 B5, 86 A7, 89 G1, 91 A5
Cassinga Angola 80 B4
Cassino Italy 63 F7
Castelló de la Plana Spain 57 H5
Castelo Branco Portugal 56 B5
Castelvetrano Italy 63 E11
Castilla-Nueva *cultural region* Spain 56 D5
Castilla-Vieja *physical region* Spain 56 E4
Castres France 55 F7
Castries *country capital* St Lucia 37 K7
Castrovillari Italy 63 H9
Catalonia *cultural region* Spain 57 H3
Catamarca Argentina 42 D4
Catanduanes *island* Philippines 95 H4
Catania Italy 63 G11
Catanzaro Italy 63 H10
Cat Island *island* Bahamas 36 E2
Catskill Mountains *mountain range* New York, USA 33 H5
Cauca *river* Colombia 40 C2
Caucasus *mountain range* Georgia/Russian Federation 47 I7, 89 F1
Causeni Moldova 65 D11
Cavan Republic of Ireland 51 C8
Caxito Angola 80 A2
Cayenne French Guiana 38 F2, 41 G2
Cayes Haiti 37 E5
Cayman Islands *island group* United Kingdom 36 B4
Cayman Islands *UK dependent territory* W West Indies 23 F11
Cazombo Angola 80 D3
Cebu *island* Philippines 95 G5
Cebu Philippines 85 G8, 95 H5
Cecina Italy 62 C5
Cedar *river* Iowa/Minnesota, USA 29 J5
Cedar City Utah, USA 27 G8
Cedar Falls Iowa, USA 29 J5
Cedar Rapids Iowa, USA 29 J5
Cedros, Isla *island* Mexico 34 A3
Ceduna South Australia, Australia 103 F6
Ceerigaabo Somalia 75 H9
Cefalù Italy 63 F11
Celebes Sea *sea* Indonesia/Philippines 85 G8, 94 G6
Celje Slovenia 61 I6
Celle Germany 58 E5
Celtic Sea *sea* NE Atlantic Ocean 46 B5, 51 C11
Central African Republic *country* C Africa 71 E6, 78 D5
Central Makran Range *mountain range* Pakistan 91 D11
Central Pacific Basin *undersea feature* C Pacific Ocean 107 E4
Central Siberian Plateau *plateau* Russian Federation 85 F3, 87 F4
Central, Sistema *mountain range* Spain 56 D4
Central Valley *valley* Chile 43 C7
Central Valley *valley* California, USA 27 B7
Ceram Sea *sea* Indonesia 95 H7
Cerignola Italy 63 G7
Cervino, Monte *mountain* Italy/Switzerland 62 A2
Cesena Italy 62 E4
Cesis Latvia 64 C4
Ceske Budejovice Czech Republic 67 B8
Cetraro Italy 63 G9
Ceuta *Spanish dependent territory* N Africa 56 D9, 70 C2, 72 D3
Cévennes *mountain range* France 55 G7
Ceylon Plain *undersea feature* N Indian Ocean 83 F3
Chabahar Iran 89 J5
Chad *country* C Africa 70 E5, 78 D3
Chad, Lake *lake* C Africa 71 E5, 77 K6, 78 C3
Chagai Hills *hill range* Afghanistan/Pakistan 91 D10
Chaghcharan Afghanistan 91 E9
Chagos Archipelago *island group* N Indian Ocean 82 E3
Chagos-Laccadive Plateau *undersea feature* N Indian Ocean 82 E4
Chalkida Greece 69 G7
Chalkidikí *peninsula* Greece 69 G6
Challans France 54 D4
Châlons-en-Champagne France 55 G3
Chalon-sur-Saône France 55 H5
Chaman Pakistan 91 E10
Chambal *river* India 92 C5
Chambéry France 55 H6
Chamonix France 55 I5
Champagne *cultural region* France 55 G3
Chandigarh India 92 C4
Chandler Arizona, USA 27 G11
Chandrapur India 93 D7
Changchun China 85 G5, 97 J3
Changde China 97 H7
Changsha China 85 F6, 97 H7
Changzhi China 97 H5
Changzhou China 97 J6
Chania Greece 69 G9
Channel Islands *island group* United Kingdom 46 C5, 51 F13
Channel Islands *island group* California, USA 27 C11
Chanthaburi Thailand 94 C4
Chaozhou China 97 I8
Chapaev Kazakhstan 90 B4
Chapala, Lago de *lake* Mexico 34 D5
Charente *river* France 54 D6
Chari *river* Central African Republic/Chad 78 D4
Charjew Turkmenistan 91 D7
Charleroi Belgium 53 D10
Charleston *state capital* West Virginia, USA 33 E8
Charleston South Carolina, USA 31 J4
Charleville Queensland, Australia 103 I5
Charleville-Mézières France 55 H2
Charlotte North Carolina, USA 23 G9, 31 J3
Charlottesville Virginia, USA 33 G8
Charlottetown Prince Edward Island, Canada 25 J7
Charters Towers Queensland, Australia 103 I3
Chartres France 55 F3
Chasong North Korea 98 B3
Châteauroux France 55 F5
Châtellerault France 55 E5
Chatham Islands *island group* New Zealand 101 G9
Chatham Rise *undersea feature* SW Pacific Ocean 107 E7
Chattahoochee *river* SE USA 31 H4
Chattanooga Tennessee, USA 31 H4
Chaumont France 55 H3
Chaves Portugal 56 B3
Cheb Czech Republic 67 A7
Cheboksary Russian Federation 86 C4
Chech'on South Korea 98 C5
Chelm Poland 67 I6
Chelmno Poland 66 E3
Chelyabinsk Russian Federation 84 C4, 86 C5
Chemnitz Germany 59 G8
Chenab *river* India/Pakistan 91 G9
Chengde China 97 I4
Chengdu China 85 F6, 97 F6
Chennai India 84 D7, 93 D9
Chenzhou China 97 H7
Cher *river* France 55 F4
Cherbourg France 54 D2
Cherepovets Russian Federation 86 B3
Cherkasy Ukraine 65 F10
Cherkessk Russian Federation 86 A5
Chernihiv Ukraine 65 E8
Chernivtsi Ukraine 65 C10
Chernobyl Ukraine 65 E8
Cherskiy Russian Federation 87 I2
Cherskogo, Khrebet *mountain range* Russian Federation 87 H3
Chervonohrad Ukraine 65 B9
Chesapeake Virginia, USA 33 H9
Chesapeake Bay *inlet* NE USA 33 H8
Chester England, United Kingdom 51 F9
Chetumal Mexico 35 H6
Cheyenne *river* South Dakota/Wyoming, USA 29 F4
Cheyenne *state capital* Wyoming, USA 28 E6
Cheyenne Wells Colorado, USA 29 F7
Chiai Taiwan 97 J8
Chiang Mai Thailand 94 B3
Chiang Rai Thailand 94 B3
Chiavari Italy 62 C4
Chiba Japan 99 H6
Chicago Illinois, USA 23 F8, 32 C5
Chiclana de la Frontera Spain 56 C8
Chiclayo Peru 40 B4
Chico *river* Argentina 43 D11, 43 D10
Chico California, USA 27 B7
Chidley, Cape *headland* Newfoundland & Labrador/Québec, Canada 23 H6, 25 H5
Chiemsee *lake* Germany 59 G12
Chieti Italy 63 F6
Chifeng China 97 I3
Chihuahua Mexico 34 C3
Chile *country* SW South America 39 C12, 43 C8
Chile Basin *undersea feature* E Pacific Ocean 107 J6
Chile Rise *undersea feature* E Pacific Ocean 107 I7
Chillán Chile 43 C7
Chiloé, Isla de *island* Chile 39 C11, 43 B9
Chilpancingo Mexico 34 E6
Chiltern Hills *hill range* England, United Kingdom 51 G11
Chimborazo *mountain* Ecuador 38 A4, 40 B3
Chimbote Peru 40 C5
Chimoio Mozambique 81 G5
China *country* E Asia 85 E5, 96 D6
Chinandega Nicaragua 35 H8
Chindwin *river* Myanmar 94 B2
Chingola Zambia 81 E3
Chinguetti Mauritania 76 D4
Chinhoyi Zimbabwe 81 F4
Chiniot Pakistan 91 G10
Chino Japan 99 G6
Chioggia Italy 62 E3
Chios Greece 69 H7
Chios *island* Greece 69 H7
Chipata Zambia 81 G4
Chiquita, Laguna Mar *lake* Argentina 42 E5
Chirchiq Uzbekistan 91 F7
Chiriqui, Gulf of *gulf* Panama 35 J9
Chisinau *country capital* Moldova 47 G6, 65 D11
Chita Russian Federation 87 H6
Chitose Japan 99 I2
Chittagong Bangladesh 84 E7, 93 H6
Chitungwiza Zimbabwe 81 F5
Chlef Algeria 73 F3
Chojna Poland 66 C4
Chokwe Mozambique 81 F6
Cholet France 54 D4
Choma Zambia 80 E4
Chomutov Czech Republic 67 B7
Ch'onan South Korea 98 B6
Chon Buri Thailand 94 C4
Ch'ongjin North Korea 98 D3
Chongju North Korea 98 B4
Ch'ongju South Korea 98 C6
Chongqing China 85 F6, 97 G7
Chongup South Korea 98 B6
Chonos, Archipiélago de los *island group* Chile 39 C11, 43 B10
Chorzow Poland 67 E7
Ch'osan North Korea 98 B3
Choshi Japan 99 H6
Chos Malal Argentina 43 C7
Choybalsan Mongolia 97 H2
Choyr Mongolia 97 G3
Christchurch New Zealand 101 F8, 105 E9
Christmas Island *island* E Indian Ocean 83 H4
Chubut *river* Argentina 43 D9
Chukchi Sea *sea* Arctic Ocean 20 B1, 85 K2
Chula Vista California, USA 27 D12
Chumphon Thailand 94 B5
Ch'ungju South Korea 98 C6
Chur Switzerland 60 D5
Churchill Manitoba, Canada 25 F6
Churchill *river* Manitoba, Canada 25 E6
Chuuk *island group* Micronesia 100 C3
Chuxiong China 97 F8
Ciechanow Poland 66 G4
Ciego de Ávila Cuba 36 C3
Cienfuegos Cuba 36 C3
Cijara, Embalse de *reservoir* Spain 56 D5
Cilacap Indonesia 94 D9
Cincinnati Ohio, USA 32 D7
Cirebon Indonesia 94 D8
Ciro Marina Italy 63 H9
Citta di Castello Italy 62 E5
Ciudad Bolivar Venezuela 41 E2
Ciudad del Este Paraguay 42 H3
Ciudad Guayana Venezuela 41 E2
Ciudad Juárez Mexico 23 D9, 34 C2
Ciudad Madero Mexico 35 E5
Ciudad Obregón Mexico 34 B3
Ciudad Real Spain 56 E6
Ciudad-Rodrigo Spain 56 C4
Ciudad Victoria Mexico 34 E4
Ciutadella de Menorca Balearic Islands, Spain 57 K5
Civitanova Marche Italy 62 F5
Civitavecchia Italy 63 D7
Clamecy France 55 G4
Clarence New Zealand 105 F8
Clarion Fracture Zone *undersea feature* E Pacific Ocean 107 G4
Clarksville Tennessee, USA 31 H3
Clearwater Florida, USA 31 I6
Clearwater Mountains *mountain range* Idaho, USA 26 E3
Clermont Queensland, Australia 103 I4
Clermont-Ferrand France 55 G5
Cleveland Ohio, USA 23 G8, 33 E6
Clipperton Fracture Zone *undersea feature* C Pacific Ocean 107 G4
Cloncurry Queensland, Australia 103 H4
Clonmel Republic of Ireland 51 C10
Cloudy Bay *bay* New Zealand 105 F8
Clovis New Mexico, USA 30 C4
Cluj-Napoca Romania 47 F6, 69 F2
Clutha *river* New Zealand 105 C12
Clyde *river* Scotland, United Kingdom 51 E6
Clyde, Firth of *inlet* Scotland, United Kingdom 51 E7
Coast Mountains *mountain range* Canada/USA 23 C5, 24 B5
Coast Ranges *mountain range* W USA 23 B7, 27 B7
Coats Land *physical region* Antarctica 21 B2
Coatzacoalcos Mexico 35 F6
Cobán Guatemala 35 G7
Coburg Germany 59 E8
Cochabamba Bolivia 39 D6, 40 E6
Cochin India 93 C10
Coco *river* Honduras/Nicaragua 35 I7
Cocos Islands *island group* E Indian Ocean 83 G4
Cod, Cape *headland* Massachusetts, USA 23 H8, 33 J5
Cody Wyoming, USA 28 C4
Coesfeld Germany 59 B6
Coeur d'Alene Idaho, USA 26 E2
Coffs Harbour New South Wales, Australia 103 J6
Cognac France 54 E6
Coiba, Isla de *island* Panama 35 J9
Coihaique Chile 43 C10
Coimbatore India 93 C10
Coimbra Portugal 56 B5
Colby Kansas, USA 29 F7
Colchester England, United Kingdom 51 I10
Coleraine Northern Ireland, United Kingdom 51 D7
Colima Mexico 34 D6
Coll *island* Scotland, United Kingdom 51 C5
Collingwood New Zealand 105 E7
Colmar France 55 I3
Cologne Germany 46 D5, 59 B7
Colombia *country* NW South America 38 B3, 40 C3
Colombo *country capital* Sri Lanka 84 D8, 93 D11
Colón Panama 35 J8
Colonna, Capo *headland* Italy 63 H10
Colonsay *island* Scotland, United Kingdom 51 D6
Colorado *river* Argentina 43 D7
Colorado *river* Mexico/USA 23 C9, 27 G9, 28 C7, 30 D5
Colorado *state* USA 28 D7

COLORADO PLATEAU–DUNHUANG . 113

Colorado Plateau *plateau* W USA 23 C8, 27 G8
Colorado Springs Colorado, USA 28 E7
Columbia *river* Canada/USA 23 C7, 26 D1
Columbia Missouri, USA 29 J7
Columbia *state capital* South Carolina, USA 23 G9, 31 J4
Columbia Basin *physical region* Washington, USA 26 D2
Columbia Plateau *plateau* Idaho/Oregon, USA 26 E5
Columbus Georgia, USA 31 H5
Columbus Mississippi, USA 31 G4
Columbus Nebraska, USA 29 H6
Columbus *state capital* Ohio, USA 23 F9, 32 E7
Comilla Bangladesh 93 H6
Como Italy 62 B3
Comodoro Rivadavia Argentina 43 D10
Como, Lake *lake* Italy 62 C2
Comoro Islands *island group* Comoros 82 C4
Comoros *country* W Indian Ocean 71 H9, 81 J3
Compiègne France 55 F2
Comrat Moldova 65 D11
Conakry *country capital* Guinea 71 A6, 76 C7
Concepción Chile 43 B7
Concepción Paraguay 42 G2
Conception, Point *headland* California, USA 27 B10
Conchos *river* Mexico 34 C3
Concord California, USA 27 B8
Concord *state capital* New Hampshire, USA 33 I5
Concordia Argentina 43 G5
Congo *country* C Africa 71 E8, 78 D6
Congo *river* Congo/Democratic Republic of Congo 71 E8, 78 D7
Congo Basin *physical region* C Africa 71 E7, 78 E6
Congo, Democratic Republic of *country* C Africa 71 F8, 79 F6
Connaught *cultural region* Republic of Ireland 51 B8
Connecticut *state* USA 33 I5
Constance Germany 59 D12
Constance, Lake *lake* Germany/Switzerland 59 D12, 60 D4
Constanta Romania 47 G7, 69 I3
Constantine Algeria 70 D2, 73 G3
Constitución Chile 43 B7
Coober Pedy South Australia, Australia 103 F6
Cook Islands *NZ dependent territory* C Pacific Ocean 101 H6
Cook, Mount *mountain* New Zealand 105 C10
Cook Strait *strait* New Zealand 105 F7
Cooktown Queensland, Australia 103 I2
Coolgardie Western Australia, Australia 102 C6
Cooma New South Wales, Australia 103 I8
Coonamble New South Wales, Australia 103 I6
Cooper Creek *seasonal river* Queensland/South Australia, 103 G5
Coorow Western Australia, Australia 102 B6
Coos Bay Oregon, USA 26 A4
Copenhagen *country capital* Denmark 46 E4, 49 C12
Copiapó Chile 42 C4
Coppermine Nunavut, Canada 24 D4
Coquimbo Chile 42 C5
Coral Sea *sea* SW Pacific Ocean 100 D6, 103 J2, 106 D5
Corcovado, Gulf of *gulf* Chile 43 C9
Córdoba Argentina 39 D9, 43 E5
Córdoba Spain 46 A7, 56 D7
Corfu *island* Greece 68 E6
Corigliano Calabro Italy 63 H9
Corinth Greece 69 F7
Corinth, Gulf of *gulf* Aegean Sea/Ionian Sea 69 F7
Cork Republic of Ireland 51 B10
Corner Brook Newfoundland & Labrador, Canada 25 J7
Corno Grande *mountain* Italy 63 F6
Coro Venezuela 40 D1
Coromandel New Zealand 104 G3
Coromandel Coast *coastal region* India 93 D10
Coromandel Peninsula *peninsula* New Zealand 104 G3
Coronel Oviedo Paraguay 42 G3
Coronel Pringles Argentina 43 F7
Coropuna, Nevado *mountain* Peru 40 D6
Corpus Christi Texas, USA 30 D7
Corrib, Lough *lake* Republic of Ireland 51 B9
Corrientes Argentina 42 F4
Corrientes, Cabo *headland* Mexico 34 C5
Corse, Cap *headland* Corsica, France 55 K8
Corsica *island* France 46 D7, 55 K9
Cortona Italy 63 D5
Coruche Portugal 56 B6
Corum Turkey 88 D1
Corumba Brazil 41 F7
Corvallis Oregon, USA 26 B4
Cosenza Italy 63 H9
Costa Rica *country* Central America 23 F13, 35 I8
Cotonou Benin 77 F7
Cotopaxi *volcano* Ecuador 40 B3
Cotswold Hills *hill range* England, United Kingdom 51 G11
Cottbus Germany 59 I6
Council Bluffs Iowa, USA 29 H6
Courland Lagoon *lagoon* Lithuania/Russian Federation 65 A6
Coventry England, United Kingdom 51 G10
Covilha Portugal 56 B5
Cowan, Lake *seasonal lake* Western Australia, Australia 102 D6
Cozumel, Isla *island* Mexico 35 H5
Cradock South Africa 80 D8
Craiova Romania 69 G3
Crawley England, United Kingdom 51 H11
Creil France 55 F2
Cremona Italy 62 C3
Cres *island* Croatia 68 B3
Crescent City California, USA 27 A5
Crete *island* Greece 47 F9, 69 G9
Créteil France 55 F3
Crete, Sea of *sea* NE Mediterranean Sea 69 H9
Creuse *river* France 55 E5
Crimean Peninsula *peninsula* Ukraine 47 H6, 65 G12
Croatia *country* SE Europe 47 E7, 68 C2
Cromwell New Zealand 105 C11
Crotone Italy 63 H10
Croydon Queensland, Australia 103 H3
Crozet Basin *undersea feature* S Indian Ocean 82 D6
Crozet Islands *island group* SW Indian Ocean 82 C7
Crozet Plateau *undersea feature* SW Indian Ocean 82 C7
Csorna Hungary 67 D10
Cuamba Mozambique 81 H4
Cuando *river* S Africa 71 E10, 80 C4
Cuango *river* Angola/Democratic Republic of Congo 71 E9, 80 B2
Cuanza *river* Angola 80 B3
Cuautla Mexico 34 E6
Cuba *country* W West Indies 23 F11, 36 C3
Cubango *river* S Africa 71 E10, 80 C5
Cúcuta Colombia 38 B2, 40 C2
Cuddapah India 93 D9
Cuenca Ecuador 40 B4
Cuenca Spain 57 F5
Cuernavaca Mexico 34 E6
Cuiabá Brazil 41 G6
Culiacán Mexico 34 C4
Cumaná Venezuela 40 E1
Cuneo Italy 62 A4
Cunnamulla Queensland, Australia 103 H5
Curaçao *island* Netherlands Antilles 37 G8
Curitiba Brazil 39 G8, 41 H8
Cusco Peru 40 D6
Cuttack India 93 F7
Cuxhaven Germany 58 D3
Cyclades *island group* Greece 69 G8
Cyprus *country* W Asia 84 A6, 88 C3
Cyrenaica *cultural region* Libya 73 I5
Czech Republic *country* C Europe 46 E6, 67 B8
Czestochowa Poland 67 F6
Czluchow Poland 66 E3

D

Dachau Germany 59 D11
Dachuan China 97 G6
Daegu South Korea 98 C6
Daejon South Korea 98 B6
Dagupan Philippines 95 G3
Dakar *country capital* Senegal 70 A5, 76 C5
Dalälven *river* Norway/Sweden 49 D9
Dalandzadgad Mongolia 97 F3
Da Lat Vietnam 94 D4
Dali China 97 F8
Dalian China 97 J4
Dallas Texas, USA 23 E9, 30 E5
Dalmatia *cultural region* Croatia 68 D4
Daloa Ivory Coast 77 E7
Daly *river* Northern Territory, Australia 103 E2
Daly Waters Northern Territory, Australia 103 F2
Daman India 93 B7
Damaraland *physical region* Namibia 80 B6
Damascus *country capital* Syria 84 A6, 88 D3
Damavand, Qolleh ye *mountain* Iran 89 H3
Damietta Egypt 74 C3
Danakil Desert *desert* Ethiopia 75 F8
Da Nang Vietnam 85 F7, 94 D4
Dandong China 97 J4
Dannenberg Germany 59 G11
Danube *river* C Europe 47 F7, 59 C9, 61 J3, 67 E11, 69 F3
Danube Delta *delta* Romania/Ukraine 65 E12, 69 I3
Danville Virginia, USA 33 F9
Dapaong Togo 77 G6
Daqing China 97 J2
Darabani Romania 69 H1
Darbhanga India 92 F5
Dar es Salaam Tanzania 71 H8, 79 J8
Darfur *cultural region* Ethiopia/Sudan 70 F5, 75 C8
Darganata Turkmenistan 91 D7
Dargaville New Zealand 104 F2
Darhan China 97 G2
Darien, Gulf of *gulf* S Caribbean Sea 35 K8, 40 C2
Darjeeling Bhutan 92 G5
Darling *river* SW Australia 100 C7, 103 H6
Darmstadt Germany 59 C9
Darnah Libya 73 J4
Darnley, Cape *headland* Antarctica 21 E2
Daroca Spain 57 G4
Dart *river* England, United Kingdom 51 E12
Dartmoor *moorland* England, United Kingdom 51 E12
Daru Papua New Guinea 100 C5
Darvishan Afghanistan 91 D10
Darwin *state capital* Northern Territory, Australia 100 B6, 103 E1
Dashhowuz Turkmenistan 91 C6
Datong Mongolia 97 H4
Daugavpils Latvia 64 D5
Davangere India 93 C9
Davao Philippines 85 G8, 95 H5
Davenport Iowa, USA 29 J6
David Panama 35 J9
Davis Strait *strait* Baffin Bay/Labrador Sea 22 H4, 25 H3, 44 C2
Davos Switzerland 60 D5
Dawson Yukon Territory, Canada 24 B3
Dax France 54 D7
Dayr az Zawr Syria 89 E3
Dayton Ohio, USA 32 D7
Daytona Beach Florida, USA 31 J6
De Aar South Africa 80 D8
Deán Funes Argentina 42 E5
Death Valley *valley* California, USA 23 C8, 27 D9
Debrecen Hungary 67 H10
Debre Markos Ethiopia 75 E9
Debre Zeyit Ethiopia 75 F9
Decatur Alabama, USA 31 H4
Decatur Illinois, USA 32 B7
Deccan *plateau* India 84 D7, 93 C7
Decin Czech Republic 67 B6
Dee *river* Scotland, United Kingdom 50 F5
Deggendorf Germany 59 G10
Dehra Dun India 92 D4
Deh Shu Afghanistan 91 D10
Delano California, USA 27 C9
Delaware *state* USA 33 H7
Delaware Bay *inlet* NE USA 33 H7
Delémont Switzerland 60 B4
Delft Netherlands 53 D6
Delfzijl Netherlands 52 I2
Delhi India 92 D4
Delicias Mexico 34 C3
Delmenhorst Germany 58 D4
Del Rio Texas, USA 30 C6
Deltona Florida, USA 31 J6
Demchok *disputed region* China/India 92 D3, 97 B6
Demerara Plain *undersea feature* W Atlantic Ocean 45 D7
Den Helder Netherlands 52 E3
Denia Spain 57 H6
Denizli Turkey 88 C2
Denmark *country* N Europe 46 D4, 49 B12
Denmark Strait *strait* Greenland/Iceland 20 B5, 25 J1, 44 E2
Denov Uzbekistan 91 E8
Denpasar Indonesia 95 F9
Denver *state capital* Colorado, USA 23 D8, 28 E7
Dera Ghazi Khan Pakistan 91 F10
Dera Ismail Khan Pakistan 91 F10
Derbent Uzbekistan 91 E8
Derby England, United Kingdom 51 G9
Derby Western Australia, Australia 100 A6, 102 D3
Derry *see* Londonderry
Derzhavinsk Kazakhstan 90 E4
Dese Somalia 75 F8
Deseado *river* Argentina 43 D10
Des Moines *river* C USA 29 I5
Des Moines *state capital* Iowa, USA 29 I6
Desna *river* Russian Federation/Ukraine 65 E8
Dessau Germany 59 G6
Desventurados, Islas de los *island group* Chile 39 A8
Detmold Germany 59 D6
Detroit Michigan, USA 23 F8, 32 F5
Deva Romania 69 F2
Deventer Netherlands 52 G5
Devon Island *island* Nunavut, Canada 25 F2
Devonport Tasmania, Australia 103 H9
Deyang China 97 G6
Dezful Iran 89 G4
Dezhou China 97 I5
Dhahran Saudi Arabia 89 G6
Dhaka *country capital* Bangladesh 84 E7, 93 H6
Dhamar Yemen 89 F9
Dhanbad India 93 F6
Dhaulagiri *mountain* Nepal 92 E4
Dhole India 93 C7
Dhuusa Marreeb Somalia 75 H10
Diamantina *seasonal river* Queensland/South Australia, Australia 103 G5
Dickinson North Dakota, USA 29 F3
Diekirch Luxembourg 53 G12
Diepholz Germany 58 C5
Dieppe France 55 E2
Diest Belgium 53 E9
Diffa Niger 77 J6
Digne France 55 I7
Dijon France 55 H4
Dili *country capital* East Timor 85 G9, 95 H9
Dilling Sudan 75 C8
Dillon Montana, USA 29 B3
Dilolo Democratic Republic of Congo 79 E9
Dinajpur Bangladesh 92 G5
Dinant Belgium 53 E11
Dinaric Alps *mountain range* Bosnia & Herzegovina 68 D4
Dingle Bay *bay* Republic of Ireland 51 A10
Diourbel Senegal 76 C5
Dire Dawa Ethiopia 71 H6, 75 F9
Dirk Hartog Island *island* Western Australia, Australia 102 A5
Dirranbandi Queensland, Australia 103 I6
Disappointment, Lake *seasonal lake* Western Australia, Australia 102 C4
Divinópolis Brazil 41 H7
Diyarbakir Turkey 89 E2
Djambala Congo 78 C7
Djanet Algeria 73 G6
Djelfa Algeria 73 F4
Djibouti *country* E Africa 71 H5, 75 G8
Djibouti *country capital* Djibouti 71 H6, 75 G8
Dnieper *river* E Europe 47 G6, 65 E7
Dnieper Lowlands *physical region* Ukraine Belarus 65 E8
Dniester *river* Moldova/Ukraine 47 F6, 65 D10
Dniprodzerzhynsk Ukraine 65 G10
Dnipropetrovsk Ukraine 47 H6, 65 G10
Doberai, Jazirah *peninsula* Indonesia 95 I7
Doboj Bosnia & Herzegovina 68 D3
Dobrich Bulgaria 69 I4
Dodecanese *island group* Greece 69 H8
Dodge City Kansas, USA 29 G8
Dodoma *country capital* Tanzania 71 G8, 79 I8
Dogo *island* Japan 98 E6
Dogondoutchi Niger 77 H6
Doha *country capital* Qatar 84 B6, 89 H6
Dolisie Congo 78 C7
Dolomites *mountain range* Italy 62 D2
Dombås Norway 49 B7
Dominica *country* E West Indies 23 I12, 37 J6
Dominican Republic *country* C West Indies 23 H11, 37 G4
Domo Ethiopia 75 H9
Domodossola Italy 62 B2
Don *river* Russian Federation 47 H5, 86 A5
Don *river* Scotland, United Kingdom 50 F5
Donaueschingen Germany 59 C12
Donauwörth Germany 59 D10
Don Benito Spain 56 D6
Doncaster England, United Kingdom 51 G9
Dondo Angola 80 B3
Dondo Mozambique 81 G5
Donegal Republic of Ireland 51 C7
Donegal Bay *bay* NE Atlantic Ocean 51 B8
Donets *river* Russian Federation/Ukraine 65 H9
Donetsk Ukraine 47 H6, 65 H10
Dongara Western Australia, Australia 102 B6
Dongchuan China 97 F8
Donghae South Korea 98 C5
Dong Hoi Vietnam 94 D3
Dongola Sudan 75 C6
Dongsheng China 97 G4
Dongying China 97 I5
Donostia-San Sebastián Spain 57 F2
Dordogne *river* France 55 F6
Dordrecht Netherlands 53 E6
Dorfen Germany 59 G11
Dornbirn Switzerland 60 D4
Dorotea Sweden 49 E6
Dortmund Germany 59 B6
Dortmund-Ems-Canal *canal* Germany 59 B6
Dos Hermanas Spain 56 D8
Dosso Niger 77 H6
Dossor Kazakhstan 90 B4
Dostyk Kazakhstan 90 I5
Dothan Alabama, USA 31 H5
Douala Cameroon 71 D7, 78 B5
Douglas Isle of Man 51 E8
Dourados Brazil 41 G7
Douro *river* Portugal/Spain 46 A7, 56 B4 *see also* Duero
Dover England, United Kingdom 51 I11
Dover *state capital* Delaware, USA 33 H7
Dover, Strait of *strait* France/United Kingdom 51 I11, 55 E1
Dovrefjell *plateau* Norway 49 B7
Dozen *island* Japan 98 E6
Drachten Netherlands 52 G2
Drakensberg *mountain range* Lesotho/South Africa 71 F12, 81 E8
Drake Passage *strait* E Atlantic Ocean 45 C12
Drama Greece 69 G5
Drammen Norway 49 C9
Drau *river* Austria 61 H5
Drava *river* C Europe 61 J6, 67 E12, 68 D2
Dresden Germany 59 H7
Drina *river* Bosnia & Herzegovina/Serbia & Montenegro 68 E3
Drobeta-Turnu Severin Romania 69 F3
Drogheda Republic of Ireland 51 D8
Drohobych Ukraine 65 B9
Dronning Maud Land *physical region* Antarctica 21 C1
Drummond Montana, USA 28 B3
Drummondville Québec, Canada 25 I8
Druskininkai Lithuania 65 B6
Duba Saudi Arabia 88 D5
Dubai United Arab Emirates 89 I6
Dubasari Moldova 65 D11
Dubawnt Lake *lake* Nunavut, Canada 24 E5
Dubbo New South Wales, Australia 103 I7
Dublin *country capital* Republic of Ireland 46 B4, 51 D9
Dubno Ukraine 65 C9
Dubrovnik Croatia 68 D4
Dubuque Iowa, USA 29 J5
Duchess Queensland, Australia 103 G4
Dudinka Russian Federation 87 F4
Duero *river* Portugal/Spain 57 F3 *see also* Douro
Dufourspitze *mountain* Italy/Switzerland 60 C6, 62 B3
Duisburg Germany 59 B6
Duluth Minnesota, USA 29 I3
Dumaguete Philippines 95 G5
Dumfries Scotland, United Kingdom 51 E7
Dumont d'Urville Sea *sea* S Pacific Ocean 21 D5
Dunaujvaros Hungary 67 E11
Dundalk Republic of Ireland 51 D8
Dundee Scotland, United Kingdom 51 F5
Dunedin New Zealand 101 F9, 105 D12
Dunfermline Scotland, United Kingdom 51 F6
Dungeness *headland* England, United Kingdom 51 I12
Dungun Malaysia 94 C6
Dunhuang China 96 E4

114 . DUNKERQUE–FUKUOKA

Dunkerque France 55 F1
Dunkirk New York, USA 33 F5
Dun Laoghaire Republic of Ireland 51 D9
Dunsandel New Zealand 105 E10
Durance *river* France 55 H7
Durango Mexico 34 D4
Durango Colorado, USA 28 C8
Durazno Uruguay 43 G6
Durban South Africa 71 G12, 81 F8
Durg India 93 E7
Durgapur India 93 G6
Durham England, United Kingdom 51 G7
Durham North Carolina, USA 31 J3
Durham Downs Queensland, Australia 103 H5
Durres Albania 68 E5
D'Urville Island *island* New Zealand 105 F7
Dushanbe *country capital* Tajikistan 84 D5, 91 F8
Düsseldorf Germany 59 D7
Duyun China 97 G7
Dzhalal-Abad Kyrgyzstan 91 G7
Dzhankoy Ukraine 65 G12
Dzuunmod Mongolia 97 G2

E

East Cape *headland* New Zealand 104 I4
East China Sea *sea* W Pacific Ocean 85 G6, 97 K6, 98 B8
Easter Fracture Zone *undersea feature* E Pacific Ocean 107 I6
Eastern Desert *desert* Egypt 74 D4
Eastern Ghats *mountain range* India 84 D7, 93 D10
Eastern Sayans *mountain range* Mongolia/Russian Federation 85 E4, 87 F6
East Falkland *island* Falkland Islands 39 E13, 43 F12
East Frisian Islands *island group* Germany 58 B3
East Kilbride Scotland, United Kingdom 51 E6
East London South Africa 71 F12, 80 E8
East Mariana Basin *undersea feature* W Pacific Ocean 106 D4
East Pacific Rise *undersea feature* SE Pacific Ocean 107 H8
East Siberian Sea *sea* Arctic Ocean 20 D1, 85 J2
East Timor *country* SE Asia 85 G9, 95 H9
Eau Claire Wisconsin, USA 32 A4
Eberswalde-Finow Germany 58 H5
Ebetsu Japan 99 I2
Eboli Italy 63 G8
Ebolowa Cameroon 78 C6
Ebro *river* Spain 57 G3
Écija Spain 56 D7
Eckernförde Germany 58 E2
Ecuador *country* N South America 38 A3, 40 B3
Ed Damazin Sudan 75 D8
Ed Dueim Sudan 75 D8
Ede Netherlands 53 F6
Edessa Greece 69 F6
Edinburgh Scotland, United Kingdom 46 C4, 51 F6
Edirne Turkey 88 B1
Edmonton Alberta, Canada 23 D6, 24 C7
Edward, Lake *lake* Democratic Republic of Congo/Uganda 79 G6
Edwards Plateau *plateau* Texas, USA 30 C5
Éfaté *island* Vanuatu 101 E6
Eger Hungary 67 G10
Egersund Norway 49 A10
Eggenfelden Germany 59 G11
Egmont, Cape *headland* New Zealand 105 E6
Egmont, Mount *mountain* New Zealand 105 F6
Egypt *country* NE Africa 70 F3, 74 D4
Eidfjord Norway 49 B8
Eifel *mountain range* Germany 59 A8
Eigg *island* Scotland, United Kingdom 50 D5
Eight Degree Channel *channel* India/Maldives 93 B11
Eighty Mile Beach *coastal region* Western Australia, Australia 102 C3
Eindhoven Netherlands 53 F7
Eisenstadt Austria 61 K3
Eivissa *island* Balearic Islands, Spain 46 B7, 57 I6
Eivissa Balearic Islands, Spain 57 I6
Ejin Qi China 97 F4
Ekibastuz Kazakhstan 90 G3
El Alamein Egypt 74 C3
Elat Israel 88 D4
Elazig Turkey 88 E2
Elba *island* Italy 63 C6
Elbasan Albania 69 E5
Elbe *river* Czech Republic/Germany 46 D5, 58 F4, 67 B7
Elbert, Mount *mountain* Colorado, USA 28 D7
Elblag Poland 66 F3
Elbrus *mountain* Russian Federation 47 I7, 86 A6
Elburz Mountains *mountain range* Iran 89 G3
El Calafate Argentina 43 C12
Elche Spain 57 G6
Elda Spain 57 G6
Elde *river* Germany 58 F4
Eldoret Kenya 79 H6
Eleuthera Island *island* Bahamas 36 D2
El Faiyum Egypt 74 C4
El Fasher Sudan 75 B8
El Fula Sudan 75 B8
El Geneina Sudan 75 A8
El Gîza Egypt 70 G3, 74 C3
El Goléa Algeria 73 F5
Elk Poland 66 H3
El Kharga Egypt 74 C4
Elko Nevada, USA 27 E6
Ellensburg Washington, USA 26 C2
Ellesmere Island *island* Nunavut, Canada 22 G4, 25 F1
Ellesmere, Lake *lake* New Zealand 105 E10
Elliston South Australia, Australia 103 F7
Ellsworth Land *physical region* Antarctica 21 A3
El Mahbas Morocco 73 C5
El Minya Egypt 74 C4
El Mreyyé *desert* Mauritania 77 E4
El Obeid Sudan 71 G5, 75 C8
El Oued Algeria 73 G4
El Paso Texas, USA 23 D9, 30 B5
El Puerto de Santa Maria Spain 56 C8
El Salvador *country* Central America 23 E12, 35 G7
Eltanin Fracture Zone *undersea feature* SE Pacific Ocean 107 G8
Elvas Portugal 56 B6
Elx *see* Elche
Emamshahr Iran 89 H3
Emba Kazakhstan 90 C4
Emden Germany 58 B4
Emerald Queensland, Australia 103 I4
Emmen Netherlands 52 I3
Emperor Seamounts *undersea feature* N Pacific Ocean 106 D2
Emporia Kansas, USA 29 H7
Empty Quarter *see* Ar Rub' al Khali
Ems *river* Germany 58 B4
Encarnación Paraguay 42 G4
Enderby Land *physical region* Antarctica 21 D2
Enderby Plain *undersea feature* S Indian Ocean 82 C8
Enerhodar Ukraine 65 G11
Enewetak Atoll *island* Marshall Islands 100 E3
Enggano *island* Indonesia 94 C8
England *national region* United Kingdom 51 F9
English Channel *channel* NE Atlantic Ocean 46 B5, 51 G12
Enid Oklahoma, USA 30 D3
Enna Italy 63 F11
En Nahud Sudan 75 C8
Ennis Republic of Ireland 51 B9
Enniskillen Northern Ireland, United Kingdom 51 C8
Enns *river* Austria 61 I4
Enschede Netherlands 52 I5
Ensenada Mexico 34 A1
Entebbe Uganda 79 H6
Enugu Nigeria 77 I7
Épinal France 55 I3
Equatorial Guinea *country* C Africa 71 D7, 78 B6
Erd Hungary 67 E10
Erdenet Mongolia 97 F2
Erenhot China 97 H3
Erfurt Germany 59 F7
Erg Chech *desert* Algeria/Mali 70 C3, 72 D6, 77 F3
Erg Iguidi *desert* Algeria/Mauritania 70 B3, 72 D6, 77 F2
Ergun He *see* Argun
Erie Pennsylvania, USA 33 F6
Erie, Lake *lake* Canada/USA 23 G8, 25 H9, 33 E6
Erimo-misaki *headland* Japan 99 I3
Eritrea *country* E Africa 70 H5, 75 E7
Erlangen Germany 59 E9
Ermelo South Africa 81 F7
Ermoupoli Greece 69 G8
Ernakulam India 93 C10
Erode India 93 D10
Er-Rachidia Morocco 73 D4
Ertis *river* NW Asia 90 G3 *see also* Irtysh
Erzgebirge *mountain range* Germany 59 G8
Erzurum Turkey 89 E2
Esbjerg Denmark 49 A12
Escanaba Michigan, USA 32 C3
Esch-Sur-Alzette Luxembourg 52 G13
Escondido California, USA 27 D11
Esenguly Turkmenistan 91 B8
Esfahan Iran 84 B6, 89 H4
Eshkashem Afghanistan 91 F8
Esil Kazakhstan 90 E3
Eskisekhir Turkey 88 C2
Española, Isla *island* Galapagos Islands 40 B9
Esperance Western Australia, Australia 102 D7
Espichel, Cabo *headland* Portugal 56 A6
Espiritu Santo *island* Vanuatu 101 E6
Espoo Finland 49 G9
Esquel Argentina 43 C9
Essen Germany 46 D5, 59 B6
Essequibo *river* Guyana 41 F2
Estados, Isla de los *island* Argentina 43 E13
Estepona Spain 56 D8
Estonia *country* NE Europe 47 F4, 64 C3
Estoril Portugal 56 A6
Estrela, Serra da *mountain range* Portugal 56 B5
Estremoz Portugal 56 B6
Esztergom Hungary 67 E10
Etawah India 92 D5
Ethiopia *country* E Africa 71 H6, 75 F10
Ethiopian Highlands *mountain range* Ethiopia 71 H6, 75 E9
Etna, Mount *volcano* Italy 46 E8, 63 G11
Etosha Pan *salt lake* Namibia 80 B5
Euboea *island* Greece 69 G7
Eugene Oregon, USA 26 B4
Eugenia, Punta *headland* Mexico 34 A3
Eupen Belgium 53 G10
Euphrates *river* SW Asia 84 B6, 89 F4
Eureka California, USA 27 A6
Europe *continent* 46–69
Europoort Netherlands 53 D6
Euskirchen Germany 59 B7
Evansville Indiana, USA 32 C8
Everard, Lake *seasonal lake* South Australia, Australia 103 F6
Everest, Mount *mountain* China/Nepal 92 F4
Everett Washington, USA 26 C1
Everglades, The *wetland* Florida, USA 23 F10, 31 J7
Evje Norway 49 B10
Évora Portugal 56 B6
Évreux France 55 E3
Evros *river* Greece/Turkey 69 H5
Exe *river* England, United Kingdom 51 F12
Exeter England, United Kingdom 51 F12
Exmoor *moorland* England, United Kingdom 51 E11
Exmouth Gulf *gulf* Western Australia, Australia 102 A4
Eyre, Lake *lake* Australia 100 C7
Eyre North, Lake *seasonal lake* South Australia, Australia 103 G5
Eyre South, Lake *seasonal lake* South Australia, Australia 103 G6

F

Faenza Italy 62 D4
Faeroe Islands *Danish dependent territory* N Atlantic Ocean 44 F3, 46 C2
Fagaras Romania 69 G2
Fagne *hill range* Belgium 53 D11
Fairbanks Alaska, USA 26 H1
Fair Isle *island* Scotland, United Kingdom 51 G2
Fairmont Minnesota, USA 29 I4
Faisalabad Pakistan 84 D6, 91 G10
Faizabad India 92 E5
Falam Myanmar 94 A2
Falkland Escarpment *undersea feature* SW Atlantic Ocean 45 D11
Falkland Islands *island group* S South America 45 D11
Falkland Islands *UK dependent territory* S South America 39 E12, 43 F12
Falköping Sweden 49 D10
Falster *island* Denmark 49 C13
Falun Sweden 49 D9
Famenne *physical region* Belgium 53 F11
Fano Italy 62 E5
Farah Afghanistan 91 D10
Farewell, Cape *headland* Greenland 23 I5
Farewell, Cape *headland* New Zealand 105 D7
Farghona Uzbekistan 91 F7
Fargo North Dakota, USA 29 H3
Faribault Minnesota, USA 29 I4
Faridabad India 92 D4
Färjestaden Sweden 49 E11
Farmington New Mexico, USA 30 A3
Faro Portugal 56 B8
Fastiv Ukraine 65 E9
Fauske Norway 48 E4
Faxaflói *bay* Iceland 48 A3
Faya Chad 78 D2
Fayetteville North Carolina, USA 31 J3
Fayetteville Arkansas, USA 31 F3
Fdérik Mauritania 76 D3
Fear, Cape *headland* North Carolina, USA 31 K4
Fehmarn *island* Germany 58 F2
Fehmarn Belt *strait* Denmark/Germany 58 F2
Feilding New Zealand 105 G6
Feira de Santana Brazil 41 J5
Feldkirch *mountain* Switzerland 60 D4
Fen He *river* China 97 H5
Fenoarivo Mozambique 81 K5
Fens, The *marsh* England, United Kingdom 51 H10
Feodosiya Ukraine 65 G12
Fergana Valley *physical region* Tajikistan/Uzbekistan 91 F7
Fergus Falls Minnesota, USA 29 H3
Ferkessédougou Ivory Coast 77 F7
Fermo Italy 63 F5
Fernandina, Isla *island* Galapagos Islands 40 A9
Fernando di Noronho *island group* E South America 45 D8
Ferrara Italy 62 D4
Ferret, Cap *headland* France 54 D7
Ferrol Spain 56 B1
Fès Morocco 70 C2, 72 D4
Feyzabad Afghanistan 91 F8
Fezzan *physical region* Libya 73 H6
Fianarantsoa Madagascar 71 I11, 81 J6
Fier Albania 68 E6
Figueira da Foz Portugal 56 A5
Figueres Spain 57 J2
Figuig Morocco 72 E4
Fiji *country* C Pacific Ocean 101 F6
Filadélfia Paraguay 42 F2
Filchner Ice Shelf *ice shelf* Antarctica 21 B2
Filipstad Sweden 49 D9
Fimbul *ice shelf* Antarctica 21 C1
Finland *country* N Europe 47 F3, 48 G7
Finland, Gulf of *gulf* NE Baltic Sea 47 F4, 49 H9, 64 C3
Finsteraarhorn *mountain* Switzerland 60 C5
Fiordland *physical region* New Zealand 105 A11
Firozabad India 92 D5
Fishguard Wales, United Kingdom 51 E10
Fitz Roy Argentina 43 D10
Fitzroy *river* Western Australia, Australia 102 D3
Fitzroy Crossing Western Australia, Australia 102 D3
Flagstaff Arizona, USA 27 G10
Flamborough Head *headland* England, United Kingdom 51 H8
Flanders *cultural region* Belgium 53 A8
Flattery, Cape *headland* Washington, USA 26 B1
Flensburg Germany 58 D2
Flinders *river* Queensland, Australia 103 H3
Flinders Island *island* Tasmania, Australia 103 I8
Flinders Ranges *mountain range* South Australia, Australia 103 G6
Flin Flon Manitoba, Canada 24 E7
Flint Michigan, USA 32 D5
Florence Italy 46 D7, 62 D5
Florence Alabama, USA 31 G4
Florencia Colombia 40 C3
Flores Guatemala 35 H6
Flores *island* Indonesia 95 G9
Flores Sea *sea* Indonesia 85 G9, 95 F9
Florianópolis Brazil 41 H8
Florida *state* USA 31 J6
Florida Uruguay 43 G6
Florida Keys *island group* Florida, USA 31 J8
Florida, Straits of *strait* Atlantic Ocean/Gulf of Mexico 23 F11, 31 J8, 36 C2
Florø Norway 49 A7
Foca Bosnia & Herzegovina 68 D4
Focsani Romania 69 H2
Foggia Italy 63 G7
Föhr *island* Germany 58 C2
Foix France 55 F8
Follonica Italy 63 D6
Fongafale *country capital* Tuvalu 101 F5
Fonyod Hungary 67 E11
Forbach France 55 I2
Forli Italy 62 D4
Formentera *island* Balearic Islands, Spain 57 I6
Formia Italy 63 F7
Formosa Argentina 42 G3
Forsayth Queensland, Australia 103 H3
Forster-Tuncurry New South Wales, Australia 103 J7
Fortaleza Brazil 38 I4, 41 J4
Fort Collins Colorado, USA 28 E6
Fort-de-France Martinique 37 J7
Fort Dodge Iowa, USA 29 I5
Forth, Firth of *inlet* Scotland, United Kingdom 51 F6
Fortín Madrejón Paraguay 42 F2
Fort Lauderdale Florida, USA 31 J7
Fort McMurray Alberta, Canada 24 D6
Fort Nelson British Columbia, Canada 24 C5
Fort Peck Lake *lake* Montana, USA 28 D2
Fort-Shevchenko Kazakhstan 91 A5
Fort Smith Northwest Territories, Canada 24 D5
Fort Smith Arkansas, USA 31 E4
Fort Wayne Indiana, USA 32 D6
Fort William Scotland, United Kingdom 50 D5
Fort Worth Texas, USA 23 E9, 30 E5
Foshan China 97 H8
Foulwind, Cape *headland* New Zealand 105 D8
Foumban Cameroon 78 B5
Fouta Djallon *mountain range* Guinea 76 D3
Foveaux Strait *strait* New Zealand 105 A12
Foxe Basin *sea* NW Atlantic Ocean 22 G5, 25 G4
Fox Glacier New Zealand 105 C9
Fram Basin *undersea feature* Arctic Ocean 20 C3
Franca Brazil 41 H7
France *country* W Europe 46 C6, 54–55
Franceville Gabon 78 C7
Francistown Botswana 71 F11, 80 E5
Frankenwald *physical region* Germany 59 F8
Frankfort *state capital* Kentucky, USA 32 D8
Frankfurt am Main Germany 46 D5, 59 C8
Frankfurt an der Oder Germany 59 I5
Fränkische Alb *mountain range* Germany 59 E10
Franz Josef Land *island group* Russian Federation 87 E2
Fraser *river* British Columbia, Canada 24 B7
Fraserburgh Scotland, United Kingdom 50 F4
Fraser Island *island* Queensland, Australia 103 J5
Frauenfeld Switzerland 60 D4
Fray Bentos Uruguay 43 G6
Fredericton New Brunswick, Canada 25 I8
Frederikshavn Denmark 49 B11
Fredrikstad Norway 49 C9
Freeport Bahamas 36 C1
Freeport Texas, USA 31 E6
Freetown *country capital* Sierra Leone 71 A6, 76 C7
Freiberg Germany 59 H7
Freiburg im Breisgau Germany 59 B11
Freising Germany 59 F11
Fréjus France 55 I8
Fremantle Western Australia, Australia 102 B7
Fremont California, USA 27 B8
French Guiana *French dependent territory* N South America 38 F3, 41 G2
French Polynesia *French dependent territory* C Pacific Ocean 101 I7
Fresno California, USA 27 C9
Fribourg Switzerland 60 B5
Friedrichshafen Germany 59 D12
Frisian Islands *island group* N Europe 58 F13
Frome, Lake *seasonal lake* South Australia, Australia 103 G6
Frontera Mexico 35 G6
Frøya *island* Norway 49 B6
Frydek-Mistek Czech Republic 67 E8
Fuengirola Spain 56 D8
Fuenlabrada Spain 56 E5
Fuerte *river* Mexico 34 B3
Fujairah United Arab Emirates 89 I6
Fuji Japan 99 G7
Fujieda Japan 99 G7
Fuji, Mount *mountain* Japan 99 G7
Fujinomiya Japan 99 G7
Fukue-jima *island* Japan 98 C8
Fukui Japan 99 F6
Fukuoka Japan 85 H6, 98 D7

LONGYEARBYEN–MELVILLE PENINSULA . 119

Longyearbyen Svalbard 20 C4
Löningen Germany 58 C4
Lop Nur *seasonal lake* China 96 D4
Lorca Spain 57 G7
Lord Howe Island *island* Australia 100 D7
Lord Howe Rise *undersea feature* SW Pacific Ocean 106 D6
Lorient France 54 C4
Los Alamos New Mexico, USA 30 B3
Los Andes Chile 43 C6
Los Angeles Chile 43 C7
Los Angeles California, USA 23 B8, 27 D11
Los Mochis Mexico 34 B4
Lot *river* France 55 F6
Louangphabang Laos 94 C3
Louga Senegal 76 C5
Louisiana *state* USA 31 F6
Louisville Kentucky, USA 32 C8
Lourdes France 54 E8
Loutra Edipsou Greece 69 F7
Lovech Bulgaria 69 G4
Lowell Massachusetts, USA 33 J5
Lower California *peninsula* Mexico 23 C9, 34 A2
Lower Hutt New Zealand 105 F7
Lower Lough Erne *lake* Republic of Ireland 51 C8
Lower Tunguska *river* Russian Federation 85 E3, 87 F4
Lowicz Poland 66 F5
Loyalty Islands *island group* New Caledonia 101 E6
Loznica Serbia & Montenegro 68 E3
Luacano Angola 80 D3
Lualuba *river* Democratic Republic of Congo 71 F8, 79 F7
Luanda *country capital* Angola 71 E9, 80 A2
Luan He *river* China 97 I4
Luanshya Zambia 81 E3
Lubango Angola 80 A4
Lübben Germany 59 H6
Lübbenau Germany 59 H6
Lubbock Texas, USA 30 C4
Lübeck Germany 58 E3
Lublin Poland 67 H6
Lubliniec Poland 67 E6
Lubny Ukraine 65 F9
Lubumbashi Democratic Republic of Congo 71 F9, 79 G9
Lucca Italy 62 C5
Lucenec Slovakia 67 F9
Lucerne Switzerland 60 C5
Lucknow India 92 E5
Lüderitz Namibia 80 B7
Ludhiana India 92 C3
Ludington Michigan, USA 32 C4
Ludvika Sweden 49 D9
Ludwigsburg Germany 59 D10
Ludwigshafen am Rhein Germany 59 C9
Ludwigslust Germany 58 F4
Luena Angola 80 C3
Lugano Switzerland 60 D6
Lugo Italy 62 D4
Lugo Spain 56 C2
Lugovoy Kazakhstan 91 F6
Luhansk Ukraine 65 I10
Lukenie *river* Democratic Republic of Congo 78 E7
Luleå Sweden 49 F5
Luleälven *river* Sweden 48 E4
Lumsden New Zealand 105 B12
Lun Mongolia 97 F2
Lund Sweden 49 C12
Lundy *island* England, United Kingdom 51 E11
Lüneburg Germany 58 E4
Lüneburg Heath *physical region* Germany 58 D4
Luo He *river* China 97 G5
Luoyang China 97 H5
Lusaka *country capital* Zambia 71 F10, 81 E4
Lut, Dasht-e *desert* Syria 89 I4
Luton England, United Kingdom 51 H10
Lutsk Ukraine 65 C9
Luxembourg *country* W Europe 46 D5, 53 G12
Luxembourg *country capital* Luxembourg 46 D5, 53 G12
Luxor Egypt 70 G3, 74 D4
Luz, Costa de la *coastal region* Spain 56 C8
Luzhou China 97 G7
Luzon *island* Philippines 85 G7, 95 G3
Luzon Strait *strait* Philippines/Taiwan 95 G3, 97 J9
Lviv Ukraine 47 F6, 65 B9
Lycksele Sweden 49 E6
Lyme Bay *bay* England, United Kingdom 51 F12
Lynchburg Virginia, USA 33 F8
Lyon France 46 C6, 55 H5
Lysychansk Ukraine 65 H10

M

Ma'an Jordan 88 D4
Maarianhamina *see* Mariehamn
Maas *river* W Europe 53 G7 *see also* Meuse
Maastricht Netherlands 53 F9
McAllen Texas, USA 30 D7
Macao China 97 I8
Macapá Brazil 41 G3
McClintock Channel *channel* Nunavut, Canada 24 E3
McDermitt Nevada, USA 27 D6
Macdonnell Ranges *mountain range* Northern Territory, Australia 103 F4
Macedonia *country* SE Europe 47 F7, 69 F5
Macedonia *cultural region* Greece 69 F5
Maceió Brazil 39 I5, 41 J5
Machakos Kenya 79 I7
Machala Ecuador 40 B4
Machilipatnam India 93 E8
Macia Mozambique 81 F6
Mackay Queensland, Australia 100 D6, 103 I4
Mackay, Lake *seasonal lake* Northern Territory/Western Australia, Australia 102 E4
Mackenzie *river* Northwest Territories, Canada 22 D5, 24 C4
Mackenzie Mountains *mountain range* Yukon Territory/ Northwest Territories, Canada 22 D4, 24 B4
McKinley, Mount *mountain* Alaska, USA 22 C4, 26 H2
Macleod, Lake *lake* Western Australia, Australia 102 B5
Macomer Italy 63 B8
Mâcon France 55 H5
Macon Georgia, USA 31 I4
Madagascar *country* SE Africa 71 H11, 81 J4
Madagascar *island* SE Africa 82 C5
Madagascar Basin *undersea feature* W Indian Ocean 82 C5
Madagascar Plateau *undersea feature* W Indian Ocean 82 C6
Madeira *Portuguese dependent territory* NW Atlantic Ocean 70 A2, 72 B4
Madeira *river* Bolivia/Brazil 38 D4, 41 E4
Mädelegabel *mountain* Germany 59 E13
Madison *state capital* Wisconsin, USA 32 B5
Madras *see* Chennai
Madre de Dios *river* Bolivia/Peru 39 C6, 40 D5
Madre, Laguna *lagoon* Mexico 35 E4
Madrid *country capital* Spain 46 B7, 57 E4
Madura *island* Indonesia 95 E9
Madurai India 93 D10
Maebashi Japan 99 H6
Mafeteng South Africa 80 E8
Mafia *island* Tanzania 79 J8
Magadan Russian Federation 87 J4
Magdalena *river* Colombia 40 C2
Magdeburg Germany 59 F6
Magellan, Strait of *strait* Argentina/Chile 39 D13, 43 D12
Mageroya *island* Norway 48 G1
Maggiore, Lake *lake* Italy/Switzerland 60 C6, 62 B2
Magnitogorsk Russian Federation 86 C5
Mahajanga Madagascar 71 I10, 81 J4
Mahakan *river* Indonesia 95 F7
Mahalapye Botswana 80 E6
Mahanadi *river* India 93 F7
Mahia Peninsula *peninsula* New Zealand 105 I6
Mahilyow Ukraine 65 E7
Mahón Balearic Islands, Spain 57 K5
Maiduguri Nigeria 71 E6, 77 J6
Main *river* Germany 59 E9
Main-Donau-Canal *canal* Germany 59 F10
Maine *state* USA 33 J3
Maine, Gulf of *gulf* NE USA 33 J4
Mainland *island* Orkney Islands, Scotland, United Kingdom 50 F3
Mainland *island* Shetland Islands, Scotland, United Kingdom 50 G1
Mainz Germany 59 C9
Maizuru Japan 99 F7
Majorca *see* Mallorca
Majuro *country capital* Marshall Islands 101 F4
Makassar Indonesia 85 G9, 95 G8
Makassar Strait *strait* Indonesia 95 F8
Makeni Sierra Leone 76 D7
Makhachkala Russian Federation 86 A6
Makiyivka Ukraine 65 H10
Makokou Gabon 78 C6
Makumbako Tanzania 79 H8
Makurdi Nigeria 77 I7
Malabar Coast *coastal region* India 93 C9
Malabo *country capital* Equatorial Guinea 71 D7, 78 B5
Malacca, Strait of *strait* Indonesia/Malaysia 83 G3, 94 B6
Maladzyechna Belarus 65 D6
Málaga Spain 46 A8, 56 E8
Malaita *island* Solomon Islands 100 E5
Malakal Sudan 75 D9
Malang Indonesia 95 E9
Malanje Angola 80 B2
Mälaren *lake* Sweden 49 E9
Malargüe Argentina 43 C7
Malatya Turkey 88 E2
Malawi *country* S Africa 71 G9, 81 G3
Malay Peninsula *peninsula* Malaysia/Thailand 94 B5
Malaysia *country* SE Asia 85 F8, 94 C6
Malbork Poland 66 F3
Maldives *country* N Indian Ocean 84 D8, 93 B12
Maldives *island group* N Indian Ocean 83 E3
Male *country capital* Maldives 84 D8, 93 B12
Malegaon India 93 C7
Malheur Lake *lake* Oregon, USA 26 D4
Mali *country* W Africa 70 C4, 77 F5
Malindi Kenya 79 J7
Mallaig Scotland, United Kingdom 50 D5
Mallawi Egypt 74 C4
Mallorca *island* Balearic Islands, Spain 46 C7, 57 J5
Malmberget Sweden 48 F4
Malmédy Belgium 53 G10
Malmö Sweden 46 E5, 49 C12
Malopolska *cultural region* Poland 67 G7
Malta *country* C Mediterranean Sea 46 E9, 63 F13
Malta *island* C Mediterranean Sea 63 F13
Malta Channel *channel* S Mediterranean Sea 63 F13
Malunda Indonesia 95 F8
Malung Sweden 49 D9
Mamberamo *river* Indonesia 95 K7
Mamoré *river* Bolivia/Brazil 40 E6
Mamou Guinea 76 D6
Mamoudzou Mayotte 81 J3
Man Ivory Coast 76 E7
Manacor Balearic Islands, Spain 57 J5
Manado Indonesia 95 H7
Managua *country capital* Nicaragua 23 F12, 35 I8
Manakara Madagascar 81 J6
Manama *country capital* Bahrain 84 B6, 89 H6
Mananjary Madagascar 81 J6
Manaus Brazil 38 E4, 41 F4
Manchester England, United Kingdom 46 C4, 51 F9
Manchester New Hampshire, USA 33 J5
Manchurian Plain *physical region* China 85 G5, 97 I3
Mandalay Myanmar 85 E7, 94 B2
Mandalgovi Mongolia 97 G3
Mandurah Western Australia, Australia 102 B7
Manfredonia Italy 63 G7
Manfredonia, Gulf of *gulf* SW Adriatic Sea 63 G7
Mangalore India 93 C9
Mangaweka New Zealand 105 G6
Manhattan Kansas, USA 29 H7
Manicouagan Reservoir *reservoir* Québec, Canada 25 I7
Maniitsoq Greenland 20 A4
Manila *country capital* Philippines 85 G7, 95 G4
Manisa Turkey 88 B2
Man, Isle of *island* United Kingdom 46 C4, 51 E8
Manitoba *province* Canada 25 E7
Manitoba, Lake *lake* Manitoba, Canada 24 E8
Manizales Colombia 40 C2
Mannar, Gulf of *gulf* India/Sri Lanka 93 D11
Mannheim Germany 59 C9
Manokwari Indonesia 95 J7
Manpo North Korea 98 B3
Manresa Spain 57 I3
Mansa Zambia 81 F3
Mansfield England, United Kingdom 51 G9
Mansfield Ohio, USA 32 E6
Manta Ecuador 40 B3
Mantova Italy 62 D3
Manukau Harbour *harbour* New Zealand 104 F4
Manurewa New Zealand 104 G3
Manzanares Spain 57 E6
Manzanillo Cuba 36 D4
Manzhouli China 97 H2
Manzini Swaziland 81 F7
Maoke, Pegunungan *mountain range* Indonesia 95 K8
Maoming China 97 H8
Maputo *country capital* Mozambique 71 G11, 81 F7
Maputo Bay *bay* W Indian Ocean 81 G7
Maqat Kazakhstan 90 B4
Maracaibo Venezuela 40 D1
Maracaibo, Lake *lake* Venezuela 38 C2, 40 C1
Maracay Venezuela 38 C2, 40 D1
Maradah Libya 73 J5
Maradi Niger 77 I6
Maragheh Iran 89 F2
Marajó, Baía de *bay* Brazil 41 H3
Marajó, Ilha de *island* Brazil 38 G3, 41 H3
Marañón *river* Peru 38 B4, 40 C4
Maratea Italy 63 G9
Marbella Spain 56 D8
Marburg Germany 59 C7
Marche-en-Famenne Belgium 53 F11
Marchena, Isla *island* Galapagos Islands 40 B8
Mar Chiquito, Laguna *lake* Argentina 39 D9
Mar del Plata Argentina 39 E10, 43 G7
Margarita, Isla de *island* Venezuela 41 E1
Margow, Dasht-e *desert* Afghanistan 91 D10
Marhanets Ukraine 65 G11
Mariana Trench *undersea feature* W Pacific Ocean 106 C4
Maribor Slovenia 61 J5
Marie Byrd Land *physical region* Antarctica 21 B4
Mariehamn Finland 49 F9
Mariental Namibia 80 C6
Mariestad Sweden 49 D10
Marijampole Lithuania 65 B6
Marikostinovo Bulgaria 69 F5
Marília Brazil 41 G7
Maringá Brazil 41 G7
Maritime Alps *mountain range* France/Italy 55 I7
Maritsa *river* SW Europe 69 H5
Mariupol Ukraine 65 H11
Marka Somalia 75 G11
Markermeer *lake* Netherlands 52 E4
Marktoberdorf Germany 59 E12
Marktredwitz Germany 59 G9
Marmara, Sea of *sea* Aegean Sea/Black Sea 69 I5
Marmaris Turkey 88 C2
Marmolada *mountain* Italy 62 E2
Marne *river* France 55 H3
Maroantsetra Madagascar 81 K4
Maroochydore-Mooloolaba Queensland, Australia 103 J5
Maroua Cameroon 78 C4
Marquesas Fracture Zone *undersea feature* C Pacific Ocean 107 G5
Marquesas Islands *island group* French Polynesia 101 J5
Marrakech Morocco 70 B2, 72 D4
Marree South Australia, Australia 103 G6
Marsa Al Burayqah Libya 73 J5
Marsabit Kenya 79 I6
Marsala Italy 63 E11
Marseille France 46 C7, 55 H8
Marshall Islands *country* W Pacific Ocean 100 D3
Martaban, Gulf of *gulf* Myanmar 94 B3
Martapura Indonesia 95 F8
Martha's Vineyard *island* Massachusetts, USA 33 J6
Martigny Switzerland 60 B6
Martin Slovakia 67 F8
Martinique *French dependent territory* E West Indies 37 J6
Martinique Passage *channel* Dominica/Martinique 37 J6
Mary Turkmenistan 91 D8
Maryborough Queensland, Australia 103 J5
Maryland *state* USA 33 G7
Maryville Missouri, USA 29 I6
Masai Steppe *physical region* Tanzania 71 H8, 79 I7
Masan South Korea 98 C6
Masasi Tanzania 79 I9
Masbate *island* Philippines 95 G4
Mascarene Basin *undersea feature* W Indian Ocean 82 D4
Maseru *country capital* Lesotho 71 F12, 80 E8
Mashhad Iran 84 C5, 89 I2
Masindi Uganda 79 H6
Masirah *island* Oman 89 J7
Masirah, Gulf of *gulf* NW Arabian Sea 89 J7
Mason City Iowa, USA 29 I5
Massa Italy 62 C5
Massachusetts *state* USA 33 I5
Massawa Eritrea 75 F7
Massena New York, USA 33 H4
Massif Central *plateau* France 46 C6, 55 F6
Masterton New Zealand 105 G7
Masty Belarus 65 C7
Masuda Japan 98 D7
Masvingo Zimbabwe 81 F5
Matadi Democratic Republic of Congo 78 C8
Matagalpa Nicaragua 35 I7
Matam Senegal 76 D5
Matamoros Mexico 35 E4
Matanzas Cuba 36 B3
Mataram Indonesia 95 F9
Mataranka Northern Territory, Australia 103 F2
Mataró Spain 57 J3
Mataura *river* New Zealand 105 B12
Matera Italy 63 H8
Mato Grosso, Planalto de *plateau* Brazil 39 E6, 41 G6
Matosinhos Portugal 56 B4
Matsue Japan 98 E6
Matsumoto Japan 99 G6
Matsuyama Japan 98 E7
Matterhorn *mountain* Italy/Switzerland 60 B6
Matto Japan 99 F6
Maturín Venezuela 41 E1
Maui *island* Hawaii, USA 27 B12
Maun Botswana 80 D5
Mauritania *country* W Africa 70 A4, 76 D4
Mauritius *island* W Indian Ocean 82 D5
Maxixe Mozambique 81 G6
Mayagüez Puerto Rico 37 H5
Maydan Shahr Afghanistan 91 F9
Maykop Russian Federation 86 A5
Mayotte *French dependent territory* S Africa 71 I9, 81 J3
May Pen Jamaica 36 D5
Mazabuka Zambia 81 E4
Mazara del Vallo Italy 63 E11
Mazar-e Sharif Afghanistan 91 E8
Mazatlán Mexico 34 C4
Mazeikiai Lithuania 64 B5
Mazuria *cultural region* Poland 66 F4
Mazyr Belarus 65 D8
Mbabane *country capital* Swaziland 71 G11, 81 F7
Mbaiki Central African Republic 78 D5
Mbaké Senegal 76 C5
Mbale Uganda 79 H6
Mbandaka Democratic Republic of Congo 71 E7, 78 D6
M'banza Congo Angola 80 B2
Mbarara Uganda 79 G6
Mbeya Tanzania 79 H8
Mbuji-Mayi Democratic Republic of Congo 71 F8, 79 F8
Mdantsane South Africa 80 E8
Mead, Lake *lake* Arizona/Nevada, USA 27 F9
Mecca Saudi Arabia 84 B7, 88 E7
Mechelen Belgium 53 D8
Meckenheim Germany 59 B8
Mecklenburg Bay *bay* S Baltic Sea 58 F2
Medan Indonesia 85 E8, 94 B6
Medellín Colombia 38 B2, 40 C2
Medford Oregon, USA 26 B5
Medias Romania 69 G2
Medicine Hat Alberta, Canada 24 C8
Medina Saudi Arabia 88 E6
Medina del Campo Spain 56 D4
Mediterranean Sea *sea* E Atlantic Ocean 63 C11, 68 D9
Meekatharra Western Australia, Australia 102 C5
Meerut India 92 D4
Megisti Greece 69 J8
Meiningen Germany 59 E8
Meizhou China 97 I8
Mekele Ethiopia 75 F8
Meknès Morocco 72 D4
Mekong *river* SE Asia 85 F7, 94 C2, 97 E6
Mekong, Mouths of the *delta* Vietnam 94 D5
Melaka Malaysia 94 C7
Melanesia *island group* W Pacific Ocean 100 C4, 106 C5
Melanesian Basin *undersea feature* W Pacific Ocean 106 D4
Melbourne *state capital* Victoria, Australia 100 D8, 103 H8
Melbourne Florida, USA 31 J6
Melilla *Spanish dependent territory* NW Africa 57 F9, 70 C2, 72 E3
Melitopol Ukraine 65 G11
Mellerud Sweden 49 C10
Melo Uruguay 43 H6
Melun France 55 F3
Melville Island *island* Northern Territory, Australia 103 E1
Melville Island *island* Northwest Territories/Nunavut, Canada 22 F4, 24 D2
Melville Peninsula *peninsula* Nunavut, Canada 25 F4

UNGAVA PENINSULA–WINSCHOTEN . 127

Ungava Peninsula *peninsula* Québec, Canada 23 G6, 25 G5
Ungheni Moldova 65 D11
Uniontown Pennsylvania, USA 33 F7
United Arab Emirates *country* SW Asia 84 C7, 89 H6
United Kingdom *country* NW Europe 46 C4, 51 E7
United States of America *country* N North America 26–33
Upington South Africa 80 C7
Upper Lough Erne *lake* Republic of Ireland/United Kingdom 51 C8
Uppsala Sweden 49 E9
Upua New Zealand 104 F2
Ural *river* Kazakhstan/Russian Federation 47 J4, 84 B4, 86 C5, 90 B4
Ural Mountains *mountain range* Asia/Europe 47 I1, 84 C3, 86 D4
Urawa Japan 99 H6
Urbino Italy 62 E5
Urengoy Russian Federation 87 E4
Urganch Uzbekistan 91 D7
Uritskiy Kazakhstan 90 E3
Urmia, Lake *lake* Iran 89 F2
Urosevac Serbia & Montenegro 69 E5
Uroteppa Tajikistan 91 F7
Uruguay *country* S South America 39 E9, 43 G6
Uruguay *river* S South America 39 E9, 41 G8, 42 G4
Urumqi China 84 E5, 96 D3
Usak Turkey 88 C2
Usedom *island* Germany 58 H3
Ushuaia Argentina 43 D13
Ussuri *river* China/Russian Federation 97 K2
Ussuriysk Russian Federation 87 J7
Ustica *island* Italy 63 E10
Ust-Ilimsk Russian Federation 87 G5
Usti nad Labem Czech Republic 67 B6
Ustka Poland 66 D2
Ust-Kamchatsk Russian Federation 87 K3
Ustrzyki Dolne Poland 67 H8
Ustyurt Plateau *plateau* Kazakhstan/Uzbekistan 91 B6
Usumacinta *river* Guatemala/Mexico 35 G6
Utah *state* USA 27 G8
Utica New York, USA 33 H5
Utiel Spain 57 G5
Utrecht Netherlands 53 E5
Utsjoki Finland 48 G2
Utsunomiya Japan 99 H6
Uvs Nuur *lake* Mongolia 96 E2
Uyo Nigeria 77 I8
Uzbekistan *country* C Asia 84 C5, 91 D7
Uzhhorod Ukraine 65 A10

V

Vaal *river* South Africa 71 F12, 80 D7
Vaasa Finland 49 F7
Vac Hungary 67 F10
Vacaville California, USA 27 B8
Vadodara India 93 B6
Vadsø Norway 48 H2
Vaduz *country capital* Liechtenstein 46 D6, 60 D5
Vah *river* Slovakia 67 E9
Valdecañas, Embalse de *reservoir* Spain 56 D5
Valdepeñas Spain 57 E6
Valdés, Península *peninsula* Argentina 43 E9
Valdivia Chile 43 C8
Valdosta Georgia, USA 31 I5
Valence France 55 H6
Valencia Spain 46 B7, 57 H5
Valencia Venezuela 38 C2, 40 D1
Valencia, Gulf of *gulf* Spain 57 H6
Valenciennes France 55 G1
Valentine Nebraska, USA 29 F5
Valera Venezuela 40 D1
Valga Estonia 64 C4
Valladolid Spain 46 B7, 56 D3
Valledupar Venezuela 40 C1
Vallejo California, USA 27 B8
Vallenar Chile 42 C4
Valletta *country capital* Malta 46 E9, 63 F13
Valmiera Estonia 64 C4
Valparaíso Chile 43 C6
Valverde del Camino Spain 56 C7
Van Turkey 89 F2
Vanadzor Armenia 89 F1
Vancouver British Columbia, Canada 23 C6, 24 B7
Vancouver Washington, USA 26 B3
Vancouver Island *island* British Columbia, Canada 23 C6, 24 A7
Vancouver, Mount *mountain* Yukon Territory, Canada 24 A4
Van Diemen Gulf *gulf* Northern Territory, Australia 103 E1
Vänern *lake* Sweden 46 E4, 49 C10
Vänersborg Sweden 49 C10
Vangaindrano Madagascar 81 J6
Van, Lake *lake* Turkey 89 F2
Vannes France 54 C4
Vanrhynsdorp South Africa 80 C8
Vantaa Finland 49 H9
Vanua Levu *island* Fiji 101 F6
Vanuatu *country* SW Pacific Ocean 100 E6
Varanasi India 93 E5
Varangerfjorden *fjord* Norway 48 H2
Varano, Lake *lagoon* Italy 63 G7
Varazdin Croatia 68 C2
Varberg Sweden 49 C11
Varde Denmark 49 A12
Varese Italy 62 B3
Varkaus Finland 49 H7
Varna Bulgaria 69 I4
Vasa *see* Vaasa
Vaslui Romania 69 H2
Västerås Sweden 49 E9
Vasto Italy 63 F6
Vatican City *country* S Europe 46 D7, 63 E7
Vatican City *country capital* Vatican City 63 E7
Vatnajökull *glacier* Iceland 48 C2
Vättern *lake* Sweden 46 E4, 49 D10
Växjö Sweden 49 D11
Veenendaal Netherlands 53 F6
Vega *island* Norway 49 C5
Vejle Denmark 49 B12
Veles Macedonia 69 F5
Vélez-Málaga Spain 56 E8
Veliko Turnovo Bulgaria 69 H4
Vellore India 93 D9
Velsen-Noord Netherlands 52 E4
Venado Tuerto Argentina 43 F6
Vendas Novas Portugal 56 B6
Venezuela *country* N South America 38 D2, 40 D2
Venezuela, Gulf of *gulf* Colombia/Venezuela 40 D1
Venice Italy 62 E3
Venice, Gulf of *gulf* NW Adriatic Sea 62 E3
Venlo Netherlands 53 G7
Ventspils Estonia 64 B4
Vera Argentina 42 F5
Veracruz Mexico 35 F6
Veraval India 93 A7
Vercelli Italy 62 B3
Verdalsøra Norway 49 C6
Verde, Costa *coastal region* Spain 56 D1
Verden Germany 58 D4
Vereeniging South Africa 81 E7
Verkhoyanskiy Khrebet *mountain range* Russian Federation 87 H4
Vermont *state* USA 33 I4
Vernon Texas, USA 30 D4
Vernon, Mount Illinois, USA 32 B7
Veroia Greece 69 F6
Verona Italy 62 D3
Versailles France 55 F3
Verviers Belgium 53 G10
Vesoul France 55 H4
Vesterålen *island group* Norway 47 F1, 48 D3
Vestfjorden *fjord* Norway 48 D4
Vestmannaeyjar Iceland 48 B3
Vestmann Islands *island group* Iceland 48 B3
Vestvagøy *island* Norway 48 D3
Vesuvius *volcano* Italy 63 F8
Veszprem Hungary 67 E10
Vetlanda Sweden 49 D11
Veurne Belgium 53 A8
Viana do Castelo Portugal 56 B3
Viareggio Italy 62 C5
Viborg Denmark 49 B11
Vibo Valentia Italy 63 H10
Vicenza Italy 62 D3
Vichy France 55 G5
Victoria *river* Northern Territory, Australia 103 E2
Victoria *state* Australia 103 H7
Victoria British Columbia, Canada 24 B7
Victoria Falls *waterfall* Zambia/Zimbabwe 71 F10, 80 E5
Victoria Island *island* Northwest Territories/Nunavut, Canada 22 E4, 24 D3
Victoria, Lake *lake* E Africa 71 G7, 79 H7
Victoria Land *physical region* Antarctica 21 C4
Victoria River Roadhouse Northern Territory, Australia 103 E2
Vidin Bulgaria 69 F3
Viedma Argentina 43 E8
Vienna *country capital* Austria 46 E6, 61 J3
Vienne *river* France 55 E5
Vientiane *country capital* Laos 85 F7, 94 C3
Vierwaldstätter See *lake* Switzerland 60 C5
Vietnam *country* SE Asia 85 F7, 94 D4
Vignemale *mountain* France 54 E8
Vigo Spain 56 B3
Vijayawada India 93 E8
Vik Iceland 48 B3
Vikna *island* Norway 49 C6
Vila do Conde Portugal 56 B4
Vila Nova de Gaia Portugal 56 B4
Vila Real Portugal 56 B4
Vila Real de Santo António Portugal 56 B8
Vilhelmina Sweden 49 E6
Viljandi Estonia 64 C4
Villach Austria 61 H5
Villahermosa Mexico 35 G6
Villa María Argentina 43 E6
Villaputzu Italy 63 B9
Villarrica Paraguay 42 G3
Villarrobledo Spain 57 F6
Villavicencio Colombia 40 C2
Villeurbanne France 55 H5
Vilnius *country capital* Lithuania 47 F5, 65 C6
Vilyuy *river* Russian Federation 85 G3, 87 H4
Viña del Mar Chile 43 C6
Vinaròs Spain 57 H4
Vincent, Gulf St *gulf* South Australia, Australia 103 F7
Vindhya Range *mountain range* India 93 C6
Vinh Vietnam 94 D3
Vinnytsya Ukraine 65 D10
Vinson Massif *mountain* Antarctica 21 B3
Virginia *state* USA 33 F8
Virginia Beach Virginia, USA 33 H9
Virgin Islands *US dependent territory* E West Indies 37 I5
Virovitica Croatia 68 D2
Vis *island* Croatia 68 C4
Visakhapatnam India 93 E8
Visby Sweden 49 E11
Viscount Melville Sound *strait* Northwest Territories/Nunavut, Canada 24 D3
Viseu Portugal 56 B4
Visoko Bosnia & Herzegovina 68 D3
Vistula *river* Poland 47 E5, 66 E4, 67 G7
Viterbo Italy 63 D6
Viti Levu *island* Fiji 101 F6
Vitim *river* Russian Federation 87 H6
Vitória Brazil 41 I7
Vitória da Conquista Brazil 41 I6
Vitoria-Gasteiz Spain 57 F2
Vitsyebsk Belarus 47 G4, 65 E6
Vittangi Sweden 48 F4
Vittoria Italy 63 F12
Vjose *river* Greece 69 F6
Vlaardingen Netherlands 53 D6
Vladikavkaz Russian Federation 86 A6
Vladimir Russian Federation 86 B4
Vladivostok Russian Federation 85 H5, 87 J7
Vlieland *island* West Frisian Islands 52 E2
Vlissingen Netherlands 53 C7
Vlore Albania 68 E6
Vltava *river* Czech Republic 67 B7
Vocklabruck Austria 61 H3
Voghera Italy 62 B3
Voinjama Liberia 76 D7
Vojvodina *cultural region* Serbia & Montenegro 68 E2
Volga *river* Russian Federation 47 G4, 86 B5
Volgograd Russian Federation 47 I5, 86 B5
Völkermarkt Austria 61 I5
Vologda Russian Federation 86 C4
Volos Greece 69 F6
Volta, Lake *lake* Ghana 71 C6, 77 G7
Volyn-Podolian Upland *hill range* Ukraine 65 D9
Vorkuta Russian Federation 86 D4
Voronezh Russian Federation 47 H5, 86 B4
Voru Estonia 64 D4
Vosges *mountain range* France 55 I3
Voss Norway 49 A8
Voznesensk Ukraine 65 E11
Vranje Serbia & Montenegro 69 F4
Vratsa Bulgaria 69 G4
Vrbas Serbia & Montenegro 68 E2
Vryburg South Africa 80 D7
Vukovar Croatia 68 D3

W

Waal *river* Netherlands 53 E6
Waalwijk Netherlands 53 E7
Wabash *river* N USA 32 C7
Waco Texas, USA 30 E5
Waddan Libya 73 I5
Waddenzee *sea* Netherlands 52 E2
Waddington, Mount *mountain* British Columbia, Canada 24 B7
Wadi Halfa Sudan 75 C5
Wad Medani Sudan 75 D8
Wagga Wagga New South Wales, Australia 103 I7
Wagin Western Australia, Australia 102 C7
Wah Pakistan 91 G9
Waiau *river* New Zealand 105 B12
Waidhofen an der Ybbs Austria 61 I3
Waigeo *island* Indonesia 95 I7
Waikato *river* New Zealand 104 G4
Waikerie South Australia, Australia 103 G7
Waimangaroa New Zealand 105 D8
Waiouru New Zealand 105 G6
Waipara New Zealand 105 E9
Waipu New Zealand 104 F2
Waipukurau New Zealand 105 H6
Wairoa New Zealand 105 H5
Waitakere New Zealand 104 F3
Wakasa-wan *bay* Japan 99 F6
Wakatipu, Lake *lake* New Zealand 105 B11
Wakayama Japan 99 F7
Wake Island *US dependent territory* SW Pacific Ocean 101 E2
Wakkanai Japan 99 I1
Walachia *cultural region* Romania 69 G3
Walbrzych Poland 67 D6
Wales *national region* United Kingdom 51 E10
Walgett New South Wales, Australia 103 I6
Wallis & Futuna *French dependent territory* C Pacific Ocean 101 F5
Walpole Western Australia, Australia 102 C7
Walvis Bay Namibia 71 E11, 80 B6
Walvis Ridge *undersea feature* SE Atlantic Ocean 45 G9
Wanaka New Zealand 105 C11
Wanaka, Lake *lake* New Zealand 105 B11
Wandel Sea *sea* Arctic Ocean 20 C4
Wanganui *river* New Zealand 105 G6
Wanganui New Zealand 105 G6
Wanxian China 97 G6
Warangal India 93 D8
Warburg Germany 59 D6
Warnemünde Germany 58 G3
Warrego *seasonal river* New South Wales/Queensland, Australia 103 H5
Warren Michigan, USA 32 E5
Warri Nigeria 77 I8
Warsaw *country capital* Poland 47 F5, 66 G5
Warta *river* Poland 66 D4, 67 F6
Warwick Queensland, Australia 103 J6
Washington *state* USA 26 C2
Washington D.C. *country capital* District of Columbia, USA 23 G9, 33 G7
Washington, Mount *mountain* New Hampshire, USA 33 I4
Wash, The *bay* England, United Kingdom 51 H9
Waterbury Connecticut, USA 33 I6
Waterford Republic of Ireland 51 C10
Waterloo Iowa, USA 29 J5
Watertown New York, USA 33 H4
Watertown South Dakota, USA 29 H4
Watford England, United Kingdom 51 H11
Watsa Democratic Republic of Congo 79 G6
Watson Lake Yukon Territory, Canada 24 B5
Watzmann *mountain* Germany 59 G12
Wau Sudan 75 C10
Wawa Ontario, Canada 25 G8
Weald, The *physical region* England, United Kingdom 51 H11
Weddell Plain *undersea feature* C Southern Ocean 45 E12
Weddell Sea *sea* SE Southern Ocean 45 D13
Wedel Germany 58 E3
Weert Netherlands 53 G8
Wei He *river* China 97 G6
Weinan China 97 H6
Welkom South Africa 80 E7
Wellesley Islands *island group* Queensland, Australia 103 G3
Wellington *country capital* New Zealand 101 F8, 105 F7
Wellington, Isla *island* Chile 39 C12, 43 C11
Wellsford New Zealand 104 F3
Wels Austria 61 H3
Wenzhou China 97 J7
Werra *river* Germany 59 E8
Weser *river* Germany 58 C4
Wessel Islands *island group* Northern Territory, Australia 103 G1
West Cape *headland* New Zealand 105 A12
Western Australia *state* Australia 102 C5
Western Desert *desert* Egypt 74 B4
Western Dvina *river* W Europe 47 F4, 65 D5
Western Ghats *mountain range* India 84 D7, 93 B7
Western Sahara *disputed region* Morocco 70 A3, 72 B6
Westerschelde *inlet* S North Sea 53 C7
West Falkland *island* Falkland Islands 39 E13, 43 F12
West Frisian Islands *island group* Netherlands 52 E2
West Indies *island group* Caribbean Sea 23 G11, 36 E2, 45 C6
West Mariana Basin *undersea feature* W Pacific Ocean 106 C4
West Palm Beach Florida, USA 31 J7
Westport New Zealand 105 D8
West Siberian Plain *physical region* Russian Federation 84 D3, 86 D4
West Virginia *state* USA 33 E7
Wetar *island* Indonesia 95 H9
Wetzlar Germany 59 C8
Wewak Papua New Guinea 100 C5
Wexford Republic of Ireland 51 D10
Weymouth England, United Kingdom 51 F12
Whakatane New Zealand 104 H4
Whangarei New Zealand 104 F2
Wharton Basin *undersea feature* E Indian Ocean 83 G5
Wheatland Wyoming, USA 28 E5
Wheeler Peak *mountain* New Mexico, USA 30 B3
Whitehorse Yukon Territory, Canada 24 B4
White Mountains *mountain range* Maine/New Hampshire, USA 33 I4
White Nile *river* Sudan 71 G6, 75 D8
White Sea *sea* Russian Federation 20 D5, 47 G2, 86 C3
White Volta *river* Burkina, Ghana 77 G7
Whitney, Mount *mountain* California, USA 23 C8, 27 D9
Whyalla South Australia, Australia 103 G7
Wichita Kansas, USA 29 H8
Wichita Falls Texas, USA 30 D4
Wick Scotland, United Kingdom 50 F3
Wicklow Mountains *mountain range* Republic of Ireland 51 D9
Wielkopolska *cultural region* Poland 66 E4
Wiener Neustadt Austria 61 J3
Wiesbaden Germany 59 C8
Wight, Isle of *island* England, United Kingdom 51 G12
Wilcannia New South Wales, Australia 103 H6
Wildon Switzerland 61 J5
Wildspitze *mountain* Austria 61 E5
Wilhelmshaven Germany 58 C3
Wilkes Land *physical region* Antarctica 21 D4
Willemstad Netherlands Antilles 37 G8
Wilhelm II Land *physical region* Antarctica 21 E3
Williston North Dakota, USA 29 E2
Willmar Minnesota, USA 29 H4
Wilmington Delaware, USA 33 H7
Wilmington North Carolina, USA 31 K4
Wilson North Carolina, USA 31 J3
Wilson, Mount *mountain* Colorado, USA 28 C7
Wiluna Western Australia, Australia 102 C5
Windhoek *country capital* Namibia 71 E11, 80 B6
Windsor Ontario, Canada 25 G9
Windward Islands *island group* E West Indies 37 J8
Windward Passage *channel* Cuba/Haiti 37 E4
Winnemucca Nevada, USA 27 D6
Winnipeg Manitoba, Canada 23 E7, 25 E8
Winnipeg, Lake *lake* Manitoba, Canada 23 E7, 24 E7
Winnipegosis, Lake *lake* Manitoba, Canada 24 E7
Winona Minnesota, USA 29 J4
Winschoten Netherlands 52 I2